I0337733

Cover Image: *Tara of Serenity and Peace* (Rab.zhi.ma) drawn by Ruth Perini (2025)

Yoga Upanishad Series

1. *Yoga Chudamani Upanishad* by Swami Satyadharma 2003

2. *Yoga Tattwa Upanishad* by Swami Satyadharma
   translated by Ruth Perini 2015, 2018

3. *Yoga Darshana Upanishad* by Swami Satyadharma
   translated by Ruth Perini 2018

4. *Yoga Kundali Upanishad* by Swami Satyadharma
   translated by Ruth Perini 2019

5. *Nadabindu & Dhyanabindu Upanishads*
   by Swami Satyadharma, translated by Ruth Perini 2019

6. *Shandilya Upanishad* by Ruth Perini 2020

7. *Trishikhi Brahmanopanishad* by Ruth Perini 2021

8. *Advayataraka & Mandalabrahmana Upanishads*
   by Ruth Perini 2023

ISBN: 978-0-6489107-6-3

Dedication

To all friends, practitioners and teachers of yoga,

and to all seekers of spiritual wisdom, regardless

of time or place, creed, gender, age or race.

Yoga Upanishad Series *Volume 9*

Varaha Upanishad

The Path to Supreme Knowledge

Original Sanskrit text with

Transliteration, Translation

and Commentary

by Ruth Perini (Srimukti)

CONTENTS

		page
Introduction		1
Opening Invocation		9
FIRST CHAPTER		
Verses		
1.	Sage Ṛbhu's boon	10
2-4.	Twenty-four Tattvas	14
5-7.	Thirty-six Tattvas	16
8-11.	The Ninety-six Tattvas	18
15-17.	Knowledge of the Ninety-six Tattvas	22
SECOND CHAPTER		
Verses		
1-3.	The Transcendent Brahma Vidyā	24
4-6.	The Witnessing Consciousness	29
7-10.	Abode of Supreme Love	31
11-19.	The Ātman	34
20-28.	One's True Nature	40
29-31.	Direct Experience	44
32-38.	Meditation on the Self	47
39-44.	I Am Brahman	51
45-48a.	All Is Consciousness	54
48b-50a.	Bright Lamp of Ātman	57
50b-54.	The Illusive Power	59
55-57.	Non-dual Brahman	62
58-63.	Beyond Waking Dreaming Sleeping	64
64-65.	Mundane Existence	67
66-71a.	End of Delusion	69
71b-74.	Radiance of Consciousness	73
75-78.	Samādhi	76
79-83.	Dissolution	79
THIRD CHAPTER		
Verses		
1-5.	The Formless One Reality	82
6-8.	I Am That	85
9-10.	Unimpeded Bliss	87
11-13.	Freedom From Darkness	88
14-19.	What is the World?	90
20-24.	Root of the Mind	93
25-30.	Ātman Alone	96

FOURTH CHAPTER

Verses

1-2.	Definition of Jīvanmukti	99
3-5.	Virtuous Desire	106
6-9.	Abundance of Sattwa	108
10-13.	Devotion to the Natural State	111
14-15.	Seat of Deep Sleep	113
16-20.	Non-dual State	115
21-30.	Who is a Jīvanmukta?	118
31-33.	Śiva	123
34-42a.	The Two Paths	125
42b-44.	Knower of Brahman	130

FIFTH CHAPTER

Verses

1-3.	Knowledge of the Body	132
4-6a.	Aging of the Body	135
6b-9.	Uḍḍiyāṇa Bandha	137
10-12a.	The Three Yogas	140
12b-14.	Yamas and Niyamas	143
15-17.	Eleven Āsanas	145
18.	Prāṇāyāma	147
19-21.	The Subtle Body	149
22-27.	The Nāḍīs	151
28-31a.	Carriers of Vital Airs	154
31b-33a.	Flow of Nectar	157
33b-36.	Illusion of Time	159
37-40.	Union of Prāṇa and Apāna	162
42-45.	Saṃpuṭa Yoga	165
46-49.	Benefits of Saṃpuṭa Yoga	167
50-53.	Parā Śaktiḥ in Mūlādhāra	169
54-59a.	Prāṇa, the abode of the Jīva	171
59b-61a.	Kumbhaka	174
61b-68a.	Raising the Vital Air	176
68b-71a.	Three Kinds of Praṇava	180
71b-75.	Four States of Nāda Yoga	182

EPILOGUE 186

APPENDICES

Introduction

Veda is a Sanskrit word meaning 'knowledge'. In the context of the Vedas, it means 'revealed knowledge which is *śruti*, 'heard' from within, not taught. These ancient spiritual texts or hymns, through which we can learn much of the perceptions and insights of the early vedic seers, are grouped into four *samhitas* or collections: *Rig Veda, Yajur Veda, Sāma Veda* and *Atharva Veda*. They were revealed to enlightened beings 3,000 to 4,500 years ago or more (the Rig-Veda contains astronomical references describing occurrences in 5,000 to 3,000 BCE), and transmitted orally by the sages from generation to generation within brahmin families.

The four Vedas were considered to be divine revelations, and each word was carefully memorised. This was to ensure accurate transmission, but also because each syllable was considered to have spiritual power, its source being the supreme, eternal sound. This was a mammoth task, as there are 20,358 verses in the four Vedas, approximately two thousand printed pages. They were composed in fifteen different metres, which demanded perfect control of the breath. Georg Feuerstein describes them as 'a composite of symbol, metaphor, allegory, myth and story, as well as paradox and riddle' and their composers as 'recipients and revealers of the invisible order of the cosmos [with] inspired insights or illumined visions'1.

Rig Veda

The Rig Veda is the oldest spiritual text in the world and still regarded as sacred, containing 1,028 hymns or songs of 10,589 verses in praise of the divine (*rig* or *ric* meaning 'praise'). Each hymn is recognised as a *mantra*, a sacred sound vibration, which releases energy from limited material awareness, thus expanding the consciousness. It is also the earliest surviving form of Sanskrit. The illumined seers composed the hymns while established in the highest consciousness, thus able to commune with luminous beings of the higher realms. There are about 250 hymns in praise of *Indra*, the divine force behind the ocean, heavens, thunder, lightning, rain and the light of the sun; 200 of *Agni*, born of the Sun, becoming the god of sacrificial fire, and over 100 of *Soma*, who gives immortality, and who is connected to the Sun, Moon, mountains, rivers and oceans. Others are dedicated to *Varuna*, who protects cosmic order; the *Ashvins*, supreme healers; *Ushas*, goddess of the dawn; *Aditi*, goddess of eternity; and *Saraswati*, goddess of the Vedas and of music and the arts.

Yajur Veda

The hymns of the Yajur-Veda, Veda of Sacrifice, consist of sacrificial formulas or prayers, including those of an internal or spiritual nature, which are chanted by the *adhvaryu* (priest), who performs the sacrifice. About a third of its 1,975 verses are taken from the Rig Veda. The rest are original and in prose form.

Sāma Veda

The Sāma Veda, Veda of Chants, gives instructions on the chanting of vedic hymns. The majority of its 1,875 verses are from the Rig Veda; only 75 verses are original. Many of the hymns were sung by special priests during sacrificial rites. Some are still sung today.

Atharva Veda

The Atharva Veda, named after the seer Atharvan, whose family were great seers in vedic times, contains 731 hymns of 5,977 verses, about one fifth of which are from the RigVeda. Much of the Atharva Veda consists of magical spells and charms for gaining health, love, peace and prosperity, or taking revenge on an enemy. Possibly for this reason, the Atharva Veda was either not accepted by the orthodox priesthood, or not given the same standing as the other Vedas.

The vedic people and their culture

The vedic people lived for over 2,500 years mainly along the banks of the Saraswati River, which was located in Northern India between the modern Ravi and Yamuna Rivers down to what is now the desert of Rajasthan. The Saraswati River dried up in about 1,900 BCE due to tectonic upheavals. Other areas of habitation included the Ganges River and its tributaries, rivers in Afghanistan (previously called Gandhara), the Himalayas and Mount Kailash in Tibet.

The vedic people had a complex multi-tiered view of the universe, in which humankind, nature and the divine are intertwined and interrelated. They had a deep knowledge of the oceans, mountains, deserts and forests of the physical world, as well as of the subtle worlds of deities and different levels of consciousness. People lived in cities or villages or were nomads, and were fully engaged in worldly life. They were an agrarian people, yet also had herds of cattle, horses and camels. Cities were constructed of stone, bricks and metal. They built chariots and ships. They were skilled workers in gold, metal, clay, stone, wood, leather and wool, and showed a very high standard in arts, crafts, astrology, medicine, music, dance and poetry.

After the Vedas

The Vedas were the foundation for the later revelations (*śruti*) in the *Brāhmaṇas* (ritual texts), the *Āranyakas* (texts on rituals and meditation for forest-dwelling ascetics) and the *Upaniṣads* (esoteric texts). Later still, the Vedas were the basis for numerous works of remembered or traditional knowledge, known as *smṛti,* including the epics: i.e. the *Mahābhārata, Rāmāyaṇa* and *Purāṇas,* and the *Sūtras,* or threads of knowledge, e.g. *Yoga Sūtras.* All these texts contain many concepts and practices, which come directly from the four Vedas.

Upaniṣads

The word *upaniṣad* is comprised of three roots: *upa* or 'near', *ni* or 'attentively', and *sad,* 'to sit'. The term describes the situation in which these unique texts were transmitted. The students or disciples sat near the realized master and listened attentively, as he expounded his experiences and understanding of the ultimate reality. These teachings are said to destroy the ignorance or illusion of the spiritual aspirant in regard to what is self and non-self, what is real and unreal, in relation to the absolute and relative reality. Only disciples were chosen, who had persevered in *sādhana catuṣṭaya*, the four kinds of spiritual effort, viz. *viveka* (discrimination between the permanent and impermanent), *vairagya* (non-attachment), *ṣadsampatti* (six virtues of serenity, self-control, withdrawal of the senses, endurance, perfect concentration and strong faith) and *mumukṣutva* (intense desire for liberation).

The Upaniṣads are derived from the Āranyakas, because they were chanted in the forest (*āranya*) after the aspirant had retired from worldly life. They are recorded in the later form of Sanskrit used in the Brāhmaṇas, and considered the last phase of *śruti*, vedic revelation. The Upaniṣads are regarded as *vedānta*, the end of the Vedas, inferring that *vedānta* is the end or completion of all perceivable knowledge, as they guide the aspirant beyond the limited mind to the *ātman* (spiritual self) and thus to *mokṣa* (liberation). Each upaniṣad reflected the teachings and tradition of a realized master, and was connected with a specific Veda and vedic school. It is estimated that there are over 200 Upaniṣads, which have been divided into seven groups: *Major*, *Vedānta*, *Śaiva, Śakta, Vaiśnava, Sannyasa* and *Yoga.*

Yoga Upaniṣads

The twenty-one Yoga Upaniṣads give an understanding of the hidden forces in nature and human beings, and describe esoteric yogic practices by which these forces can be manipulated and controlled. They emphasise that the inner journey to the one permanent reality, the *ātman*, is the essential one. Journeys to external places, such as holy sites and temples, as well as rituals and ceremonies, are not given importance. Their teachings give important information on the subtle body (*cakras, koṣas, prāṇa, kuṅḍalinī,* meditative states), and the tantric and yogic techniques, not given in the earlier upaniṣads, to attain them. Therefore, they are regarded as a significant integration of Vedanta and Tantra, which were previously considered incompatible. They are classified as 'minor' only because they postdate Adi Shankara.

Although their teachings actually predate Patañjali, the Yoga Upaniṣads were codified after the *Yoga Sūtras of Patañjali,* and form an important part of the classical yoga literature. However, they contain no references to Patañjali or his *Yoga Sūtras*. So, although the compilation of the Yoga Upaniṣads is post-Patañjali, the *vidyās*, or meditative disciplines, contained within them are pre-Patañjali. The Yoga Upaniṣads emerged at a time when the vedic and tantric cultures were coming together to share their knowledge. The wise thinkers from each culture sat down together and discussed how their insights and teachings could be combined in order to benefit humanity. Thus these upanisads combine the teachings of both tantra and yoga. It is evident in them that yoga leads to vedānta, and vedānta leads to yoga. However, they were written down by vedantic scholars and practitioners in order to show that these *vidyās* and related practices were not borrowed from Patañjali, but were known and practised from the ancient period.

Within the twenty-one Yoga Upaniṣads are six sub-groups which have their own main focus. The *Bindu Upaniṣads*, which include the *Amṛta-Bindu* (also known as the *Brahma-Bindu-Upaniṣad*), *Amṛta-Nada-Bindu*, *Nada-Bindu*, *Dhyāna-Bindu* and *Tejo-Bindu-Upaniṣads*, all concentrate on the bindu, the source or origin of all sound, and hence of creation. Bindu represents the transcendental sound manifested in the mantra *Aum*. The *Hamsa-Mantra*, *Soham*, is the main practice of the *Hamsa*, *Brahma-Vidya*, *Mahavakya* and *Paśupata-Brahma-Upaniṣads*. Concentration on *prāṇa*, the life force related to the process of inhalation and exhalation, brings the yogin to the knowledge of the transcendental self. The light of pure consciousness, which the enlightened irradiate, is the theme of the *Advaya-Taraka* and *Maṅḍala-Brahmana-Upaniṣads*. The *Kṣurika-Upaniṣad* (*kṣurika* meaning 'dagger') emphasises non-attachment as a means to liberation. The sixth group, comprised of eight late Yoga Upaniṣads from 1200 to 1300 A.D., covers teachings related to hatha and kundalini yogas. They are the *Yoga-Kuṅḍalī, Yoga-Tattwa, Yoga-Śikhā, Varāha, Śāndilya, Tri-Śikhi-Brahmana, Yoga-Darśana* and *Yoga-Chūdāmani Upaniṣads.*

Varāha-Upaniṣad

Varāha-Upaniṣad is said to have been composed between the 13th and 16th centuries CE. It is one of the thirty-two *Kṛṣṇa Yajurveda Upaniṣads*.

In the first chapter the sage Ṛbhu asks Viṣṇu in his incarnation as the Boar to explain the supreme knowledge of Brahman. Viṣṇu defines the 96 tattwas which make up the world starting with the sensory organs, organs of action, the vital airs, the mind, then the elements, states of consciousness, changes in existence, sheaths, qualities and enemies of the mind, the jīva, guṇas and the karmas, and finally stating that those who worship Him become liberated.

In the second chapter Ṛbhu asks Viṣṇu to reveal to him the transcendent Brahma Vidyā, knowledge of the Ātman, which is our true nature. This is the Advaita Vedānta theme of the Upanishads - that we are all pure consciousness. Viṣṇu says that the way is to fulfil one's duties, please the guru, and practise the spiritual virtues and disciplines. Eventually one should identify with the Self, the witnessing consciousness.

The third chapter describes the nature of the formless One Reality, the indivisible sat (being, existence) cit (awareness, consciousness) ānanda (happiness, bliss), not limited in space, time and object. Practising in silence 'I am That' removes suffering. Viṣṇu exhorts Ṛbhu to worship his feet to attain the light and freedom of liberation, where there is no beginning or ending.

The fourth chapter commences with the definition of Jīvanmukti, describing the seven stages of wisdom, all of which, according to Vedānta, have been achieved by a jīvanmukta. This chapter also includes the topic of the Ultimate Reality in the Mandukyopanishad. Praṇava is Om, composed of the three sounds A, U and M which symbolize the gross, subtle and causal aspects of Brahman. Two approaches to liberation are described: that of the bird, as followed by the sage Śuka, and that of the ant, as followed by the sage Vāmadeva. The former course leads to instant liberation, whereas the latter results in gradual liberation.

The theme of the fifth chapter is Yoga, presented as a discussion between Ṛbhu and his student Nidāgha. Vedantic methods, such as 'I am That', are supported by the yogic methods of calming the mind through meditation, yama, niyama, prāṇāyāma, āsana, bandha and Bhakti Yoga. In the calm mind the difference between consciousness and thoughts becomes obvious. The three yogas of laya, haṭha and mantra are recommended. Verses 22 to 68 are devoted to the subtle body, viz. the nāḍīs, vital airs, cakras and the raising of the kuṇḍalinī. The chapter concludes with a description of the four states of Nāda Yoga, viz. ārambha, ghaṭa, paricaya and niṣpatti.

वराह उपनिषद्
Varāha-Upaniṣad

Opening Invocation

श्रीमद्वाराहोपनिषद्वद्याखङ्डसुखाकृति ।

त्रिपान्नारातणाख्यं तद्रामचन्द्रपदं भजे ।।१।।

ॐ सहनाववत्विति शानति ।।

śrīmadvarāhopaniṣadvadyākhaṅḍasukhākṛti
tripānnārāyaṇākhyaṃ tadrāmacandrapadaṃ bhaje (1)
Om sahanāvavatviti śāntiḥ

Vocabulary
bhaje: I worship; *rāmacandra-padam*: name Rāmacandra; *akhyam*: called; *tripāt-nārāyaṇa*: triple Narāyaṇa; *kṛti*: causing; *akhaṅḍa*: endless; *sukha*: joy; *vadya*: words; *śrīmad*: holy; *varāhopaniṣad*: Varāha-Upaniṣad; *iti*: saying thus; *saha nau avavatu*: may we both have; *śāntiḥ Om*: peace of Om.

Translation
I worship the name Rāmacandra, called the triple Narāyaṇa, causing endless joy in the words of the holy Varāha-Upaniṣad. Saying thus, may we both have the peace of Om.

|| प्रथमोऽध्यायः ||

prathamo'dhyāyaḥ

First Chapter

Verse 1: Sage Ṛbhu's boon

हरिः ॐ ।

अथ ऋभुर्वै महामुनिर्देवमानेन द्वादशत्सरं तपश्चार ।

तदवसाने वराहरूपी भगरान्प्रादुरभूत ।

स होवाचोत्तिष्ठोत्तिष्ठ वरं वृणेष्वेति ।

सोदतिष्ठत् ।

तस्मै नमस्कृत्योवाच भगवन्कामिभिर्यद्यत्कामितं

तत्तत्त्वत्सकाशात्स्वप्नेऽपि न याचे ।

समस्तवेदशास्त्रेतिहासपुराणानि समस्त्विद्याजालानि

ब्रह्मादयः सुराः सर्वे त्वद्रूपज्ञान्मुकतिमाहुः ।

अतस्त्वद्रूपप्रातिपदिकं ब्रह्मविद्यां ब्रूहीति होवाच ।

तथेति स होवाच वराहरूपी भगवान् ।

चतुर्विंशतितत्त्वानि केचिदिच्छन्ति वादिनः ।

केचित्षद्त्रिंशत्तत्त्वानि केचित्षण्णवतीनि च ||१||

atha Ṛbhurvai mahāmunirdevamānena dvādaśavatsaraṃ
tadvasāne varāharūpī bhagavānprādurabhūt
sa hovācottiṣṭhottiṣṭha varaṃ vṛṇeṣeti
sodatiṣṭhat
tasmai namaskṛtyovāca bhagavankāmibhiryadyatkāmitaṃ
tattattvatsakāśātsvapne'pi na yāce
samastavedaśāstretihāsapurāṇāni samastvidyājālāni
brahmādayaḥ surāḥ sarve tvadrūpajñānānmuktimāhuḥ
atastvadrūpaprātipadikaṃ brahmavidyaṃ brūhīti hovāca
tatheti sa hovāca varāharūpī bhagavān

caturviṃśatitattvāni kecidicchanti vādinaḥ
kecitṣadtriṃśattattvāni kecitṣaṇṇavatīni ca (1)

Vocabulary

atha: now; *mahāmuniḥ Ṛbhuḥ*: great sage Ṛbhu; *cāra*: wandered; *tapaḥ*: austerities; *dvādaśavat-saram*: for a period of twelve years; *deva-mānena*: in honour of the gods; *tadvasāne*: at the end of that time; *bhagavān*: Lord; *prādurabhūt*: appeared before; *varāha-rūpī*: form of a boar; *sa ha uvāca*: he said; *uttiṣṭha*: arise; *vṛṇeṣu*: you may choose; *varam*: boon; *sa-udatiṣṭhat*: he arose; *namskṛti*: bowing down; *tasmai*: to him; *uvāca*: he said; *na yāce*: I will not ask for; *yadyat*: whatever; *kāmitam*: is desired; *kāmibhiḥ*: by the worldly; *api*: even if; *tattvatsakāśāt*: it appears; *svapne*: in a dream; *samasta*: all; *veda-śāstra-itihāsa-purāṇāni*: Vedas, Śāstras, Itihāsas and Purāṇas; *sarve*: all; *āhuḥ*: say; *muktim*: liberation; *jñānāt*: from knowledge; *tvat-rūpa*: your true nature; *ataḥ*: so; *brūhi-iti*: explain; *brahma-vidyam*: supreme knowledge of Brahma; *prātipadikam*: expresses; *ha uvāca*: thus he spoke.

tatheti: very well; *varāha-rūpī bhagavān*: boar-shaped Lord; *kecit*: some; *icchanti vādinaḥ*: like to assert; *caturviṃśati-tattvāni*: twenty-four elements; *ṣadtriṃśat-tattvāni*: thirty-six elements; *ca ṣaṇṇavatīni*: and ninety-six.

Translation

Now the great sage Ṛbhu wandered about [performing] austerities for a period of twelve years in honour of the gods. At the end of that time the Lord appeared before [him] in the form of a boar.

He [the Lord] said: “Arise, arise! You may choose a boon!”

He arose. Bowing down to Him he said: “O Lord, I will not ask for whatever is desired by the worldly, even if it appears in a dream. All the Vedas, Śāstras, Itihāsas and Purāṇas [and] mass of spiritual knowledge, from Brahma and divine beings, all say [that] liberation [comes] from the knowledge of your true nature. So [please] explain the supreme knowledge of Brahman [which] expresses your nature." Thus he spoke.

"Very well," said the boar-shaped Lord. "Some like to assert [that there are] twenty-four elements, some thirty-six and some ninety-six.

Commentary
Ṛbhu was a Vaiṣṇava sage, said to be a direct son of Brahma. His non-dualist teaching is included in the *Viṣṇu-Purāṇa.*

Viṣṇu is the second deity of the *Trimurti*. Brahma, the creator, is the first deity, and Śiva, the transformer is the third. The name Viṣṇu means 'pervader', as he pervades and maintains everything in the universe.

He is the the Supreme Consciousness, who is everywhere, pervading everything and everyone, maintaining and supporting the whole world, often depicted 'in his formless state resting on the cosmic serpent Ananta, Lord Shesha, floating in the infinite ocean of unmanifest existence' [1] becoming one of ten physical forms at times of crisis.

His ten incarnations (*avatāra*, descent) are *Matsya* (fish), *Kurma* (tortoise), *Varāha* (boar), *Narasimha* (man-lion), *Vāmana* (dwarf), *Paraśu Rāma* (Rāma with the ax), *Rāma* (also called Rāmacandra), *Kṛṣṇa* (Krishna), *Buddha* (awakened one) and *Kalki* (base one).

This upaniṣad takes place during his incarnation as Varāha, the boar, whose 'mission was to destroy the demon Hiranyākṣa (Golden-Eyed) who had flooded the entire Earth'.[2]

It was considered that it took twelve years of constant self-discipline and austerities to eliminate the inner impurities. According to the *Haṭha Yoga Pradīpikā*:

'The yogi who meditates on the Self, takes moderate and pure food and practises *siddhāsana* for twelve years, attains perfection.' [3]

'Of all the eighty-four *āsanas*, *siddhāsana* should always be practised. It purifies the 72,000 *nāḍīs*.' [4]
Siddhāsana is a cross-legged seated position, where the heel of the left foot presses the perineum and the heel of the right foot presses the pubis.

Because Ṛbhu has completed this process, Viṣṇu offers him a boon. Ṛbhu wants nothing worldly, only the freedom that comes from realising one's own true nature.

Over the next fifteen verses Viṣṇu describes in detail the composition of the human body and mind and their functions and capabilities.

Verses 2 to 4: Twenty-four Tattvas

तेषां क्रं प्रवक्ष्यामि सावधानमनाः शृणु ।
ज्ञानेन्द्रियाणि पञ्चैव श्रोत्रत्वग्लोचनादयः ॥२॥
कर्मेन्द्रियाणि पञ्चैव वाक्पाण्यङ्घ्र्यादयः क्रमात् ।
प्राणादतस्तु पञ्चैव पञ्च शब्दादयस्तथा ॥३॥
मनोबुद्धिरहंकारश्चित्तं चेति चतुष्टयम् ।
चतुर्विंशतितत्त्वानि तानि ब्रह्मविद् विदुः ॥४॥

teṣāṃ kraṃ pravakṣyāmi sāvadhānamanāḥ śṛṇu
jñānendriyāṇi pañcaiva śrotratvaglocanādayaḥ (2)
karmendriyāṇi pañcaiva vākpāṇyaṅghryādayaḥ kramāt
prāṇādayastu pañcaiva pañca śabdādayastathā (3)
manobuddhirahaṃkāraścittaṃ ceti catuṣṭayam
caturviṃśatitattvāni tāni brahmavid viduḥ (4)

Vocabulary

pravakṣyāmi: I shall relate; *teṣāṃ kraṃ*: in their order; *śṛṇu*: listen; *sāvadhāna-manāḥ*: with an attentive mind; *pañca jñānendriyāṇi*: five sensory organs; *śrotra*: ear; *tvac*: skin; *locana*: eye; *ādayaḥ*: and so on; *kramāt*: in order; *pañca karmendriyāṇi*: five organs of action; *vāk*: mouth; *pāṇi*: hand; *aṅghri*: foot; *tu*: then; *pañca prāṇa-ādayaḥ*: five vital airs beginning with; *śabda-ādayaḥ*: sound and the others; *manas*: rational, perceptive mind; *buddhi*: discerning intuitive mind; *ahaṃkāra*: individual self; *ca*: and; *citta*: seat of consciousness; *iti*: are; *catuṣṭayam*: four; *viduḥ*: knows; *tāni caturviṃśati-tattvāni*: these twenty-four principles; *brahma-vit*: knows Brahman.

Translation

I shall relate [them] in their order. Listen with an attentive mind. [There are] five sensory organs: ear, skin, eye and so on. [There are] in order five organs of action: mouth, hand, foot and so on; then five vital airs beginning with sound and the others [are] five. *Manas, buddhi, ahaṃkāra* and *citta* are four. [Whoever] knows these twenty-four principles knows Brahman.

Commentary

Having agreed to explain the supreme knowledge of Brahma, Viṣṇu urges Ṛbhu to listen attentively. This is called *śravaṇa*, 'attentive listening to the sacred teachings, followed by pondering (*manana*)'[5]. It is the first limb of Bhakti Yoga, and the sixth *niyama* (internal discipline) in the second limb of the eightfold path of yoga.

'Tattva' translates as 'that-ness'. It means the essence, truth, reality or principle of something or part of it. The *Śiva-Samhitā* states that 'when all the tattvas have disappeared then the tattva itself becomes manifest'[6], which is the essence of the self, one's true nature.

These verses list the tattvas or components of the human being. They are the five sensory organs, viz. ears, skin, eyes, tongue and nose; the five organs of action, viz. vocal cords, hands, feet, genital organ and anus; the five vital airs, viz. *prāṇa* which moves up from the diaphragm to the larynx, *apāna* which moves down from the navel to the perineum, *udāna* which moves in the arms, legs and head, *samāna* which moves sideways between the navel and perineum, and *vyāna*, the reserve of pranic energy moving through the whole body; and the four components of the individual mind, viz. perception, discernment, individual identity and the seat of all layers of consciousness.

Verses 5 to 7: Thirty-six Tattvas

एतैस्तत्त्वैः समं पञ्चीकृतभूतानि पञ्च च ।
पृथिव्यापस्तथा तेजो वायुराकाशमेव च ।।५।।
देहत्रयं स्थूलसुक्ष्मकारणानि विदुर्बुधाः ।
अवस्था त्रितयं चैव जाग्रत्स्वप्न सुषुप्तयः ।।६।।
आहत्य तत्त्वजातानां षट्त्रिंशन्मुनयो विदुः ।
पूर्वोक्तैस्तत्त्वजातैस्तु समं तत्त्वानि योजयेत् ।।७।।

etaistattvaiḥ samaṃ pañcīkṛtabhūtāni pañca ca
pṛthivyāpastathā tejo vāyurākāśameva ca (5)
dehatrayaṃ sthūlasukṣmakāraṇāni vidurbudhāḥ
avasthā tritayaṃ caiva jāgratsvapna suṣuptayaḥ (6)
āhatya tattvajātānāṃ ṣaṭtriṃśanmunayo viduḥ
pūrvoktaistattvajātaistu samaṃ tattvāni yojayet (7)

Vocabulary

budhāḥ: wise; *viduḥ*: know; *samam*: as well as; *etaiḥ-tattvaiḥ*: these principles; *pṛthivi*: earth; *āpaḥ*: water; *tejaḥ*: fire; *vāyuḥ*: air; *ca ākāśam*: ether; *ca dehatrayam*: and three bodies; *sthūla*: gross; *sukṣma*: subtle; *kāraṇāni*: causal; *tritayam*: three; *avasthā*: states of consciousness; *jāgrat*: waking; *svapna*: dreaming; *ca suṣuptayaḥ*: sleeping; *munayaḥ*: sages; *viduḥ*: know; *āhatya*: total; *tattva-jātānām*: collection of *tattvas*; *ṣaṭ-triṃśat*: thirty-six; *yojayet*: combined; *jātaiḥ*: with the collection; *ukta*: spoken of; *pūrva*: previously.

Translation

The wise know [that] as well as these principles [there are] five quintuplicated elements: earth, water, fire, air and ether; three bodies: gross, subtle [and] causal; and three states of consciousness: waking, dreaming and sleeping. The sages know [that] the total collection of *tattvas* is thirty-six. These principles are combined with the collection spoken of previously.

Commentary

Viṣṇu adds another twelve tattwas to the list of twenty-four totalling thirty-six.

Earth has the quality of weight, solidity and cohesion; water has the quality of fluidity; air has the quality of constant movement; fire has the quality of heat; and ether has the quality of emptiness and space.

Every object consists of the gross, that is, it can be perceived by the senses; the subtle, which is the energy flowing through it; and the causal, its unmanifest creative source.

The living being fluctuates between one of these three states of consciousness: waking, dreaming or sleeping. The sages abide in the fourth state, *turīya*, where they are both aware of and transcend the other three states.

Verses 8 to 14: The Ninety-six Tattvas

षद्भावविकृतिश्चास्ति जायते वर्धतेऽपि च ।
परिणामं क्षयं नाशं षड्भावविकृतिं विदुः ।।८।।
अशना च पिपासा च शोकमोहै जरा मृतिः ।
एते षडूर्मयः प्रोक्ताः षट्कोशानतह वच्मि ते ।।९।।
त्वक्च रक्तं मांसमेदोमज्जास्थानी निबोधत ।
कामग्रोधै लोभमोहै मदो मात्सर्यमेव च ।।१०।।
एतेऽरिषड्वा विश्वश्च तैजसः प्राज्ञ एव च ।
जीवत्रयं सत्त्वरजस्तमांसि च गुणज्ञयम् ।।११।।
प्रारब्धागामीसञ्चितानि कर्मत्रयमितीरितम् ।
वचनादानगमनविसर्गानन्दपञ्चकम् ।।१२।।
संकल्पोऽध्यवशयश्च अभिमानोऽवधारणा ।
मुदिता करुणा मैत्री उपेक्शा च चतुष्टयम् ।।१३।।
दिवाकरप्रचेतोऽश्विनौवह्नीन्द्रेपेन्द्रमुत्युकाः ।
तथा चन्द्रश्चतुर्वक्त्रो रुद्रः क्षेत्रज्ञ ईश्वरः ।।१४।।

ṣaḍbhāvavikṛtiścāsti jāyate vardhate'pi ca
pariṇāmaṃ kṣayaṃ naśaṃ ṣaḍbhāvavikṛtiṃ viduḥ (8)
aśanā ca pipāsā ca śokamohai jarā mṛtiḥ
ete ṣaḍūrmayaḥ proktāḥ ṣaṭkośānatha vacmi te (9)
tvakca raktaṃ māṃsamedomajjāsthānī nibodhata
kāmagrodhai lobhamohai mado mātsaryameva ca (10)
ete'riṣaḍvā viśvaśca taijasaḥ prājña eva ca
jīvatrayaṃ sattvarajastamāṃsi ca guṇajñayam (11)
prārabdhāgāmīsañcitāni karmatrayamitīritam
vacanādānagamanavisargānandapañcakam (12)
saṃkalpo'dhyavasāyaśca abhimāno'vadhāraṇā
muditā karuṇā maitrī upekśā ca catuṣṭayam (13)
divākarapraceto'śvinauvahnīndrependramṛtyukāḥ
tathā candraścaturvaktro rudraḥ kṣetrajña īśvaraḥ (14)

Vocabulary

ca-asti: and there are; *ṣaḍ-bhāva-vikṛtiḥ*: six changes in existence; *jāyate*: one is born; *ca api*: and also; *vardhate*: grows; *viduḥ*: wise; *ṣaḍ-bhāva-vikṛtiṃ*: six changes in existence; *pariṇāmam*: transformation; *kṣayam*: decay; *nāśam*: destruction; *nibodhata*: know; *ṣaṭkośān*: six sheaths; *tvag*: skin; *raktam*: blood; *māṃsa*: flesh; *medaḥ*: fat; *majjāsthāni*: marrow in bones; *kāma*: passion; *krodhai*: anger; *lobha*: greed; *mohai*: delusion; *madāḥ*: pride; *ca mātsaryam*: and jealousy; *ete vā*: these indeed; *ṣaḍ ari*: six enemies; *trayam*: three [parts]; *jñayam*: known as.

iti-īritam: it is said; *karma-trayam*: three karmas; *vacana*: talking; *ādāna*: grasping; *gamana*: walking; *visarga*: voiding; *ānanda*: sensual pleasure; *pañcakam*: five; *saṃkalpaḥ*: volition; *adhyavasāyaḥ*: perseverance; *abhimānaḥ*: arrogance; *avadhāraṇā*: determination; *ca catuṣṭayam*: and this set of four; *muditā*: sympathetic joy; *karuṇā*: compassion; *maitrī*: friendliness; *upekśā*: indifference; *dik*: direction; *vāta*: wind; *ārka*: Sun; *pracetaḥ*: Varuṇa; *aśvinau*: *-kāḥ*: subtle forms of; Aśvins; *vahni*: Agni; *indra*: Indra; *Upendra*: Upendra; *mṛtyu*: Death; *tathā*: then; *candra*: Moon; *caturvaktraḥ*: Brahma; *kṣetrajñaḥ*: knower of the soul; *īśvaraḥ*: higher consciousness.

Translation

And [within the tattwas] there are six changes in existence. One is born and also grows. The wise [know that] in the six changes in existence, [there are] transformation, decay and destruction. Hunger, thirst, pain, delusion, age and death are said to be the six waves of existence. Know [that] the six sheaths are skin, blood, flesh, fat marrow [and] bones. Passion, anger, greed, delusion, pride and jealousy, these are indeed the six enemies. *Viśva*, *Taijasaḥ* and *Prājña* [are] the three [parts] of the *jīva*. *Sattva*, *rajas* and *tamas* are known as the *guṇas*.

It is said [that] *prārabdha*, *āgāmī* [and] *sañcita* [are] the three karmas. Talking, grasping, walking, voiding [and sensual] pleasure [are] the five [actions]; volition, perseverance, arrogance, determination, and this set of four: sympathetic joy, compassion, friendliness [and] indifference; [four] directions, Vāyu, Sun, Varuṇa, Aśvins, Agni, Indra, Upendra and Mṛtyu; then the Moon, Brahma, Rudra, Kṣetrajña [and] Īśvara.

Commentary

The theme of these verses is impermanence, and all that is outside is also inside: macrocosm mirrored in the microcosm. Any change in a tattva is listed as a tattva in its own right.

There are six stages in the human life cycle: birth, childhood, adolescent, adult, old age and death. The six sufferings are hunger, thirst, grief, delusion, age and death. The body is made up of six components: skin, blood, flesh, fat marrow and bone. The six enemies of the mind are lust, anger, greed, delusion, arrogance and jealousy, which prevent us seeing the light of our true nature.

The triad of *jīvas* includes Viśva, Taijasaḥ and Prājña. They are the witnesses who experience the different states of consciousness. Viśva is the seer or witness of the waking state. Tejas is the seer of the dreaming state in which are the subtle dimensions of consciousness. Prajnā, the seer of the state of deep sleep, is aware of the causal dimensions of consciousness.

The three *guṇas* manifest in the *divya loka*, the divine plane beyond time and space. They pervade all nature in both a mundane and pure form. Verse 11 refers to their mundane form. *Sattva* is attachment to goodness and knowledge; *rajas* is attachment to activity and competition; *tamas* is attachment to dullness and inertia. In their transcendental state, sattva is luminosity, rajas is creativity and tamas is total stillness. 'The three gunas also correspond to experiences: waking or conscious state; dreaming or subconscious state, neither awake nor asleep; deep sleep, no awareness of the world, senses, name, form or idea.'[7]

Prārabdha karmas are past actions, the consequences of which materialise in the present life. *Āgāmī karmas* are current actions, the consequences of which will take place in the future. *Sañcita karmas* are all actions done in previous births, a portion of which is allotted to bear fruit in each birth. Actions, emotions and thoughts are tattvas, and have karmic consequences.

The remaining tattvas are the four directions and the Vedic deities who are within the human body, *viz.* 'Vāyu (air, ear), Sun (light, eye), Varuṇa (water, tongue), Aśvins (nose), Agni (fire),' Indra (mind, soul), Upendra (Viṣṇu), Mṛtyu (decay), Moon (nectar of immortality), Brahma (creation), Rudra (transformation through dissolution), Kṣetrajña (knower of the soul) and Īśvara (higher consciousness).

Verses 15 to 17: Knowledge of the Ninety-six Tattwas

आहत्य तत्त्वजातानां षण्णवत्यस्तु कीर्तिताः ।
पूर्वोक्ततत्त्वजातानां वैलक्षण्यमनामयम् ।।१५।।
वराहरूपिणं मां ये भजन्ति मयि भक्तिः ।
विमुक्ताज्ञतत्कार्या जीवन्मुक्ता भवन्ति ते ।।१६।।
ये षण्णवतितत्त्वज्ञा यत्र कुत्राश्रमे रतः ।
जटी मुण्डी शिकही वापि मुच्यते नात्र संशयः ।।१७।।

āhatya tattvajātānāṃ ṣaṇṇavatyastu kīrtitāḥ
pūrvoktatattvajātānāṃ vailakṣaṇyamanāmayam (15)
varāharūpiṇaṃ māṃ ye bhajanti mayi bhaktiḥ
vimuktājñānatatkāryā jīvanmukta bhavanti te (16)
ye ṣaṇṇavatitattvajña yatra kutrāśrame rataḥ
jaṭī muṇḍī śikhī vāpi mucyate nātra saṃśayaḥ (17)

Vocabulary
āhatya: altogether; *astu kīrtitāḥ*: there are said to be; *jātānām*: aggregate; *ṣaṇṇavati tattva*: ninety-six tattvas; *ye*: those who; *bhajanti*: worship; *mām*: me; *bhaktiḥ*: devotion; *mayi*: in me; *varāha-rūpiṇam*: form of the boar; *anāmayam*: without disease; *vailakṣaṇyam*: diverges from; *pūrvokta*: aforesaid; *tattva-jātānām*: aggregate of tattwas; *tat-kāryā*: this having been done; *te bhavanti jivanmukta*: they become *jīvanmuktas*; *vimukta-ajñāna*: freed from ignorance; *ye jña*: those who know; *ṣaṇṇavati tattva*: ninety-six tattvas; *rataḥ*: intent; *yatra kurta-āśrame*: on whichever stage of life; *jaṭī*: matted; *muṇḍī*: shaven; *va-api*: or even; *śikhī*: tuft; *na saṃśayaḥ*: without a doubt; *mucyate*: become liberated; *atra*: here.

Translation
Altogether there are said to be an aggregate of ninety-six tattvas. Those who worship me [with] devotion in me [as] the

form of the boar, [who], without disease, diverges from the aforesaid aggregate of tattwas, this having been done, they become *jīvanmuktas*, freed from ignorance. Those who know the ninety-six tattvas, intent on whichever stage of life, [their hair] matted, shaven or even [in] a tuft, without a doubt become liberated here.

Commentary

Viṣṇu, as the boar, is beyond all categories of existence. Whoever worships him in this incarnation, devoid of ignorance and suffering, becomes liberated, a *jīvanmukta*, in this lifetime, irrespective of stage and role in life.

Definitions of a *jīvanmukta*: 'a soul who is liberated while living; purified by true knowledge of the supreme reality, is freed from future births and all ceremonial rites while yet embodied; in Vedanta, who has experienced all 7 stages of wisdom (*jñāna bhūmikā*)' [8].

Swami Satyananda uses the word *vivekakhyāti*, right knowledge. He says:
'Vivekakhyati brings about consciousness of seven stages, each one higher than the previous one. Prantabhumi means a particular range or province. It appears that during the process of vivekakhyati the purusha or consciousness passes through different stages of experience. Those experiences are contemplative: firstly, realization of what is to be avoided; secondly, awareness of the means for that removal; thirdly, awareness of spiritual evolution; fourthly, awareness of fulfilment and accomplishment; fifthly, awareness of the purpose of experience and liberation; sixthly, awareness of the fulfilment of the work of the gunas; lastly, awareness of one's own self. Through these seven stages, a higher kind of awareness is developed which is called vivekakhyati.'[9]

||द्वितीयोऽध्यायः||

dvitīyo 'dhyāyaḥ

Second Chapter

Verses 1 to 3: The Transcendent Brahma Vidyā

ऋभुर्नाम महायोगी क्रोडरूप रमापतिम् ।
वरिष्ठां ब्रह्मविद्यां त्वमधीहि भगवन्मम ।
एवं स पृष्टो भगवान्प्राह भक्तार्तिभञ्जनः ||१||
स्ववर्णाश्रमधर्मेण तपसा गुरुतोषणात् ।
साधनं प्रभवेत्पुंसा वैराग्यदिचतुष्टयम् ||२||
नित्यानित्यविवेकश्च इहामुत्र विरागता ।
शमादिषड्कसंपत्तिर्मुमुक्षा तां समभ्यसेत् ||३||

ṛbhurnāma mahāyogī kroḍarūpa ramāpatim
variṣṭhāṃ brahmavidyāṃ tvamadhīhi bhagavanmama
evaṃ sa pṛṣṭo bhagavānprāha bhaktārtibhañjanaḥ (1)
svavarṇāśramadharmeṇa tapasā gurutoṣaṇāt
sādhanaṃ prabhavetpuṃsā vairāgyādicatuṣṭayam (2)
nityānityavivekaśca ihāmutra virāgatā
śamādiṣaṅkasaṃpattirmumukṣā tāṃ samabhyaset (3)
evaṃ jitendriyo bhūtvā sarvatra mamatāmatim
vihāya sākṣicaitanye mayi kuryādahaṃmatim (4)

Vocabulary
mahāyogī: great yogin; *ṛbhuḥ-nāma*: called Ṛbhu; *ramā-patim*: husband of Lakshmi; *kroḍa-rūpa*: form of a boar; *bhagavan*: o Lord; *tvam*: you; *adhīhi*: please reveal; *mama*: to me; *variṣṭhām brahmavidyām*: transcendent Brahma Vidyā; *pṛṣṭaḥ*: having been asked; *evam*: thus; *bhagavān*: Lord; *bhañjanaḥ*: removes; *bhakta-ārti*: suffering of devotees; *prāha*: instructed; *dharmeṇa*: through one's duty; *sva-varṇa-āśrama*: one's caste and stage of life; *tapasā*:

through austerity; *guru-toṣaṇāt*: through the act of pleasing the *guru*; *catuṣṭayam sādhanam*: four spiritual disciplines; *vairagya-ādi*: non-attachment etc; *prabhavet*: arise; *puṃsā*: in person; *vivekaḥ*: discrimination; *nitya-anitya*: permanent and impermanent; *virāgatā*: indifference; *ihāmutra*: in this world and others; *ṣaṅka-saṃpattiḥ*: six virtues; *śama-ādi*: equanimity etc; *mumukṣā*: desire for final liberation; *samabhyaset tām*: one should practice these.

Translation

The great yogin called Ṛbhu [asked] the spouse of Lakshmi in the form of a boar: "O Lord, please reveal to me the transcendent Brahma Vidyā". Having been asked thus, the Lord, [who] removes the suffering of his devotees, instructed: "Through one's duty [according to] caste [and] stage of life, through austerity [and] through the act of pleasing the *guru*, the four spiritual disciplines, non-attachment etc, arise in a person. [They are] discrimination [between] the permanent and impermanent, indifference to [what is] in this world and others, the six virtues, equanimity etc, [and] the desire for final liberation. One should practise these.

Commentary

Brahma-vidyā means knowledge of the Absolute, the rare state of self-realisation.

The Absolute is pure consciousness without qualities, and, according to Vedānta, the essence of the human being, the True Self, which can only be realised by transcending the mind. Self-realisation is not a cognitive process or mere experience. The True Self is not the limited ego personality. It is the transcendental Reality synonymous with enlightenment or liberation.

Lakṣmī is the spouse of Viṣṇu. She was born from the ocean, and is loved for her auspicious and beautiful nature.

Similarly, Viṣṇu, out of compassion for the suffering of those who are ignorant of their True Self, agrees to teach Ṛbhu the way to Self-realisation.

Viṣṇu says that first one has to do one's duty according to one's caste and stage of life, self-discipline, and through service and obedience to the *guru*, and meditation on the guru. The four principal castes are priest (*brāhmaṇa*), warrior or ruling class (*kṣatriya*), merchant (*vaiṣya*) and servant (*śudra*).[10] The four stages of life are studentship (*brahmacarya*), householdership (*gṛhastha*), forest dwelling (*vānaprastha*) and complete renunciation (*saṃnyāsa*). *Āśramadharma* are the special duties of each order of life. [11]

The first two spiritual disciplines are *nitya-anitya viveka*, discrimination between the eternal and the transient; and *vairagya*, non-attachment, dispassion towards that which is unreal. Viveka and vairagya are the two wings of the bird which soars to liberation.

The third is the group of *ṣat sampatti*, six virtues/attainments. They are *śama*, control of the mind when the mind is fixed on its aim; *dama*, control of the senses; *uparati*, withdrawal from or non-dependence of the mind on anything external, the ability to internalise; *titikṣā*, forebearance, endurance without complaint; *śraddha*, faith, unwavering belief in the scriptures and the guru's teaching; *samādhāna*, perfect establishment of the higher mind (buddhi) in Brahman (the expanding reality). This combination of six virtues can halt the fluctuations of the mind, eventually controlling it, so that it becomes calm, and free from anger, greed and hatred.

The fourth is *mumukśutvā*, intense longing for freedom from *ahaṃkāra* (limited sense of self which attaches us to the body) by realising one's true nature.

Swami Sivananda recommends ways to strengthen the spiritual disciplines. For all of them daily practice and dispassion are necessary.

Śama: For mind control one should destroy vicious desires by developing virtuous desires, then reduce them to one strong desire. 'Peace is in the heart of a desireless person who has controlled the senses and the mind.'[12] Practise the *yamas* and *niyamas*, as well as *prāṇāyama* which weakens *rajas* and *tamas*, making the mind steady and one-pointed. Bhakti yoga: 'in this Kali Yuga the easiest way to control the mind and emotions and attain serenity is kirtan or singing the name of the Lord.' Cultivate the sattwic qualities of compassion, universal love and patience. Sattwic food. Be the witness to the thoughts as they come and go without identifying with them. Think positive thoughts. [13]

Dama: Observing silence controls the organs of speech. Practising trataka, gazing at a point, helps to control the eyes. Use the senses in a spiritual way. Listen to kirtan, chanting. Eating simple food will help to control the tongue, the organ of taste. Walking barefoot helps to discipline the skin, the organ of touch. Fix the mind on the *ishta devata*. Practise contentment.

Uparati: When one has grasped viveka, vairagya, śama and dama, the mind naturally loses interest in objects of sensual desire and enjoyment - it comes naturally. Practise *pratyāhāra*, withdrawal of the senses from sense objects, necessary for concentration.

Titikṣa: 'The power of endurance develops the willpower. The ability to face difficulties with calm endurance in pleasure and pain, heat and cold, is one of the most essential qualifications for an aspirant on the path of *samatvam*, equanimity. Every difficult that comes is an opportunity to grow stronger and to develop the will.'p.41 It must be practised with discrimination, dispassion and faith.

Śraddha: Faith and trust in the spiritual teachings are crucial to spiritual life. Faith is not irrational. The sages understood that the True 'Reality lies beyond reason, beyond the mind (*manas*), even beyond illumined reason or wisdom (*buddhi*).'[14] Thus they have shown practical ways to transcend the limitations of the individual self.

'One should practise these' *abhyāsa*: practice, repetition. 'The *Śiva-Samhitā* (4.9) declares: "Through practice comes perfection; through practice one will attain liberation."[15]

Verses 4 to 6: The Witnessing Consciousness

एवं जितेन्द्रियो भूत्वा सर्वत्र ममतामतिम् ।
विहाय साक्षिचैतन्ये मयि कुर्यादहंमतिम् ॥४॥
दुर्लभं प्राप्य मानुष्यं तत्रापि नरविग्रहम् ।
ब्राह्मण्यं च महाविष्णोर्वेदान्तश्रवणादिना ॥५॥
अतिवर्णाश्रं रूपं सच्चिदानन्दलक्षणम् ।
यो न जानाति सोऽविद्वान्कदा मुक्तो भविष्यति ॥६॥

evaṃ jitendriyo bhūtvā sarvatra mamatāmatim
vihāya sākṣicaitanye mayi kuryādahaṃmatim (4)
durlabhaṃ prāpya mānuṣyaṃ tatrāpi naravigraham
brāhmaṇyaṃ ca mahāviṣṇorvedāntaśravavaṇādinā (5)
ativarṇāśraṃ rūpaṃ saccidānandalakṣaṇam
yo na jānāti so'vidvānkadā mukto bhaviṣyati (6)

Vocabulary

bhūtvā: having become; *jitendriyaḥ*: one who has control over the senses; *vihāya*: given up; *matim*: concept; *mamatā*: mine; *sarvatra*: at all times; *aham*: I; *kuryāt*: should be; *mayi*: in me; *sākṣi-caitanye*: witnessing consciousness; *prāpya*: having attained; *durlabham*: with great difficulty; *mānuṣyam*: human state; *api*: even; *nara-vigraham*: form of a man; *yaḥ*: whoever; *na jānāti*: does not learn; *vedānta-śravavaṇa-ādinā*: through hearing *vedānta* and others; *mahā-viṣṇuḥ*: great Viṣṇu; *rūpam*: form; *ati-varṇa-āśram*: beyond caste and stage of life; *kadā*: when; *saḥ*: he; *vidvān*: ignorant; *bhaviṣyati*: will become; *muktaḥ*: liberated.

Translation

Having become one who has control over the senses [and] given up the concept [of] 'mine' at all times, [your] concept [of] 'I' should be in me, the witnessing consciousness. Having attained with great difficulty the human state, even in the form of a man [who is] a *brāhmaṇa*, whoever does not learn, through hearing *vedānta* and others, the goal of existence-consciousness-bliss, the great Viṣṇu, [as] the form beyond caste and stage of life, when will he, ignorant, become liberated?

Commentary

Having incarnated as a human in this lifetime, fulfilled one's duty to guru, family and role in life, developed the above disciplines and attainments, and now conquered the senses, one should renounce the limited self-identity, and identify with the Self, the ātman, the witnessing consciousness.

Swami Satyananda in his commentary on the Ishavasya Upanishad defines *sat-cit-ānanda* thus: *sat*: 'that which is, was and will never cease to exist'; *cit*: 'consciousness, supreme principle, the force which is conscious'; *ānanda*: expression of the Supreme, blossoming. [16]

Swami Sarvapriyananda describes the difference between pure consciousness and reflected consciousness. 'Vedānta says as long as we identify with the reflected consciousness, we are trapped in samsāra – as long as you emphasise the erroneous identification with the reflected consciousness and all its activities and relationships. Only when you negate that identification with the reflected consciousness, do you see that 'I am pure consciousness; I am of the nature of pure consciousness and completely unattached'. How do you negate it? I am not that. I am the witness of that. You can drop the thoughts of everything, and still be aware. That awareness is pure consciousness. Negation of error.' [17]

Verses 7 to 10: Abode of Supreme Love

अहमेव सुखं नान्यदन्यच्चेत्रैव तत्सुखम् ।
अमदर्थं न हि प्रेयो मदर्थं न स्वतः प्रियम् ॥७॥
परप्रेमास्पदतया मा न भूवमहं सदा ।
भूयासमिति यो द्रष्टा सोऽहं विष्णुर्मुनीश्वर ॥८॥
न प्रकाशोऽहमित्युक्तिर्यत्प्रकाशैकबन्धना ।
स्वप्रकाशं तमात्मानमप्रकाशः कथं स्पृशेत् ॥९॥
स्वयं भातं निराधारं ये जानन्ति सुनिश्चितम् ।
ते हि विज्ञानसंपन्ना इति मे निश्चिता मतिः ॥१०॥

ahameva sukhaṃ nānyadanyaccetraiva tatsukham
amadarthaṃ na hi preyo madarthaṃ na svataḥ priyam (7)
parapremāspadatayā mā na bhūvamahaṃ sadā
bhūyāsamiti yo draṣṭā so'haṃ viṣṇurmunīśvara (8)
na prakāśo'hamityuktiryatprakāśaikabhandhanā
svaprakāśaṃ tamātmānamaprakāśaḥ kathaṃ spṛśet (9)
svayaṃ bhātaṃ nirādhāraṃ ye jānanti suniścitam
te hi vijñānasaṃpannā iti me niścitā matiḥ (10)

Vocabulary

aham-eva: I alone; *sukham*: happiness; *na-anyat-anyat*: nothing else; *cetraiva*: if there is; *hi*: then; *tat-sukham*: that happiness; *amadartham*: not for my sake; *na preyaḥ*: not dear; *madartham*: for my sake; *na svataḥ*: not for oneself; *priyam*: dear; *para-prema-āspadatayā*: because [I am] the abode of Supreme Love; *bhūvam*: existence; *na mā*: not mine; *saḥ yaḥ*: one who; *āsam sadā bhūya*: I have always been; *aham*: I am; *viṣṇuḥ-muni-īśvara*: Viṣṇu-silent witness-Supreme Consciousness.

katham: how; *aprakāśaḥ*: non-light; *spṛśet*: can touch; *tam-ātmānam*: that ātman; *svaprakāśam*: with its own light; *yat uktiḥ*: this statement; *aham*: I; *na prakāśaḥ*: not the light;

bhandhanā: is produced; *prakāśa-eka*: one light; *ye jānanti*: those who know; *suniścitam*: with certainty; *svayaṃ bhātam*: my own light; *nirādhāram*: without support; *hi saṃpannā*: indeed endowed with; *vijñāna*: supreme wisdom; *iti*: this is; *me niścitā matiḥ*: my definite conviction.

Translation

I alone [am] happiness, nothing else. If there is, then that happiness [which is] not for my sake is not dear [to me]. [That happiness which is] for my sake [and] not for oneself is dear [to me]. Because [I am] the abode of Supreme Love, existence is not mine. I am one who has always been. I am Viṣṇu, the silent witness, the Supreme Consciousness.

How can the non-light touch that ātman with its own light? This statement 'I am not the Light' is produced [by] the one Light. Those who know with certainty [that I am] my own light, without support, are endowed with supreme wisdom. This is my definite conviction.

Commentary

The only true permanent happiness is through Viṣṇu. All other happiness is temporary and, dependent on external circumstances, is easily swayed by other emotions, such as anxiety, sadness, fear etc.

To know the ātman, Swami Satyadharma in *Yoga Kundali Upanishad* says to 'meditate on your own ātman, the pure consciousness, resting in the body, like a light inside a jar, until just the essence remains. Think of the ātman as the size of your thumb. See or imagine it as a form of light, without any emanation of smoke, shining within. Unchangeable, imperishable and eternal.' [18]

Swami Satyananda says: 'Once one attains enlightenment through the process of yoga, there is no darkness in any realm of life. There is no ignorance, the light within becomes very clear. The light is very quiet, there is tranquillity, no tension, and everything id full of bliss. In fact, when you have attained the light of enlightenment it can be seen; you do not have to prove that you have it.' [19]

'Vishnu is also associated with the Vaishvanara form of Agni as the spiritual light within the heart or Narayana.' [20]

Verses 11 to 19: Ātman is Brahman

स्वपूर्णात्मातिरेकेण जगज्जीवेश्वरादयः ।
नसन्ति नास्ति माया च तेभ्यश्चाहं विलक्षणः ।।११।।
अज्ञानान्धतमोरूप कर्मधर्मादिलक्षणं ।
स्वयंप्रकाशात्मानं नैव मां स्प्रष्टुमर्हति ।।१२।।
सर्वसाक्षिणमात्मानं वर्णाश्रमविवर्जितम् ।
ब्रह्मरूपतया पश्यन्ब्रह्मैव भवति स्वयम् ।।१३।।
भासमानमिदं सर्वं मानरूपं परं पदम् ।
पश्यन्वेदान्तमानेन सद्य एव विमुच्यते ।।१४।।
देहात्मज्ञानवज्ज्ञानं देहात्मज्ञानबाधकम् ।
आत्मन्येव भवेद्यस्य स नेच्छन्नापि मुच्यते ।।१५।।
सत्यज्ञानान्दपूर्णालक्षणं तमसः परम् ।
ब्रह्मानन्दं सदा पश्यन्कथं बध्ये कर्मणा ।।१६।।
त्रिधामसाक्षिणं सत्यज्ञानानन्दादिलक्षणां ।
तवमहंशब्दलक्ष्यार्थमसक्तं सर्वदोषता ।।१७।।
सर्वगं सत्चिदात्मानं ज्ञानचक्षुर्निरीक्षते ।
अज्ञानचक्षुर्नेक्षेत भास्वन्तं भानुमन्धवत् ।।१८।।
प्रज्णानमेव तद्ब्रह्म सत्रप्रज्ञानलक्षणम् ।
एवं ब्रह्मपरिज्ञानादेव मर्त्योऽमृतो भवेत् ।।१९।।

svapūrṇātmātirekeṇa jagajjīveśvarādayaḥ
na sānti nāsti māyā ca tebhyaścāhaṃ vilakṣaṇaḥ (11)
ajñānāndhatamorūpa karmadharmādilakṣaṇam
svayaṃprakāśātmānaṃ naiva māṃ sprasṭumarhati (12)
sarvasākṣiṇamātmānaṃ varṇāśramavivarjitam
brahmarūpatayā paśyanbrahmaiva bhavati svayam (13)
bhāsamānamidaṃ sarvaṃ mānarūpaṃ paraṃ padam
paśyanvedāntamānena sadya eva vimucyate (14)

dehātmajñānavajjñānaṃ dehātamajñānabādhakam
ātmanyeva bhavedyasya sa necchannāpi mucyate (15)
satyajñānānandapūrṇālakṣaṇaṃ tamasaḥ param
brahmānandaṃ sadā paśyankathaṃ bahye karmaṇā (16)
tridhāmasākṣiṇaṃ satyajñānānandādilakṣaṇam
tavamahaṃśabdalakṣyārthamasaktaṃ sarvadoṣatā (17)
sarvagaṃ saccidātmānaṃ jñānacakṣurnirīkṣate
ajñānacakṣurnekṣeta bhāsvantaṃ bhānumandhavat (18)
prajñānameva tadbrahma satyaprajñānalakṣaṇam
evaṃ brahmaparijñānādeva martyo 'mṛto bhavet (19)

Vocabulary

ātma-atirekeṇa: with the exception of; *sva-pūrṇa*: complete by itself; *jagat*: world; *jīva*: living beings; *īśvara*: Supreme Lord; *ādayaḥ*: and others; *na sānti*: do not exist; *ca na-asti*: and nor does exist; *aham*: I; *tebhyaḥ*: those; *vilakṣaṇaḥ*: characteristics; *rūpa*: form; *andha-tamaḥ*: intense darkness; *ajñāna*: ignorance; *lakṣaṇam*: character; *karma-dharma-ādi*: *karma* [and] *dharma* etc; *na eva arhati*: does not deserve; *sprаṣṭum mām*: to touch me; *svayam-prakāśā-ātmānam*: self-shining ātman; *paśyan*: seeing; *sarva-sākṣiṇam-ātman*: ātman, witness of all; *vivarjitam*: free from; *varṇa-aśrama*: caste and life stages; *brahma-rūpatayā*: in the formation of Brahman; *bhavati*: one becomes; *brahma svayam*: Brahman oneself; *paśyan*: seeing; *vedānta-mānena*: through the testament of Vedānta; *idam*: this; *bhāsa-mānam*: appearance of light; *sarvam mānarūpam*: whole form; *paraṃ padam*: Supreme Seat; *sadya*: instantly; *vimucyate*: one is liberated;

yasya: whoever; *bādhakam*: refuting; *jñānavat*: knowledge of the kind; *deha-ātma*: ātman in the body; *bhavet*: has; *jñānam*: knowledge; *ātmani-eva*: of the ātman alone; *mucyate*: refuting; *api*: even if; *na icchan*: not desiring; *sadā*: always; *paśyan*: seeing; *lakṣaṇam*: nature; *satya-jñāna-ānanda-pūrṇā*: truth knowledge bliss fullness; *tamasaḥ*: from darkness; *param ānandam*: supreme bliss; *brahma*: Brahman; *katham*: how; *badhyeta*: can one be bound; *karmaṇā*: by karma; *jñāna-cakṣuḥ*: eyes of spiritual wisdom; *nirīkṣate*: perceives; *sarvagaṃ saccidātmānam*: omnipresent spirit; *sākṣiṇaṃ*: witness; *tridhāma*: three states; *lakṣaṇam*: characteristics; *satya-jñāna-ānanda-ādi*: truth wisdom bliss and so on; *ajñāna-cakṣuḥ*: eyes without spiritual wisdom; *na-īkṣeta*: does not see; *bhāsvantaṃ bhānumandhavat*: radiant light of the splendour of the sun; *prajñānam-eva*: supreme knowledge alone; *tat-brahma*: that Brahman; *lakṣaṇam*: characteristics; *satya-prajñāna*: truth wisdom; *parijñānāt-eva*: only through knowing; *brahma evam*: Brahman thus; *martyaḥ*: mortal; does become; *amṛtaḥ*: immortal.

Translation

With the exception of the ātman [which is] complete by itself, the world [of] living beings, the Supreme Lord and others do not exist and nor does *māyā* exist. I do not have those characteristics. [Whatever has] the form of the intense darkness of ignorance in the character of *karma* [and] *dharma* etc does not deserve to touch me, the self-shining ātman. Seeing the ātman, the witness of all, free from caste and life stages, in the formation of Brahman, one becomes Brahman oneself. Seeing through the testament of Vedānta this appearance of light [as] the whole form of the Supreme Seat, one is instantly liberated.

Whoever, refuting knowledge of the kind [that] the ātman [is] in the body, has knowledge of the ātman alone is liberated even if not desiring [it]. Always seeing the nature of truth, knowledge, bliss and fullness [which is furthest] from darkness, the supreme bliss of Brahman, how can one be bound by karma? [One who has] the eyes of spiritual wisdom perceives the omnipresent spirit [as] the witness of the three states, with the characteristics [of] truth, wisdom, bliss and so on, [which is] the inner meaning of the words 'your' [and] 'I' [and] detached from all faults. [One whose] eyes are without spiritual wisdom does not see the radiant light of the splendour of the sun. Supreme knowledge alone [is] that

Brahman [with] the characteristics of truth [and] wisdom. Only through knowing Brahman thus, does a mortal become immortal.

Commentary

Swami Satyananda, in his introduction to the *Aitareya Upanishad*, says:

'As stated in the Vedas, in the beginning there is no creation except Atman, and that creation is willed by Him only. This whole universe is nothing but the projection of His will based on pure consciousness; therefore consciousness is Brahman. He has made it, right from Indra, the ruler of the gods, and Prajapati, the protector, to the smallest gross creation. He is everywhere but devoid of all characteristics of the world, such as names, forms, activities, waking, dreaming, and deep sleep states. He is fearless, decayless and deathless. To attain the Absolute, which is the chief aim of life, is not possible by any means other than true knowledge of the secondless Self. One possessing a deep, direct realisation of this Atman obtains immortality.' [21]

In this context Īśvara is the Supreme Lord who is powerful and capable, and therefore with attributes. What is *māyā*, usually translated as illusion? Swami Niranjan describes māyā as 'a combination or symptom of the two experiences of pain and pleasure, which we encounter in our external life and in our mental and emotional life. The whole life experience is also considered to be false and unreal, because the spiritual traditions have believed the soul to be beyond the experiences of pain and pleasure. They have described the soul as the real nature, the real identity of an individual, which is not subject to birth or death, decay or disease.' [22]

'The experiences of pain and pleasure are known as māyā. The *vrittis* are aspects of māyā, wrong or false notions about self identity. The pain and pleasure that one experiences in life are transitory. Despite that, there is total identification, we are under their total influence.' [23] 'Without māyā, the ego reality ceases to exist.' [24]

Karma is 'law of cause and effect that shapes the destiny of each individual with actions inevitably bearing their fruit as the law operates inexorably throughout the universe.'[25] In this context 'karma means the primal seed of desire. The concept of karma which has evolved is that this primal seed of desire guides the destiny, thought, action and behaviour of every individual.' [26]

Dharma is one's duty, the role one plays in life. It is one of the *purusharthas*, the four goals of human life, *viz. dharma, artha* (material support), *kama* (sensory enjoyment) and *moksha* (final liberation). Viṣṇu says '*dharma* etc does not deserve to touch me, the self-shining ātman', as he is the Supreme Self, who, like the sun, makes his own light and is beyond human roles and duties.

Usually we see only the surface of objects, including people and events. Few have the inner perception to see through the layers to the depths. This perception binds us to māyā. Swami Satyananda says: 'Beyond the body there is the mind, and beyond the mental personality there is the higher spirituality. The higher spirituality is always operating, it is always there. It is never absent in us, even if we are unaware of it. We breathe 24 hours a day, our heart is unconsciously beating, but we are unconscious of it.' [27]

Knowledge of the higher consciousness is spoken of in the following upaniṣads.

The *Ishavasya Upanishad* says in verses 6 and 7:
'He who constantly sees all beings in the Higher Self, or in the spiritual consciousness, and the Self in all beings, does not hate.'

‘When all beings become one in one’s own higher consciousness, then what delusion and what grief is there for one who is constantly seeing oneness?’ [28]

The *Muṇḍaka-Upanishad* says:
'The knot of the heart is released of he who is a realiser of the Self, the higher and lower Brahman; all doubts disappeared, all karmas vanished.' [29]

Spiritual wisdom is compared with the sun by Swami Niranjananda and David Frawley.

‘To attain, to have the knowledge of the luminous atma is the esoteric aspect of yoga.’ ‘Surya Tantra is the way to see, realise and know the vitality and and energy hidden in the sun; the sun is the lens through which part of the radiance of the atman is seen, as it is a symbol of the surce of light, vitality and energy.’ [30]

‘Brahma, Vishnu and Shiva are identified with the three aspects of solar energy as creating, sustaining, and transforming the universe. Vishnu, the preserver, is worshipped as the Sun, particularly as *Surya-Narayana*, the Sun as the cosmic person who enters into the hearts of all beings. Brahma, the Creator, has a solar aspect. Shiva, the transformer, is honored as the Supreme deity behind the Sun, particularly as Rudra, who represents the highest light and colour of the Sun.' [31]

Verses 20 to 28: One's True Nature

तद्ब्रह्मानन्दमद्वन्द्वं निर्गुणं सत्यचिद्धनम् ।
विदित्वा स्वात्मनो रूपं न बिभेति कुश्चन ॥२०॥
चिन्मात्रं सर्वगं नित्यं संपूर्णं सुखमद्वयम् ।
साक्षाद्ब्रह्मैव नान्योऽस्तीत्येवं ब्रह्मविदां स्थितिः ॥२१॥
अज्ञास्य दुःखौघमयं ज्ञास्यानन्दमयं जगत् ।
अन्धं भुवनमन्धस्य प्रकाशं तु सुचक्षुषाम् ॥२२॥
अनन्ते सच्चिदानन्दे मयि वाराहरूपिणि ।
स्थितेऽद्वितीयभावः स्यात्को बन्धः कष्च मुच्यते ॥२३॥
स्वरूपं तु चिन्मात्रं सर्वदा सर्वदेहिनाम् ।
नैव देहादिसंघातो घटवद्दृशिगोचरः ॥२४॥
स्वात्मनोऽन्यदिवाभातं चराचरमिदं जगत् ।
स्वात्ममात्रतया बुद्ध्वा तदस्मीति विभावय ॥२५॥
स्वस्वरूपं स्वं भुङ्क्ते नास्ति भोज्यं पृथक् स्वतः ।
अस्ति चेदस्तितारूपं ब्रह्मैवास्तित्वलक्षणम् ॥२६॥
ब्रह्मविज्ञानसंपन्नः प्रतीतमखिलं जगत् ।
पश्यन्नपि सदा नैव पश्यति स्वात्मनः पृथक् ॥२७॥
मत्स्वरूपपरिज्ञानात्कर्मभिर्न स बधयते ॥२८॥

tadbrahmānandamadvandvaṃ nirguṇaṃ satyaciddhanam
viditvā svātmano rūpaṃ na bibheti kuścana (20)
cinmātraṃ sarvagaṃ nityaṃ saṃpūrṇaṃ sukhamadvayam
sākṣādbrahmaiva nānyo'stītyevaṃ brahmavidāṃ sthitiḥ (21)
ajñāsya duḥkhaughamayaṃ jñāsyānandamayaṃ jagat
andhaṃ bhuvanamandhasya prakāśaṃ tu sucakṣuṣām (22)
anante saccidānande mayi vārāharūpiṇi
sthite'dvitīyabhāvaḥ syātko bandhaḥ kaṣca mucyate (23)
svarūpaṃ tu cinmātraṃ sarvadā sarvadehinām

naiva dehādisaṃghāto ghaṭavaddṛśigocaraḥ (24)
svātmano'nyadivābhātaṃ carācaramidaṃ jagat
svātmamātratayā buddhvā tadasmīti vibhāvaya (25)
svasvarūpaṃ svayaṃ bhuṅkte nāsti bhojyaṃ pṛthak svataḥ
asti cedastitārūpaṃ brahmaivāstitvalakṣaṇam (26)
brahmavijñānasaṃpannaḥ pratītamakhilaṃ jagat
paśyannapi sadā naiva paśyati svātmanaḥ pṛthak (27)
matsvarūpaparijñānātkarmabhirna sa badhayate (28)

Vocabulary

viditvā: knowing; *sva-ātmanaḥ*: one's own ātman; *rūpam*: form; *tat*: that; *advandvam*: non-dual; *brahma-ānandam*: bliss of Brahman; *nirguṇam*: without qualities; *dhanam*: possessing; *satya-cit*: true consciousness; *na bibheti cana*: does not fear any; *kuś*: threat.

sthitiḥ: conviction; *brahmavidām*: of knowers of Brahman; *evam*: thus; *sākṣāt*: clearly; *na-ānyaḥ astīti*: there is nothing else; *eva*: only; *cinmātram*: consciousness alone; *sarvagam*: all-pervading; *nityam*: eternal; *saṃpūrṇam*: complete; *sukham-advayam*: ultimate joy; *jagat*: material world; *duḥkha-augha-mayam*: is a flood of suffering; *ajñāsya*: to the ignorant; *ānanda-mayam*: full of bliss; *jñāsya*: to the wise; *bhuvanam*: earth; *andhasya*: is dark; *andham*: blind; *tu*: but; *prakāśam*: bright; *sucakṣuṣām*: to those with good vision; *sthite*: has faith; *mayi*: in me; *vārāha-rūpiṇi*: in the form of a boar; *anante*: infinite; *sat-cit-ānande*: existence consciousness bliss; *syāt*: is; *advitīya-bhāvaḥ*: non-dual state; *kaḥ bandhaḥ*: what is bondage; *ca*: and; *kaḥ mucyate*: who is to be liberated; *svarūpam*: true nature; *sarva-dehinām*: of all bodies; *sarvadā*: always; *cinmātram*: consciousness alone; *deha-ādi-saṃghātaḥ*: combination of the body and its parts; *na eva*: is not; *ghaṭavat*: like a pot; *gocaraḥ*: perceived; *dṛśi*: through the eyes; *buddhvā*: knowing; *idam*: this; *carācaram*: moving and fixed; *jagat*: world; *bhātam*: appears as; *anyat-iva*: other than; *sva-ātmanaḥ*: one's own Self; *svātma-mātratayā*: not more or less than one's own ātman; *vi-*

bhāvaya: reflect on; *tat-asmi*: That I am; *bhuṅkte*: one enjoys; *svayam*: by oneself; *svasvarūpam*: one's own real form; *na asti*: there is no; *bhojyam*: enjoyment; *pṛthak*: apart from; *svataḥ*: one's own Self; *cet asti*: if there is; *astitā-rūpam*: form of reality; *brahma-eva*: Brahman alone; *astitva-lakṣaṇam*: attribute of reality; *saṃpannaḥ*: endowed with; *brahma-vijñāna*: knowledge of Brahman; *api paśyan*: even when seeing; *akhilam*: whole; *pratītam*: recognised; *jagat*: world; *na sadā*: never; *paśyati*: sees; *pṛthak*: apart; *svātmanaḥ*: from one's ātman; *pari-jñānāt*: through complete knowledge; *mat-svarūpa*: my form; *sa na badhayate*: one is not bound; *karmabhiḥ*: by *karma.*

Translation
Knowing one's own ātman [as] the form [of] that non-dual bliss of Brahman, without qualities, possessing true consciousness, one does not fear any threat.

The conviction of the knowers of Brahman [is] thus: clearly there is nothing else, only Brahman, consciousness alone, all-pervading, eternal, complete [and] ultimate joy. The material world is a flood of suffering to the ignorant [and] full of bliss to the wise, [just as] the earth is dark to the blind but bright to those with good vision. [Whoever] has faith in me, in the form of a boar, infinite existence, consciousness, bliss, is in the non-dual state. [Therefore] what is bondage and who is to be liberated?

The true nature of all bodies is always consciousness alone. The combination of the body and its parts is not like a pot perceived through the eyes. Knowing [that] this moving and fixed world appears as [something] other than one's own Self, [yet is] not more or less than one's own ātman, reflect on 'That I am'. One enjoys by oneself one's own real form. There is no enjoyment apart from one's own Self. If there is a form of reality, [then] Brahman alone [has] the attribute of reality. One who is endowed with knowledge of Brahman, even when seeing the whole recognised world, never sees [it] apart from one's ātman. Through complete knowledge [of] My form, one is not bound by karma.

Commentary

Swami Satyananda quotes from the *Katha Upanishad* (111:10) which defines the state of resting in one's true nature thus: 'When the five senses of perception together with the mind are at rest, when even the intellect has ceased to function, that, say the sages, is the supreme state.' 'This is the state where there is complete absence of both external and internal mental modifications; all that remain is awareness.' [32]

Swami Satyadharma defines our true nature as 'the transcendental state of consciousness, in which all barriers and limitations of the conscious, subconscious and unconscious are removed. In samādhi the consciousness is one indivisible field, total and complete. Within this totality of consciousness, all knowledge exists'.

'The Sanskrit term for this totality of consciousness in the individual is *ātman*, the soul or the self. The Rishi describes the ātman as eternal, which means it is the one permanent reality, unaffected by change, by time and space, or by birth and death. This ātman, this pure consciousness, within each individual, is the same as the pure consciousness everywhere, on all the planes of existence, whether manifest or unmanifest. Being the basis or the substratum of all beings and all existence, the ātman is in itself unchangeable and devoid of any faults or imperfections.

Being the state of perfect oneness, the ātman differs from the limited states of consciousness, by which the relative worlds of duality, dreams and illusions are perceived. But there is no differentiation within its own transcendental state.'[33]

Verses 29 to 31: Direct Experience

यः शरीरेन्द्रियादिभ्यो विहीनं सर्वसाक्षिणम् ।
परमार्थैकविज्ञानं सुखात्मानम् स्वयम्प्रभम् ॥२९॥
स्वस्वरूपतया सर्वं वेद स्वानुभवेन यः ।
स धीरः स तु विज्ञेयः सोऽहं तत्त्वं ऋभो भव ॥३०॥
अतः प्रपञ्चानुभवः सदा न हि स्वरूपबोधानुभवः
सदा खलु ।
इति प्रपश्यन्परिपूर्णवेदनो न बन्धमुक्तो न च बद्ध
एव तु ॥३१॥

yaḥ śarīrendriyādibhyo vihīnaṃ sarvasākṣiṇam
paramārthaikavijñānaṃ sukhātmānaṃ svayam-prabham (29)
svasvarūpatayā sarvaṃ veda svānubhavena yaḥ sa dhīraḥ sa tu vijñeyaḥ so'haṃ tattvaṃ ṛbho bhava (30)
ataḥ prapañcānubhavaḥ sadā na hi svarūpabodha-anubhavaḥ sadā khalu
iti prapaśyanparipūrṇavedano na bandhamukto na ca baddha eva tu (31)

Vocabulary

yaḥ veda: whoever knows; *vihīnam*: free from; *śarīra-indriya-ādi-bhyaḥ*: sense organs and body; *sarva-sākṣiṇam*: witness of all; *eka-vijñānam*: one knowledge; *paramārtha*: highest truth; *svayam-prabham*: self-shining; *sukhātmānam*: blissful ātman; *yaḥ sva-anubhavena*: whoever through one's own direct experience; *sva-svarūpatayā*: state of one's true nature; *sa vijñeyaḥ*: that [one] should be known; *dhīraḥ*: courage; *ṛbho bhava*: O Ṛbhu, become; *so'ham*: I am; *tattvam*: That; *ataḥ*: hence; *prapaśyan*: understanding; *anubhavaḥ*: perception; *prapañca*: visible world; *na sadā*: not always; *khalu*: true; *hi anubhavaḥ*: indeed the experience; *svarūpa-bodha*: realisation of one's true form; *paripūrṇa-*

vedana: full knowledge; *na . . na ca eva*: neither nor at all; *bandha-muktaḥ*: liberated from bondage; *baddha*: bound.

Translation

Whoever knows [Brahman] free from sense organs and body, witness of all, the one knowledge [of] the highest truth, the self-shining blissful ātman, whoever [knows this] through direct experience the state of one's true nature, that [one] should be known as [a person of] courage. O Ṛbhu, become 'I Am That'. Hence, understanding [that] the perception of the visible world is not always true, indeed the experience of the realisation of one's true form [is] always [true and possessing] full knowledge [of the ātman], one is neither liberated from bondage nor at all bound.

Commentary

The phrase 'a person of courage' is used to describe the yogin because the spiritual path is like the razor's edge. One has to give up all one's attachments, to go to the unknown place beyond the senses – all our life we have depended on the senses for security, our comfort and joy, we depend on them. We live through the five senses for food and protection, and also experience through them pleasure and pain.

The *Bhagavad Gita* in Chapter 3, *The Yoga of Action* says: 'There is no point in restraining one's senses, while constantly engaging in thoughts about sensory objects and pleasures.' Vs6
'Great is the man who can control his senses and do his karma without any attachment.' Vs.7

How to become the witness of all? How to identify with pure consciousness, the Ultimate Reality, and not the activities of the mind, *cidābhāsa*, the reflected consciousness which is continually changing? Swami Sivananda says the way to *svarupasthiti*, being established in one's true nature, is by entering into silence. 'Silence is Atman. Silence is Brahman. Silence is centre. Silence is the *hṛdaya-guhā* (heart-cave). That is Brahman. When the mind is controlled fully, Vrittis cease. When all the modifications subside, you enter into the silence then and then alone. Realise this, this very moment. Feel the divine glory and Brahmic splendour now by closing the eyes, by withdrawing the *indriyas* (sense organs), by stilling the mind, by silencing the thoughts, by sharpening the intellect, by purifying the *citta*, by meditating on Om, by chanting Om with *bhāva* (feeling). Keep up the continuity of Brahmic consciousness throughout the 24 hours. Have an unceasing flow of Atmic consciousness. This is very, very important.'[35]

'One is neither liberated from bondage nor at all bound' means that one has transcended the duality of bondage and its opposite. The *Bhagavad Gita* in Chapter 3 says:
'Brahman, which is beginningless and endless and which is ruled by me, is beyond cause and effect.'[36]

Verses 32 to 38: Meditation on the Self

स्वस्व रूपानुसंधानान्नृत्यन्तं सर्वसाक्षिणम् ।
मुहूर्तं चिन्तेन्मां यः सर्वबन्धैः प्रमुच्यते ।।३२।।
सर्वभूतान्तरस्थाय नित्यमुक्तचिदात्मने ।
प्रत्यक्चैतन्यरूपाय मह्यमेव नमोनमः ।।३३।।
त्वं वाहमस्मि भगवो देवतेऽहं वै त्वमसि ।
तुभ्यं मह्यमनन्ताय मह्यं तुभ्यं चिदात्मने ।।३४।।
नमो मह्यं परेशाय नमस्तुभ्यं शिवाय च ।
किं करोमि क्व गच्छमि किं गृह्णामि त्यजामि किम् ।।३५।।
यन्मया पूरितं विश्वं महाकल्पाम्बुना यथा ।
अन्तःसङ्गं बहिःसङ्गमात्मसङ्गं च यस्त्यजेत् ।
सर्वसङ्गनिवृत्तात्मा स मामेति न संशयः ।।३६।।
अहिरिव जनयोगं सर्वदा वर्जयेद्यः कुणपमिव
सुनारीं त्यक्तुकामो विरागी ।
विषमिव विषयादीन्मन्यमानो दुरन्ताञ्जगति
परमहंसो वासुदेवोऽहमेव ।।३७।।
इदं सत्यमिदं सत्यं सत्यमेतदिहोच्यते ।
अहं सत्यं परं ब्रह्म मत्तः किंचिन्न विद्यते ।।३८।।

svasva rūpānusaṃdhānānnṛtyantaṃ sarvasākṣiṇam
muhūrtaṃ cintayenmāṃ yaḥ sarvabandhaiḥ pramucyate (32)
sarvabhūtāntarasthāya nityamuktacidātmane
pratyakcaitanyarūpāya mahyameva namonamaḥ (33)
tvaṃ vāhamasmi bhagavo devate'haṃ vai tvamasi
tubhyaṃ mahyamanantāya mahyaṃ tubhyaṃ cidātmane (34)
namo mahyaṃ pareśāya namastubhyaṃ śivāya ca
kiṃ karomi kva gacchami kiṃ gṛhṇāmi tyajāmi kim (35)
yanmayā pūritaṃ viśvaṃ mahākalpāmbunā yathā

antaḥsaṅgaṃ bahiḥsaṅgamātmasaṅgaṃ ca yastyajet
sarvasaṅganivṛttātmā sa māmeti na saṃśayaḥ (36)
ahiriva janayogaṃ sarvadā varjayedyaḥ kuṇapamiva
sunārīṃ tyaktukāmo virāgī
viṣamiva viṣayādīnmanyamāno durantāñjagati
paramahaṃso vāsudevo'hameva (37)
idaṃ satyamidaṃ satyaṃ satyametadihocyate
ahaṃ satyaṃ paraṃ brahma mattaḥ kiṃcinna vidyate (38)

Vocabulary

yaḥ: one who; *cintayet*: meditates on; *mām*: me; *anu-saṃdhānāt*: through concentration; *svasva rūpa*: one's own true form; *mām*: me; *nṛtyantantam*: dancing; *sarva-sākṣiṇam*: witness of all; *pramucyate*: is liberated; *sarva-bandhaiḥ*: from all bondage; *namonamaḥ*: salutations; *mahyam-eva*: to me alone; *antara-sthāya*: am within; *sarva-bhūta*: within all beings; *cidātmane*: of the nature of consciousness; *nitya-mukta*: ever liberated; *pratyak-caitanya-rūpāya*: form of innermost consciousness; *namaḥ*: reverence; *mahyam*: to me; *pareśāya*: transcendent Lord; *ca namaḥ-tubhyam*: and reverence to you; *śivāya*: auspicious one.

kiṃ karomi: what shall I do; *kva gacchami*: where shall I go; *kim gṛhṇāmi*: what shall I take; *kim tyajāmi*: what shall I renounce; *yat . . yathā*: just as . . so; *viśvam*: universe; *pūritam*: filled; *mayā*: by me; *ambunā*: ocean; *mahā-kalpa*: great cycle of time; *yaḥ tyajet*: whoever gives up; *saṅgam*: attachment; *antaḥ*: internal; *bahiḥ*: external; *ātma*: self; *nivṛtta-ātmā*: ātman devoid of; *sarva-saṅga*: all attachments; *saḥ*: that one; *na saṃśayaḥ*: without doubt; *eti*: reaches; *mām*: me; *yaḥ*: whoever; *tyaktukāmaḥ*: wishes to leave; *jagati*: worldly life; *varjayet*: should avoid; *sarvadā*: always; *ahiḥ-iva*: like a snake; *jana-yogam*: company of men; *virāgī*: indifferent to; *sunārīm*: beautiful woman; *iva*: as if; *kunapam*: corpse; *mānaḥ*: regard; *viṣaya-ādi*: all sensual enjoyments; *durantān*: endless; *viṣam-iva*: as poison; *paramahaṃsaḥ*: ascetic; *aham*: I; *vāsudevaḥ eva*: Vāsudeva alone; *idam*: this; *satyam*: Truth; *etad*: this; *iha-ucyate*: spoken here; *param brahma*: Supreme Brahman; *kiṃcit na*: nothing; *vidyate*: exists; *mattaḥ*: from me.

Translation

One who meditates through concentration on one's own real form for a *muhurta*, on me, dancing as the witness of all, is liberated from all bondage. Salutations to me alone who am within all beings, of the nature of consciousness, ever liberated, the form of innermost consciousness. I am truly you. You are I, o Glorious Divine one, to you [and] me the infinite, to me [and] you the nature of consciousness. Reverence to me, the transcendent Lord, and reverence to you, the auspicious one.

What shall I do? Where shall I go? What shall I take? What shall I renounce? Just as the universe is filled by me with the ocean of the great cycle of time, so whoever gives up attachment to the internal, attachment to the external and attachment to the self, the ātman devoid of all attachments, that one without doubt reaches me.

Whoever wishes to leave the worldy life should always avoid like a snake the company of men, [be] indifferent to a beautiful woman as if to a corpse, [and] regard endless sensual enjoyments as poison. [This is] the *paramahaṃsa* [who says] 'I [am] Vāsudeva alone'. This is the Truth. This is the Truth. This is the Truth spoken here. I am the Truth, the Supreme Brahman. Nothing exists [apart] from me.

Commentary

Viṣṇu says that only one *muhurta*, forty-eight minutes, of intense one-pointed concentration, on one's essential nature, which is the inmost recess of all beings, will free Ṛbhu from bondage. This essential nature is both Viṣṇu and pervaded by him, who, as the witness of everyone and everything, does the cosmic dance. Viṣṇu speaks as if he, Ṛbhu and all beings are equally revered and auspicious.

'The ocean of the great cycle of time' refers to eternity, existence without end, infinite time. Therefore whoever is free of all attachments, just as the ātman is free of attachment, leads one to the Supreme Self.

All worldly activities and sensory enjoyments should be avoided. Vāsudeva ('he who pervades and sports') is one of the twenty-four forms of Visnu.

The *paramahaṃsa* is one who can differentiate between reality and unreality, and knows for sure that he is none other than the Supreme Brahman.

'Fix the mind on Ātman. Fix the mind on the all-pervading, pure Intelligence and self-luminous effulgence (Svayamjyotis). Stand firm in Brahman. Then will you become 'Brahma-samstha,' established in Brahman.'[37]

Verses 39 to 44: I Am Brahman

उप समीपे यो वासो जीवात्मपरमात्मनोः ।

उपवासः स विज्ञेयो न तु दायस्य शोषणम् ।।३९।।

कायशोषणमात्रेण का तत्र ह्यविवेकिनाम् ।

वल्मीकताडनादेव मृतः किं नु महोरगः ।।४०।।

अस्ति ब्रह्मेति चेद्वेद परोक्षज्ञानमेव तत् ।

अहं ब्रह्मेति चेद्वेद साक्षात्कारः स उच्यते ।।४१।।

यस्मिन्काले स्वमात्मानं योगी जानाति केवलम् ।

तस्मात्कालात्समारभ्य जीवन्मुक्तो भयेदसौ ।।४२।।

अहं ब्रह्मेति नियतं मोक्षहेतुर्महात्मनाम् ।

द्वे पदे बन्धमोक्षाय निर्ममेति ममेति च ।।४३।।

ममेति बध्यते जन्तुर्निर्ममेति विमुच्यते ।

बाह्याचिन्ता न कर्तव्या तथैवान्तरचिन्तिका ।

सर्वचिन्तां समुत्सृज्य स्वस्थो भव सदा ऋभो ।।४४।।

upa samīpe yo vāso jīvātmaparamātmanoḥ
upavāsaḥ sa vijñeyo na tu kāyasya śoṣaṇam (39)
kāyaśoṣaṇamātreṇa kā tatra hyavivekinām
valmīkatāḍanādeva mṛtaḥ kiṃ nu mahoragaḥ (40)
asti brahmeti cedveda parokṣajñānameva tat
ahaṃ brahmeti cedveda sākṣātkāraḥ sa ucyate (41)
yasminkāle svamātmānaṃ yogī jānāti kevalam
tasmātkālātsamārabhya jīvanmukto bhayedasau (42)
ahaṃ brahmeti niyataṃ mokṣaheturmahātmanām
dve pade bandhamokṣāya nirmameti mameti ca (43)
mameti badhyate janturnirmameti vimucyate
bāhyācintā na kartavyā tathaivāntaracintikā
sarvacintāṃ samutsṛjya svastho bhava sadā ṛbho (44)

Vocabulary

vijñeyaḥ: should be known as; *yaḥ*: that which; *vāsaḥ*: abides; *upa samīpe*: near; *jīvātma-paramātmanoḥ*: *paramātman* and *jīvātman*; *na tu*: not as; *śoṣaṇam*: withering; *kāyasya*: of the body; *kāḥ tatra*: what then; *kaya-śoṣaṇa-mātreṇa*: mere drying up of the body; *hi-avivekinām*: for the ignorant; *mahoragaḥ*: great serpent; *mṛtaḥ*: die; *kiṃ nu*: just; *tāḍanāt*: by beating; *valmīka*: anthill; *eva*: alone; *ced-veda*: if one knows; *asti brahma*: 'this is Brahman'; *tat eva*: that [is] only; *parokṣa-jñānam*: indirect knowledge; *sa mucyate*; one is said; *sākṣātkāraḥ*: direct knowledge; *ced-veda*: if one knows; *aham brahma*: 'I am Brahman'.

yasmin-kāle: at whatever time; *yogī*: yogin; *jānāti*: knows; *svam-ātmānam*: his own ātman; *kevalam*: one Self; *samārabhya*: beginning; *tasmāt-kālāt*: from that time; *asau*: that; *bhayet*: becomes; *niyatam*: always in the state; *aham brahma*: I am Brahman; *mokṣa-hetuḥ*: cause of liberation; *mahātmanām*: for the high souls; *dve pade*: two words; *bandha-mokṣāya*: for bondage and liberation; *iti*: they are; *mam*: mine; *ca nirmam*: and non-mine; *jantuḥ*: person; *badhyate*: is bound by; *vimucyate*: freed from; *bāhyā-cintā*: external anxieties; *na kartavyā*: not to be had; *tathaiva*: similarly; *antara-cintikā*: any inner anxieties; *samutsṛjya*: having given up; *sarvacintām*: all anxiety; *bhava sadā*: be always; *svasthaḥ*: at ease; *ṛbho*: o Ṛbhu.

Translation

Upavāsaḥ should be known as that which abides near *param-ātman* and *jīvātman*, not as the withering of the body. What then [is the use] of the mere drying up of the body for the ignorant? Does the great serpent die just by beating the ant-hill alone? If one knows 'this is Brahman', that [is] only indirect knowledge. One is said [to have] direct knowledge if one knows 'I am Brahman'.

At whatever time the yogin knows his own ātman [to be] the one Self, beginning from that time that [person] becomes a *jīvanmukta.* Always in the state 'I am Brahman' is the cause of liberation for the high souls. [There are] two words for bondage and liberation. They are 'mine' and 'non-mine'. A person is bound by 'mine' and freed by 'non-mine'. External anxieties are not to be had [and] similarly any inner anxieties. Having given up all anxiety, be always at ease, o Ṛbhu!

Commentary

Upavāsaḥ literally means 'fasting', but it should be known as the giving up of sensory enjoyments and worldly desires, because that renunciation is what leads to the *paramātman* and *jīvātman.*

External rituals do not kill the inner enemies of the mind. They do not lead to the experience of Brahman. It is the mind which needs to be purified of all thoughts except one: 'I am Brahman', which means I am that absolute reality of which the entire universe and the person I think myself to be are manifestations of Brahman.

A *jīvātman* is an individual person or soul.
Definitions of a *jīvanmukta* are 'a soul who is liberated while living; a person, who, being purified by true knowledge of the supreme reality, is freed from future births and all ceremonial rites while yet embodied.' [38]

Verses 45 to 48a: All Is Consciousness

संकल्पमात्रकलनेन जगत्समग्रं संकल्पमात्रकलने हि

जगद्विलासः ।

संकल्पमात्रमिदमुत्सृज निर्विकल्पमाश्रित्य मामकपदं

हृदि भावयस्व ॥४५॥

मच्चिन्तनं मत्कथनमन्योन्यं मत्प्रभाषणम् ।

मदेकपरमो भूत्वा कालं नय महामते ॥४६॥

चिदिहास्तीति चिन्मात्रमिदं चिन्मयमेव च ।

चित्त्वं चिदहमेते च लोकाश्चिदिति भावय ॥४७॥

रागं नीरागतां नीत्वा निर्लेपो भव सर्वदा ।४८।

saṃkalpamātrakalanena jagatsamagraṃ
saṃkalpamātrakalane hi jagadvilāsaḥ
saṃkalpamātramidamutsṛja nirvikalpamāśritya
māmakapadaṃ hṛdi bhāvayasva (45)
maccintanaṃ matkathanamanyonyaṃ matprabhāṣaṇam
madekaparamo bhūtvā kālaṃ naya mahāmate (46)
cidihāstīti cinmātramidaṃ cinmayameva ca
cittvaṃ cidahamete ca lokāściditi bhāvaya (47)
rāgaṃ nīrāgatāṃ nītvā nirlepo bhava sarvadā (48a)

Vocabulary

samagram: entire; *jagat*: world; *kalanena*: through the effect; *saṃkalpa-mātra*: extent of volition; *hi*: hence; *kalane*: cause; *jagat-vilāsaḥ*: shining forth of the world; *utsṛja*: having abandoned; *idam*: this; *āśritya*: taking refuge in; *bhāvaya*: meditate on; *māma-kapadam*: my abode; *hṛdi*: in the heart; *mahāmate*: o wise one; *bhūtvā*: having become; *mat-eka-paramaḥ*: me the one Supreme; *naya*: spend; *kalam*: time; *mat-cintanam*: thinking about me; *mat-kathanam*: singing about me; *mat-prabhāṣaṇam*: conferring about me; *anyonyam*: with one another; *bhāvaya iti*: know that; *iha*: in this universe; *asti cit*: there is consciousness; *cinmātram*: pure intelligence; *cinmayam-eva*: consisting of consciousness alone; *ca tvam cit*: and you are consciousness; *aham cit*: I am consciousness; *ca ete lokāḥ*: and these worlds; *cit-iti*: are consciousness; *nītvā*: having changed; *rāgam*: passion; *nīrāgatām*: dispassion; *bhava*: become; *sarvadā*: forever; *nirlepaḥ*: unattached.

Translation

The entire world [exists] through the effect of the extent of volition. Hence the extent of volition is the cause of the shining forth of the world. Having abandoned this volition, taking refuge in *nirvikalpa*, meditate on My abode in [your] heart. O wise one, having become Me, the one Supreme, spend your time thinking about Me, singing about Me [and] conferring about Me with one another. Know that in this universe there is consciousness, pure intelligence consisting of consciousness alone, and you are consciousness, I am consciousness and [all] these worlds are consciousness. Having changed passion to dispassion, become forever unattached.

Commentary

Saṃkalpa means volition or desire. It is a concept formed in the mind. The material world consists of the results of desires. Once the mind is free of desires, one can rest in *nirvikalpa samādhi*, where 'the mind ceases to function and only pure consciousness remains, revealing itself to itself and there is no object of the mind; superconscious state where mental modifications cease to exist, resulting in transcendence of the manifest world'.[39]

Swami Sivananda describes *nirvikalpa samādhi* as 'that state in which one's identity with the universal reality is realised. When the mind ceases functioning, when all thoughts subside, when all consciousness of the body and the outer world is effaced from the mind, the individual soul completely merges into the supreme soul, into universal consciousness. It is the highest realisation known as the superconscious state, and as *turīya* or the fourth state.'[40]

In this state one can meditate on the psychic space of the heart centre at *anāhata cakra*. This spiritual heart is the seat or abode of the transcendental Self. Here, knowing that all is consciousness, one is in the state of equanimity.

Verses 48b to 50a: Bright Lamp of Ātman

अज्ञानजन्यकर्त्रादिकारकोत्पन्नकर्मणा ।।४८।।

श्रुत्युत्पन्नात्मविज्ञानप्रदीपो बाध्यते कथम् ।

अनात्मतां परित्यज्य निर्विकारो जगात्स्थितौ ।।४९।।

एकनिष्ठत्वयान्तस्थसंदचिन्मात्रपरो भव ।५०।

ajñānajanyakartrādikārakotpannakarmaṇā (48b)
śrutyutpannātmavijñānapradīpo bādhyate katham
anātmatāṃ parityajya nirvikāro jagātsthitau (49)
ekaniṣṭhatvayāntasthasaṃdacinmātraparo bhava (50a)

Vocabulary
katham: how; *pradīpaḥ*: bright lamp; *ātma-vijñāna*: knowledge of the ātman; *utpanna*: stemming from; *śruti*: Vedas; *bādhyate*: be impaired; *karmaṇā*: by action; *utpanna*: arising from; *karaka*: causes; *kartra-ādi*: agents and others; *ajñāna-janya*: born from ignorance; *parityajya*: having left; *anātmatām*: *anātmatām* state; *sthitau*: remaining in; *jagāt*: world; *nirvikāraḥ*: unaffected; *bhava-niṣṭha-tvayā*: devote yourself to; *eka antastha*: one inner; *para-cinmātra*: Supreme Intelligence.

Translation
How can the bright lamp [of] the knowledge of the ātman, stemming from the Vedas, be impaired by any action arising from causes [made by] agents and others [which is] born from ignorance? Having left the *anātman* state, remaining in the world unaffected, devote yourself to the one inner Supreme Intellligence.

Commentary
The spiritual light is imperishable and indestructible. The Rishis of the Vedas had knowledge of the ātman, and this knowledge was handed down through the Upanishads. No longer identifying with individual self (*anātman*), unaffected

by the duality of pain and pleasure, one can devote oneself to the Supreme Intelligence, Brahman.

Verses 50b to 54: The Illusive Power

घटाकाशमठाकाशौ महाकाशे प्रतिष्ठितौ ।।५०।।

एवं मयि चिदाकशे जीवेशौ परिकल्पतौ ।

या च प्रागात्मनो माया तथान्ते च तिरस्कृता ।।५१।।

ब्रह्मवादिमिरुद्गीता सा मायेती विवेकतः ।

मायातत्कार्यविलये नेश्वरत्वं न जीवता ।।५२।।

ततः शुद्धश्चिदेवाहं व्योमवन्निरुपाधिकः ।

जीवेश्वरादिरूपेण चेतनाचेतनात्मकम् ।।५३।।

ईक्षणादिप्रवेशान्ता सृष्टिरीशेन कल्पता ।

जाग्रदादिविमोक्षान्तः संसारो जीवकल्पितः ।।५४।।

ghaṭākāśamaṭhākāśau mahākāśe pratiṣṭhitau (50b)
evaṃ mayi cidākaśe jīveśau parikalpatau
yā ca prāgātmano māyā tathānte ca tiraskṛtā (51)
brahmavādimirudgītā sā māyetī vivekataḥ
māyātatkāryavilaye neśvaratvaṃ na jīvatā (52)
tataḥ śuddhaścidevāhaṃ vyomavannirupādhikaḥ
jīveśvarādirūpeṇa cetanācetanātmakam (53)
īkṣaṇādipraveśāntā sṛṣṭirīśena kalpatā
jāgradādivimokṣāntaḥ saṃsāro jīvakalpitaḥ (54)

Vocabulary

ghaṭa-ākāśa: ether of the pot; *maṭha-ākāśau*: ether of the monastery; *pratiṣṭhitau*: are located; *maha-ākāśe*: in the great ether; *evaṃ*: thus; *jīveśau*: living beings; *parikalpatau*: are formed; *mayi*: in me; *cit-ākaśe*: space of pure unlimited consciousness; *yāḥ*: whichever; *māyā*: illusive power; *prāga*: before; *tathā-ante*: then at the end; *tiraskṛtā*: vanishes; *sā udgītā*: this has been sung as; *māyā*: illusive power; *brahma-vādimiḥ*: by the teachers of Brahman; *vivekataḥ*: through correct understanding; *vilaye*: with the death; *tat-kārya*: its actions; *na-īśvaratvam*: neither supremacy; *na jīvatā*: nor existence; *tataḥ*: thus; *śuddhaḥ*: pure; *aham*: I; *cit-eva*: consciousness alone; *vyomavat*: like the ether; *nirupādhikaḥ*: without attributes; *rūpeṇa*: with the form of; *jīva-īśvara-ādi*: *jīva*, *Īśvara* and others; *sṛṣṭiḥ*: creation; *īkṣaṇa-ādi*: beginning with reflection; *praveśa-antā*: ending with entry; *kalpatā*: function; *īśena*: of sight; *saṃsāraḥ*: worldly existence; *jāgrat-ādi*: beginning with waking; *vimokṣa-antaḥ*: ending with liberation; *jīva-kalpitaḥ*: function of jīva.

Translation

The ether of the pot [and] the ether of the monastery are located in the great ether. Thus living beings are formed in Me, the space of pure unlimited consciousness. Whichever illusive power [exists] before [Me], the ātman, then at the end vanishes. This has been sung as *māyā* by the teachers of Brahman through their correct understanding. With the death [of] māyā [and] its actions, [there is] neither supremacy nor existence. Thus pure, I [am] consciousness alone, like the ether without attributes, consisting of the sentient and the non-sentient, with the form of *jīva*, *Īśvara* and others. Creation, beginning with reflection [and] ending with entry, [is] the function of sight. Worldly existence, beginning with waking [and] ending with liberation [is] the function of jīva.

Commentary

Swami Satyadharma elaborates on these concepts in *Yoga Darshana Upaniṣad*:

'In the scriptures, we find the analogy of the space in the pot or the space in the dwelling, being the same space as that which exists all around the pot, or all around the dwelling. Although, our mind perceives the space in the pot or in the dwelling as different from the space all around. This is an example of the false notion of duality. Similarly, due to this same false notion, the ātman, the unlimited, unborn reality, is called *jīva,* the consciousness that is born and lives in the body, and is considered to be limited in this sense, like the space that exists inside the pot, or the dwelling. And again, in the universal sense, the pure cosmic consciousness, which sustains the manifest order of existence, is called *Īśvara*.

So, the Rishi, who has established his awareness in samādhi says to his disciples: Indeed I am not the body, nor am I the prāṇa, nor am I the senses, nor am I the mind. I am Śiva, pure consciousness alone, ever the witness of my true self. This wisdom is said to be samādhi in this life.' [41]

Verses 55 to 57: Non-dual Brahman

त्रिणाचिकादियोगान्ता ईश्वरभ्रान्तिमाश्रिताः ।
लोकायतादिसांख्यान्ता जीवविश्रान्तिमाश्रिताः ।।५५।।
तस्मान्मुमुक्षुभिर्नैव मतिर्जीवेशवादयोः
लार्या किंतु ब्रह्मतत्त्वं निश्चलेन विचार्यताम् ।।५६।।
अद्वितीयब्रह्मतत्त्वं न जानन्ति यथा तथा ।
भ्रान्ता एवाखिलास्तेषां क्व मुक्तिः क्वेह वा सुखम् ।।५७।।

triṇācikādiyogāntā īśvarabhrāntimāśritāḥ
lokāyatādisāṃkhyāntā jīvaviśrāntimāśritāḥ (55)
tasmānmumukṣubhirnaiva matirjīveśavādayoḥ
kāryā kiṃtu brahmatattvaṃ niścalena vicāryatām (56)
advitīyabrahmatattvaṃ na jānanti yathā tathā
bhrāntā evākhilāsteṣāṃ kva muktiḥ kveha vā sukham (57)

Vocabulary
triṇācika-ādi: beginning with *triṇāciketa*; *yoga-antā*: ending with *yoga*; *āśritāḥ*: rest on; *īśvara-bhrāntim*: confusion about Īśvara; *lokāyata-ādi*: beginning with *lokāyata*, materialism; *sāṃkhya-antā*: ending with *sāṃkhya*, system of creation; *jīva-viśrāntim*: cessation of jīva; *tasmāt*: therefore; *na matiḥ eva*: no thought at all; *mumukṣubhiḥ*: by those desirous of liberation; *jīva-īśa-vādayoḥ*: controversies about jīva and *īśa*; *kiṃtu*: but; *niścalena*: with a steady [mind]; *brahma-tattvam*: true nature of Brahman; *kāryā vicāryatām*: should be investigated; *yathā*: to whatever extent; *na jānanti*: do not know; *advitīya*: non-dual; *tathā*: to that extent; *akhilāḥ*: all; *bhrāntāḥ*: deluded; *kva*: where; *muktiḥ*: liberation; *kva-iha*: where in this world; *sukham*: happiness.

Translation
[Teachings] beginning with *triṇāciketa* [and] ending with *yoga* rest on confusion about Īśvara. [Philosophies] beginning with *lokāyata* [and] ending with *sāṃkhya* rest on

the cessation of jīva. Therefore no thought at all by those desirous of liberation [should be given to] controversies about jīva and *īśa*, but, with a steady [mind], the true nature of Brahman should be investigated. To whatever extent [people] do not know the non-dual nature of Brahman, to that extent [they are] all deluded. Where [is] their liberation? Where in this world [is] happiness?

Commentary

The paths to liberation in this second chapter have been *bhaktiyoga*, the yoga of devotion, and *advaita vedānta*, the non-dual Brahman.

Other practices such as the fire rituals described in the *Kathopanishad* and yoga postures depend on the illusion of Īśvara being separate from Brahman; and the materialist atheist philosophies of *lokāyata* and *sāṃkhya* are created by living beings.

Wisdom, spiritual knowledge and eternal happiness are found only in the non-dual nature of Brahman. This is the theme of *Advaita Vedānta*, which can be described in one sentence *tat tvam asi*, That thou art; you are the one Self which is beyond the body, mind and states of waking, dreaming and sleeping. This is a journey from ignorance to knowledge, when one realises the divinity within, and then knows the whole world as an expression of the same divinity.

Verses 58 to 63: Beyond Waking Dreaming Sleeping

उत्तमाधमभावश्चेत्तेषां स्यादस्ति ते किम् ।
स्वप्नस्थराज्यभिक्षाभ्यां प्रबुद्धः स्पृशते खलु ।।५८।।
अज्ञाने बुद्धिविलये निद्रा सा भण्यते बुधैः ।
विलीनाज्ञानतत्कार्ये मयि निद्रा कथं भवेत् ।।५९।।
बुद्धेः पूर्णविकासोऽयं जागरः परिकीर्त्यते ।
विकारादिविहीनत्वाज्जगरो मे न विद्यते ।।६०।।
सूक्ष्मनाडिषु संचारो बुद्धेः स्वप्नः प्रजायते ।
संचारधर्मरहिते मयि स्वप्नो न विद्यते ।।६१।।
सुषुप्तिकाले सकले विलीने तमसावृते ।
स्वरूपं महदानन्दं बुङ्क्ते विश्वविवर्जितः ।।६२।।
अविशेषेण सर्वं तु यः पश्यति चिदन्वयात् ।
स एव साक्षाद्विज्ञानीं स शिवः स हरिर्विधि ।।६३।।

uttamādhamabhāvaścetteṣāṃ syādasti te kim
svapnastharājyabhikṣābhyāṃ prabuddhaḥ spṛśate khalu (58)
ajñāne buddhivilaye nidrā sā bhaṇyate budhaiḥ
vilīnājñānatatkārye mayi nidrā kathaṃ bhavet (59)
buddheḥ pūrṇavikāso'yaṃ jāgaraḥ parikīrtyate
vikārādivihīnatvājjagaro me na vidyate (60)
sūkṣmanāḍiṣu saṃcāro buddheḥ svapnaḥ prajāyate
saṃcāradharmarahite mayi svapno na vidyate (61)
suṣuptikāle sakale vilīne tamasāvṛte
svarūpaṃ mahadānandaṃ buṅkte viśvavivarjitaḥ (62)
aviśeṣeṇa sarvaṃ tu yaḥ paśyati cidanvayāt
sa eva sākṣādvijñānīṃ sa sivaḥ sa harirvidhi (63)

Vocabulary

cet: if; *teṣām syāt*: they have; *bhāvaḥ*: impression; *uttama-adhama*: high and low; *kim asti te*: what is that; *prabuddhaḥ*: woken; *khalu*: indeed; *spṛśate*: affected; *rājya-bhikṣābhyām*:

by sovereignty and beggary; *svapnastha*: in the dreaming state; *buddhi-vilaye*: when the intellect is dissolved; *ajñāne*: in ignorance; *sā bhaṇyate*: this is called; *nidrā*: sleep; *budhaiḥ*: by the wise; *katham*: how; *bhavet*: can there be; *nidrā*: sleep; *mayi*: for me; *vilīnā*: free from; *ajñāna*: ignorance; *tat-kārye*: in its deeds; *ayam pūrṇavikāsaḥ*: this fully expanded; *buddheḥ*: of the intellect; *parikīrtyate*: is called; *jāgaraḥ*: waking; *na vidyate*: does not exist; *me*: for me; *vihīnatvāt*: devoid of; *vikāra-ādi*: change etc; *svapnaḥ*: dreaming; *prajāyate*: is caused by; *saṃcāraḥ*: movement; *buddheḥ*: of the intellect; *sūkṣma-nāḍiṣu*: through the subtle *nāḍis*, channels; *rahite*: inner; *dharma*: attribute.

viśvavivarjitaḥ: freed from all; *tamas-āvṛte*: enclosed in darkness; *sakale vilīne*: when all is dissolved; *suṣupti-kāle*: at the time of deep sleep; *yaḥ paśyati*: whoever sees; *sarvam*: everything; *aviśa*: without difference; *cit-anvayāt*: because of the connection with consciousness; *eva*: indeed; *sākṣāt-vijñānīm*: one who has direct realisation; *sa sivaḥ*: he [is] Śiva; *hariḥ-vidhi*: way of Hari.

Translation

If they have the impression [of] high and low, what is that? Is one [who is] woken indeed affected by sovereignty and beggary [experienced] in the dreaming state? When the intellect is dissolved in ignorance, this is called sleep by the wise. How can there be sleep for me, free from ignorance in its deeds? The fully expanded [state] of the intellect is called the waking [state]. The waking [state] does not exist for me, [who am] devoid of change. The dreaming [state] is caused by the movement of the intellect through the subtle *nāḍis*. The dreaming [state] does not exist in me [who am without] the inner attribute of movement.

Freed from all, enclosed in darkness when all is dissolved at the time of deep sleep, one enjoys the highest bliss of one's own true nature. Whoever sees everything without difference because of the connection with consciousness is indeed one who has direct realisation. He [is] Śiva. He [is] the way of Hari.

Commentary

Opposites and comparisons such as the superiority of Īśvara and the inferiority of jīva do not exist in non-dual Brahman. Similarly dreams of wealth and poverty do not affect one's financial status. In the sleeping state the intellect dissolves into ignorance and lack of awareness. The dreaming state is the result of the mind's wandering in the subtle channels. 'The dream state is based on the focussing of attention on the inner environment of the body'.[42] The intellect is active in the waking state which is narrowly focussed on the individual identity. As Brahman does not change, the different states of waking, dreaming and sleeping do not exist there.

Mandukya Upaniṣad refers to the state of 'deep dreamless sleep, lying beyond desire. Prājña is the Lord of this territory; he abides in deep sleep in which all things have vanished, and he enjoys bliss. Prājña lies at the gateway to the dreaming and waking states.' [43]
Prājña is the 'seer who observes the state of deep sleep'. [44]

In deep sleep one is free from the sense of sight and other senses, worldly experiences and identity with the individual self. However, the *vṛttis*, mental modifications of the mind are still present although one is not aware of them. Sleep rests in *tamas* (mental dullness and darkness), so liberation cannot be attained through it.

Verses 64 to 65: Mundane Existence

दीर्घस्वप्नमिदं यत्तद्दीर्घं वा चिदत्तविभ्रमम् ।
दीर्घं वापि मनोराज्यं संसारं दुःखमागरम् ।
सुप्तेरुत्थाय सुप्त्यन्तं ब्रह्मैकं प्रविचिन्त्यताम् ।।६४।।
आरोपितस्य जगतः प्रविलापनेन चित्तं मदात्मकतया
परिकल्पितं नः ।
शत्रून्निहस्य गुरुषट्कगणान्निपाताद्गन्धद्विपो भवति
केवलमद्वितीयः ।।६५।।

dīrghasvapnamidaṃ yattaddīrghaṃ vā cidattavibhramam
dīrghaṃ vāpi manorājyaṃ saṃsāraṃ duḥkhamāgaram
supterutthāya suptyantaṃ brahmaikaṃ pravicintyatām (64)
āropitasya jagataḥ pravilāpanena cittaṃ madātmakatayā
parikalpitaṃ naḥ
śatrūnnihasya guruṣaṭkagaṇānnipātādgandhadvipo
bhavati kevalamadvitīyaḥ (65)

Vocabulary

utthāya: having risen; *supteḥ*: from sleep; *pravicintyatām*: reflecting on; *suptyantam*: at the end of sleep; *brahma-ekam*: one Brahman; *idam saṃsāram*: this one mundane existence; *vā*: like; *dīrgha-svapnam*: long dream; *yat*: which; *dīrgham*: long; *vibhramam*: delusion; *cit-atta*: consuming the mind; *vā-api*: also like; *āgaram*: ocean; *duḥkham*: suffering; *manaḥ-rājyam*: reign over the mind.

pravilāpanena: through complete dissolution; *āropitasya jagataḥ*: of the apparent world; *cittam*: mind; *parikalpitam*: takes on; *mad-ātmaka*: my form; *śatrūn*: enemies; *nihasya*: having been killed; *nipātād*: destruction; *guru-ṣaṭ-kagaṇāt*: by the six means of the *guru*; *gandha-dvipaḥ*: scent of an elephant; *bhavati*: becomes; *advitīyaḥ*: peerless; *kevalam*: alone.

Translation
Having risen from sleep, reflecting at the end of sleep on the one Brahman, [one realises that] this mundane existence [is] like a long dream, which [is] a long delusion consuming the mind, [and] also like an ocean of suffering [with] a long reign over the mind.

Through complete dissolution of the apparent world, the mind takes on My form. The enemies having been killed, their destruction [caused] by the six means [through the grace of] *guru*, [the ātman], [like] the scent of an elephant, becomes peerless alone.

Commentary
The daily life activities of the mundane existence are transitory and, like a dream, remain only in one's memory. Therefore the mind's most important activity is to reflect on that which is permanent, Brahman.

The six enemies of the mind, passion, anger, greed, delusion, pride and jealousy, can be destroyed, through the grace of guru, by mind control, sense control, ability to internalize, forebearance and equanimity.

The most difficult of all yoga practices is control of the mind. Swami Satsangananda says 'it is almost impossible to control the patterns of the mind, especially the negative aspects such as anger, jealous, greed and passion. They invade the mind from all sides.
It is Guru's grace alone that can liberate us from the bondage of the mind. It is he alone who can give us the strength and equanimity to survive the invasions of our mental patterns. It is his grace that helps us through the severest trials.'[45]

Verses 66 to 71a: End of Delusion

अद्यास्तमेतु वपुरशशङ्कतारकास्तां कस्तावत्वापि मम
चिद्वपुषो विशेषः ।
कुम्भे विनाश्यति चिरं समवस्थिते वा कुम्भाम्बरस्य
नहि कोऽपि विशेषलेशः ।।६६।।
अहिनिर्व्लयनी सर्पनिर्मोके जीववर्जितः ।
वल्मीके पतितस्तिष्ठेत्तं सर्पो नाभिमन्यते ।।६७।।
एवं स्थूलं च सूक्ष्मं च शरीरं नाभिमन्यते ।
प्रत्यग्ज्ञानशिखिध्वंसो मिथ्याज्ञाने सहेतुके ।
नेति नेतीति रूपत्वादशरीरे भवत्ययम् ।।६८।।
शास्त्रेण न स्यात्परमार्थदृष्टिः कार्यक्षमं पश्यति
चापरोक्षम् ।
प्रारब्धनाशात्प्रतिभाननाश एवं त्रिधा नश्यति
चात्ममायस ।।६९।।
ब्रह्मत्वे योजिते स्वामिञ्जीवभावो न गच्छति ।
अद्वैते बोधिते तत्त्वे वासना विनिवर्तते ।।७०।।
प्रारब्धान्ते देहहानिर्मायेति क्षीयतेऽखिला ।७१।

adyāstametu vapurśaśaṅkatārakāstaṃ kastāvatvāpi mama cidvapuṣo viśeṣaḥ
kumbhe vinaśyati ciraṃ samavasthite vā kumbhāmbarasya nahi ko'pi viśeṣaleśaḥ (66)
ahinirvlayanī sarpanirmoke jīvavarjitaḥ
valmīke patitastiṣṭhettaṃ sarpo nābhimanyate (67)
evaṃ sthūlaṃ ca sūkṣmaṃ ca śarīraṃ nābhimanyate
pratyagjñānaśikhidhvaṃso mithyājñāne sahetuke
neti netīti rūpatvādaśarīre bhavatyayam (68)
śāstreṇa na syātparamārthadṛṣṭiḥ kāryakṣamaṃ paśyati cāparokṣam

prārabdhanāśātpratibhānanāśa evaṃ tridhā naśyati
cātmamāyā (69)
brahmatve yojite svāmiñjīvabhāvo na gacchati
advaite bodhite tattve vāsanā vinivartate (70)
prārabdhānte dehahānirmāyeti kṣīyate 'khilā (71a)

Vocabulary

vapuḥ: body; *astametu*: cease to exist; *adya*: today; *vā-api*: or even; *tāvat*: as long as; *śaśaṅka-tārakāḥ*: moon and stars; *mama cit-vapuṣoḥ*: consciousness of my body ; *viśeṣaḥ*: will survive; *kumbhe*: pot; *vinaśyati*: is broken; *vā samava-sthite*: or fully formed; *ciram*: for a long time; *leśaḥ nahi*: little at all; *viśeṣa*: difference; *kumbha-ambarasya*: to the ether of the pot; *jīvavarjitaḥ*: lifeless; *ahinirvlayanī*: cast-off skin of a snake; *sarpanirmoke*: cast-off skin of a snake; *tiṣṭhet*: remains; *patitaḥ*: fallen; *valmīke*: on the anthill; *sarpaḥ*: snake; *nābhimanyate tam*: does not care about it; *evam*: thus; *nābhimanyate*: does not care about; *sthūlam*: gross; *ca sūkṣmam*: and subtle; *śarīram*: body; *mithyā-jñāne*: when false knowledge; *sahetuke*: together with its cause; *dhvaṃsaḥ*: is destroyed; *śikhi*: fire; *pratyak-jñāna*: inner knowledge; *ayam*: this; *bhavati*: becomes; *aśarīre*: bodiless; *rūpatvāt*: through the state of the form; *neti neti*: not this not this.

paśyati: one sees; *aparokṣam*: visible; *kārya-kṣamam*: made enduring; *śāstreṇa*: through the *śāstras*; *na syāt*: it does not exist; *dṛṣṭiḥ*: perception; *paramārtha*: highest truth; *prārabdha-nāśāt*: through the removal of *prārabdha karma*; *pratibhāna-nāśa*: destruction of manifestation; *evam*: thus; *tridhā*: in three ways; *ātma-māyā*: delusion about the ātman; *naśyati*: is destroyed; *svāmin*: yogin; *na gacchati*: does not go; *jīva-bhāvaḥ*: state of a jīva; *yojite*: when he is attached; *brahmatve*: state of Brahman; *advaite bodhite*: when the non-dual is known; *vāsanāḥ*: affinity; *tattve*: for objects; *vinivartatate*: ceases; *iti*: thus; *deha-hāniḥ*: loss of the body;

prārabdha-ante: at the end of karma; *māyā*: delusion; *kṣīyate*: perishes; *akhilā*: completely.

Translation

Let the body exist today or even as long as the moon and stars, consciousness of my body will survive. [Whether] a pot is broken or fully formed for a long time [makes] little difference at all to the ether of the pot. The lifeless cast-off skin of a snake remains cast off over the anthill [and] the snake does not care about it. Thus [the wise person] does not care about the gross and subtle bodies. When false knowledge together with its cause is destroyed [by] the fire [of] inner knowledge, this [person] becomes bodiless through the state of the form of 'not this not this'.

One sees the visible as made enduring, [but] according to the *śāstras* (sacred texts) it does not exist, [only] the perception of the highest truth. Through the removal of *prārabdha karma*, [there is] the destruction of the manifestation [of the world]. Thus in three ways delusion about the ātman is destroyed. The yogin does not go to the state of a jīva when he is attached to the state of Brahman. When the non-dual is known, an affinity for objects ceases. Thus [there is] loss of the body at the end of his karma [and] delusion perishes completely.

Commentary

The delusion is that the impermanent is permanent. No matter how long something lasts, be it the physical body, a pot, the slough of a snake or even that which is beyond the planet Earth, they are all transitory, whereas the consciousness that pervades them remains. Knowing this the wise person, no longer attached to mind, thought and body, attaches himself to Brahman alone. *Prārabdha karma* are past actions, the consequences of which are experienced in the present life.

Swami Vivekananda says: 'Ignorance is taking the non-eternal, the impure, the painful, and the non-Self for the eternal, the pure, the happy, and the Âtman or Self (respectively). All the different sorts of impressions have one source, ignorance. We have first to learn what ignorance is. All of us think, "I am the body, and not the Self, the pure, the effulgent, the ever blissful," and that is ignorance. We think of man, and see man as body. This is the great delusion.' [46]

Verses 71b to 74: Radiance of Consciousness

अस्तीत्युक्ते जगत्सर्वं सद्रसं ब्रह्म तद्भवेत् ॥७१॥

भातीत्युक्ते जगत्सर्वं भानं ब्रह्मैव केवलम् ।

मरुभूमौ जलं सर्वं मरुभूमात्रमेव तत् ।

जगत्त्रयमिदं सर्वं चिन्मात्रं स्वविचारतः ॥७२॥

अज्ञानमेव न कुतो जगतः प्रसङ्गे जीवेशदेशिकविकल्प-

कथातिदूरे ।

एकान्तकेवलचिदेकरसस्वभावे ब्रह्मैव केवलमहं

परिपूर्णमस्मि ॥७३॥

बोधचन्द्रमसि पूर्णविग्रहे मोहराहुमुषितात्मतेजसि ।

स्नानदानयजनादिकाः क्रिया मोचनावधि वृथैव यिष्ठते ॥७४॥

astītyukte jagatsarvaṃ sadrasaṃ brahma tadbhavet (71b)
bhātītyukte jagatsarvaṃ bhānaṃ brahmaiva kevalam
marubhūmau jalaṃ sarvaṃ marubhūmātrameva tat
jagattrayamidaṃ sarvaṃ cinmātraṃ svavicārataḥ (72)
ajñānameva na kuto jagataḥ prasaṅge jīveśadeśikavikalpa-kathātidūre
ekāntakevalacidekarasasvabhāve brahmaiva kevalamahaṃ paripūrṇamasmi (73)
bodhacandramasi pūrṇavigrahe moharāhumuṣitātmatejasi
snānadānayajanādikāḥ kriyā mocanāvadhi vṛthaiva tiṣṭhate (74)

Vocabulary

iti-ukte: when is uttered; *asti*: there is; *jagat-sarvam*: whole world; *bhavet*: becomes; *tat*: that; *sat-rasam*: essence of Truth; *brahma*: Brahman; *bhāti*: it shines forth; *kevalam*: only; *bhānam*: light; *brahma-eva*: Brahman alone; *sarvam jalam*: all the water; *marubhūmau*: in the desert; *eva*: only; *tat marubhū-mātram*: that desert itself; *sva-vicārataḥ*: enquiry into the nature of the Self; *idam sarvam*: this whole;

jagat-trayam: threefold world; *cinmātram*: consciousness alone.

ajñānam: ignorance; *prasaṅge*: in the context; *jagataḥ eva*: of the world alone; *na kutaḥ*: nowhere; *atidūre*: at a great distance from; *kathāḥ*: accounts; *vikalpa*: differences; *jīva-īśa-deśika*: *jīva īśvara guru*; *aham asmi*: I am; *paripūrṇam brahma*: completely full Brahman; *svabhāve*: whose being; *ekānta*: one; *kevala*: alone; *cit-ekarasa*: absolute consciousness.

ātma-tejasi: when the radiance; *pūrṇavigrahe candramasi*: in the full moon; *bodha*: consciousness; *musita*: is obscured; *moha-rāhu*: shadow of delusion; *kriya*: rite; *snāna-dāna-yajana-ādikāḥ*: ablution donation sacrifice and so on; *tiṣṭhate*: remains; *vṛtha*: futile; *avadhi*: duration; *mocana*: until the end.

Translation

When 'There Is' is uttered, the whole world becomes that essence of Truth, Brahman. When 'It Shines Forth' is uttered, the whole world [becomes] only the light of Brahman alone. All the water in the desert [becomes] only that desert itself. [Through] the enquiry into the nature of the Self, this whole threefold world is consciousness alone.

Ignorance [is] in the context of the world alone, nowhere [else]. At a great distance from the accounts of the differences [between] *jīva*, *īśvara* and *guru*, I am the completely full Brahman whose being is the one alone absolute consciousness.

When the radiance in the full moon of consciousness is obscured by the shadow of delusion, the rites [of] ablution, donation and sacrifice and so on remain futile for the duration [of the eclipse] until the end.

Commentary
To say 'there is' refers to Brahman, as there is nothing apart from Brahman. To say 'there shines forth' refers to the light of Brahman reflected in all forms of existence.

The pure consciousness of Brahman pervades the three worlds of the physical, mental and unconscious and the waking, dreaming and sleeping states.

When one is in the world, one differentiates between *jīva*, the individual being, *īśvara*, the supreme being, and *guru*, teacher of the science of the ultimate reality. As Brahman pervades all, this differentiation does not exist in the pure consciousness of Brahman.

Rituals and donations do not transform the darkness of ignorance into the light of knowledge.

Swami Vivekananda says: 'When the mind composed of subtle matter is quelled, the Ātman is effulgent by Its own radiance. One proof of the fact that māyā or mind is an illusion is that the mind by itself is non-intelligent and of the nature of darkness; and it is the light of the Ātman behind, that makes it appear as intelligent. When you will understand this, the mind will merge in the unbroken Ocean of Intelligences; then you will realise: This Ātman is Brahman.'[47]

Verses 75 to 78: Samādhi

सलिले सैन्धवं यद्वत्साम्यं भवति योगतः ।
तथात्ममनसोरैक्यं समाधिरिति कथ्यते ।।७५।।
दुर्लभो विषयत्यागो दुर्लभं तत्त्वदर्शनम ।
दुर्लभो सहजावस्था सद्गुरोः करुणां विना ।।७६।।
उत्पन्नशक्तिबोधस्य त्यक्निःशेषकर्मणः ।
योगिनः सहजावस्था स्वयमेव प्रकाशते ।।७७।।
रसस्य मनसश्चैव चञ्चलत्वं स्वभावतः ।
रसो बद्धो मनो बद्धं किं न सिद्ध्यति भूतले ।।७८।।
salile saindhavaṃ yadvatsāmyaṃ bhavati yogataḥ
tathātmamanasoraikyaṃ samādhiriti kathyate (75)
durlabho viṣayatyāgo durlabhaṃ tattvadarśanam
durlabho sahajāvasthā sadguroḥ karuṇāṃ vinā (76)
utpannaśaktibodhasya tyakniḥśeṣakarmaṇaḥ
yoginaḥ sahajāvasthā svayameva prakāśate (77)
rasasya manasaścaiva cañcalatvaṃ svabhāvataḥ
raso baddho mano baddhaṃ kiṃ na siddhyati bhūtale (78)

Vocabulary
yadvat: just as; *saindhavam*: rock-salt; *salile*: in water; *bhavati*: becomes; *sāmyam*: same; *tathā*: so; *yogataḥ*: through yoga; *ātma-manasoḥ*: mind and ātman; *aikyam*: one; *kathyate*: it is said; *samādhiḥ-iti*: to be *samādhi*; *vinā*: without; *karuṇām*: grace; *sadguroḥ*: true guru; *yāgaḥ*: giving up; *viṣayat*: sensual pleasure; *durlabhaḥ*: very difficult; *darśanam*: perception; *tattva*: Truth; *durlabham*: hard to obtain; *sahajā-āvasthā*: natural state; *durlabhaḥ*: rare; *yoginaḥ*: of a yogin; *prakāśate*: shines; *svayameva*: of its own accord; *śakti-bodhasya*: in whom the awakened *śakti*; *utpanna*: has arisen; *niḥśeṣa-karmaṇaḥ*: all the karmas; *tyak*: relinquished; *cañcalatvam*: fluctuation; *svabhāvataḥ*: innate tendency; *rasasya*: of quicksilver; *ca manasaḥ*: and the mind;

rasah: quicksilver; *baddhaḥ*: bound; *manaḥ baddham*: mind bound; *kim*: what; *na siddhyati*: cannot be accomplished; *bhūtale*: on [this] earth.

Translation

Just as rock-salt in water becomes the same, so [when] through yoga the mind and ātman [become] one, it is said to be *samādhi*. Without the grace of a true guru, the giving up of sensual pleasure [is] very difficult, the perception of Truth [is] hard to obtain, [and] the natural state [is] rare. The natural state of a yogin shines of its own accord [and] in whom the awakened *śakti* has arisen, [and in whom] all the karmas [have been] relinquished. Fluctuation is the innate tendency of quicksilver and the mind. [If] quicksilver [is] bound [and] mind [is] bound, what cannot be accomplished on [this] earth?

Commentary

Rock salt forms in large chunky crystals. Dissolving in water it becomes the water. Similarly, through meditation, the mind merges with the ātman, in the state of *samādhi*, 'the realisation of transcendental consciousness where all earthly karmas are finished with'. [48]

'Enlightenment is said to be something like a drop of water which, having gone into the ocean, cannot come back from the ocean. The small personality cannot come back again, but comes back with a cosmic will, becomes an unlimited person with unlimited resources and unlimited knowledge.' [49]

'*Guru* means one who has experienced the light and who has the capacity to illumine others by the light of that illumination. The guru can be anyone, but he should definitely have realised the spiritual light or knowledge. He should have become one with cosmic existence during the period of samadhi.' [50]

The guru instructs the disciple to purify the mind by removing the desire for the enjoyment of the senses (sight, sound, touch, speech and smell) in order to reveal his natural state. Thus the mind becomes stable, and does not wander here and there searching external experiences.

When *śakti*, the power of consciousness, primal energy, expands, it becomes one with the ātman which, like the sun, shines with its own light. This is one's natural original condition. This is samādhi.

Verses 79 to 83: Dissolution

मूर्छितो हरति व्याधिं मृतो जीवयति स्वयम् ।
बद्धः खेचरतां धत्ते ब्रह्मत्वं रसचेतसि ।।७९।।
इन्द्रियाणां मनो नाथो मनोनाथस्तु मारुतः ।
मारुतस्य लयो नाथस्तन्नाथं लयमाश्रय ।।८०।।
निश्चेष्टो निर्विकारश्च लयो जीवति योगिनाम् ।
उच्छिन्नसर्वसंकल्पो निःशेषाशेषचेष्टितः ।
स्वावगम्यो लयः कोऽपि मनसां वागगोचरः ।।८१।।
पुङ्खनुपुङ्खविषयेक्षणतत्परोऽपि
ब्रह्मावलोकनधियं न जहाति योगी ।
सङ्गीततालयावाद्यवशं गतापि मौलिस्यकुम्भपरि-
रक्षणन्नर्तकीव ।।८२।।
सर्वचिन्तां परित्यज्य सावधानेन चेतसा ।
नाद एवानुसंधेयो योगसाम्राज्यमिच्छता ।।८३।।

mūrchito harati vyādhiṃ mṛto jīvayati svayam
baddhaḥ khecaratāṃ dhatte brahmatvaṃ rasacetasi (79)
indriyāṇāṃ mano nātho manonāthastu mārutaḥ
mārutasya layo nāthastannāthaṃ layamāśraya (80)
niśceṣṭo nirvikāraśca layo jīvati yoginām
ucchinnasarvasaṃkalpo niḥśeṣāśeṣaceṣṭitaḥ
svāvagamyo layaḥ ko'pi manasāṃ vāgagocaraḥ (81)
puṅkhanupuṅkhaviṣayekṣaṇatatparo'pi
brahmāvalokanadhiyaṃ na jahāti yogī
saṅgītatālalayāvādyavaśaṃ gatāpi maulisyakumbha-
parirakṣaṇannartakīva (82)
sarvacintāṃ parityajya sāvadhānena cetasā
nāda evānusaṃdheyo yogasāmrājyamicchatā (83)

Vocabulary
mūrchitaḥ: filled; *harati*: removes; *vyādhim*: disease; *mṛtaḥ*: dead; *svayam jīvayati*: is restored to his own life; *baddhaḥ*: bound; *dhatte*: given; *khecaratām*: power of flying; *rasa-cetasi*: mercury and mind; *brahmatvam*: state of Brahman; *nāthaḥ*: lord; *indriyāṇām*: of the sense organs; *manaḥ*: mind; *mārutaḥ*: vital air; *mārutasya*: of the vital air; *layaḥ*: dissolution; *layam-āśraya*: refuge of dissolution; *tat-nātham*: that lord;

layaḥ yoginām: dissolution of the yogins; *jīvati*: lives; *niśceṣṭaḥ*: motionless; *ca nirvikāraḥ*: and unchangeable; *ucchinna*: cut off from; *sarva-saṃkalpaḥ*: all volition; *niḥśeṣa-aśeṣa-ceṣṭitaḥ*: indeed all actions; *sva-avagamyaḥ*: one's understanding; *vāga-gocaraḥ*: range of speech; *manasām*: of mind.

yogī: yogin; *īkṣaṇat*: viewing; *viṣaya*: sensual pleasures; *puṅkha-nu-puṅkha*: feather after feather; *na jahāti*: does not forsake; *tat paraḥ*: that highest; *brahma avalokana-adhiyam*: aim of beholding Brahman; *iva*: like; *nartakī*: female dancer; *layā*: absorbed in; *saṅgīta-tāla*: singing and cymbals; *vaśam*: composed by; *vādya*: musical instruments; *api*: also; *pari-rakṣaṇat*: maintains; *kumbha*: pot; *maulisya*: on her head.

icchatā: desire; *yoga-sāmrājyam*: power of yoga; *nāda eva*; inner sound alone; *anusaṃdheyaḥ*: should be meditated on; *sāvadhānena cetasā*: with an attentive mind; *sarva-cintām*: all worries; *parityajya*: having been given up.

Translation
[Whoever] is filled [with prāṇa] removes disease. The dead is restored to his own life. [Whoever] has bound [the mind or intellect] is given the power of flying. Then mercury and mind [are in] the state of Brahman. The lord of the sense organs is the mind. The lord of the mind is the vital air. The

lord of the vital air is dissolution. The refuge of dissolution is that lord.

The yogins' dissolution remains motionless and unchangeable, cut off from all volition [and] indeed all actions. One's understanding of dissolution [is beyond] the range of speech [and] mind.

The yogin, viewing all sensual pleasures with feather after feather does not forsake that highest aim of beholding Brahman, like the female dancer, absorbed in [the symphony of] singing and cymbals composed by musical instruments, also maintains the pot on her head.

[If there is] the desire for the power of yoga, the inner sound alone should be meditated on with an attentive mind, all worries having been given up.

Commentary

Laya yoga means the yoga of dissolution, 'when the individual consciousness dissolves into the object meditated upon'. [51] Then one has gone beyond the limitations and constraints of the body and mind. It cannot be described or conceived of. Therefore, one should seek refuge in the lord of all, Brahman. The final dissolution of the yogins is Brahman, forever actionless, changeless, free of desire and purpose.

Like the touch of a feather, the yogin sees all the transitory pleasures of the senses darting through his mind without attachment and without aversion, so focussed is he on merging with Brahman.

Nāda is 'the primal sound or first vibration from which all creation has emanated'.[52] The aspiring yogin can hear this subtle sound vibration in the meditative state when the mind is free of thought.

तृतीयोऽध्यायः
tṛtīyo'dhyāyaḥ

Third Chapter

Verses 1 to 5: The Formless One Reality

नहि नानास्वरूपं स्यादेकं वस्तु कदाचन ।
तस्मादखङ्ड एवास्मि यन्मदन्यन्न किंचन ॥१॥
दृङ्यते श्रूयते यद्यद्ब्रह्मणोऽन्यन्न तद्भवेत् ।
नित्यशुद्धविमुक्तैकमखङ्डानन्दमद्वयम् ।
सत्यं ज्ञानमनन्तं यत्परं ब्रह्माहमेव तत् ॥२॥
आनन्दरूपोऽहमखङ्डबोधः परात्परोऽहं घनचित्प्रकाशः ।
मेघा यथा व्योम न च स्पृशन्ति संसारदुःखानि न मां
स्पृशन्ति ॥३॥
सर्वं सुखं विद्धि सुदुःखनाशात्सर्वं सद्रूपमसत्यनाशात् ।
चिद्रूपमेव प्रतिभानयुक्तं तस्मादखण्डं मम रूपमेतत् ॥४॥
नहि जनिर्मरणं गमनागमौ न च मलं विमलं न च वेदनम् ।
चिन्मयं हि सकलं विराजते स्पुटतरं परमस्य तुयोगिनः ॥५॥

nahi nānāsvarūpaṃ syādekaṃ vastu kadācana
tasmādakhaṅḍa evāsmi yanmadanyanna kiṃcana (1)
dṛśyate śrūyate yadyadbrahmaṇo'nyanna tadbhavet
nityaśuddhavimuktaikamakhaṅḍānandādvayam
satyaṃ jñānamanantaṃ yatparaṃ brahmāhameva tat (2)
ānandarūpo'hamakhaṅḍabodhaḥ parātparo'haṃ
ghanacitprakāśaḥ
meghā yathā vyoma na ca spṛśanti saṃsāraduḥkhāni
na māṃ spṛśanti (3)
sarvaṃ sukhaṃ viddhi suduḥkhanāśātsarvaṃ

sadrūpamasatyanāśāt
cidrūpameva pratibhānayuktaṃ tasmādakhaṇḍaṃ mama rūpametat (4)
nahi janirmaraṇaṃ gamanāgamau na ca malaṃ vimalaṃ na ca vedanam
cinmayaṃ hi sakalaṃ virājate spuṭataraṃ paramasya tu yoginaḥ (5)

Vocabulary

nahi kadācana: at no time; *syāt*: can be; *ekaṃ vastu*: one reality; *nānā-svarūpam*: many forms; *tasmāt*: therefore; *na kiṃcana anyat*: no other; *mad*: myself; *asmi eva*: I alone am; *akhaṅḍa*: indivisible; *yadyad*: whatever; *dṛśyate*: is seen; *śrūyate*: is heard; *tat bhavet*: that is; *na anyat*: no other; *brahmaṇaḥ*: than Brahman; *aham eva*: I alone; *tat param brahma*: that Supreme Brahman; *yat*: which; *nitya*: eternal; *śuddha*: pure; *vimukta*: free; *ekam-akhaṅda-ānandam*: one indivisible bliss; *advayam*: non-dual; *satyam*: truth; *jñānam-anantam*: infinite wisdom; *aham*: I; *ānanda-rūpaḥ*: nature of bliss; *akhaṅḍa-bodhaḥ*: indivisible intelligence; *parātparaḥ*: exalted; *ghana*: unshakeable; *cit-prakāśaḥ*: light of consciousness; *ca yathā*: and just as; *meghāḥ*: clouds; *na spṛśanti*: do not touch; *vyoma*: ether; *duḥkhāni*: sufferings; *saṃsāra*: worldly life; *na māṃ spṛśanti*: do not touch me.

viddhi: know; *sarvam*: all; *sukham*: happiness; *nāśāt*: through elimination; *suduḥkha*: great suffering; *sat-rūpam*: nature of truth; *asatya*: untruth; *cit-rūpam*: nature of consciousness; *eva*: alone; *yuktam*: is connected; *pratibhāna*: inner light; *tasmāt*: therefore; *etat rūpam*: this form; *mama*: of mine; *akhaṇḍam*: indivisible; *paramasya yoginaḥ*: to the supreme yogin; *na*: no; *janiḥ-maraṇam*: birth or death; *gamana-āgamau*: going or coming; *malam vimalam*: impurity or purity; *vedanam*: knowledge; *hi*: as; *sakalam*: all; *virājate*: shines; *spuṭataram*: clearly; *cinmayam*: pure consciousness.

Translation

At no time can the One Reality be of many forms. Therefore, [as there is] no other [besides] myself, I alone am indivisible. Whatever is seen [and] heard, that is no other than Brahman. I alone [am] that Supreme Brahman which [is] eternal, pure, free, the one indivisible bliss, non-dual, truth [and] infinite wisdom. I [am] the nature of bliss, the indivisible intelligence. I [am] the exalted unshakeable light of consciousness and just as clouds do not touch the ether, [so] the sufferings of worldly life do not touch me.

Know [that] all happinesss [is] through the elimination of great suffering; all is of the nature of truth through the elimination of untruth. The nature of consciousness alone is connected with the inner light. Therefore this form of mine is indivisible. To the supreme yogin [there is] no birth or death, no going or coming, no impurity or purity and no knowledge, as [to him] all shines clearly as pure consciousness.

Commentary

The nature of the One Reality is the indivisible *sat* (being, existence) *cit* (awareness, consciousness) *ānanda* (happiness, bliss), not limited in space, time and object. Identification with this removes suffering.

Swami Vivekananda describes the One Reality thus:

'But there is the real existence in and through everything; and that reality, as it were, is caught in the meshes of time, space, and causation. There is the real man, the infinite, the beginningless, the endless, the ever-blessed, the ever-free. He has been caught in the meshes of time, space, and causation. So has everything in this world. The reality of everything is the same infinite. This is not idealism; it is not that the world does not exist. It has a relative existence, and fulfils all its requirements But it has no independent existence. It exists because of the Absolute Reality beyond time, space, and causation.'[53]

Verses 6 to 8: I Am That

सत्यचिद्धनमखण्डमद्वयं सर्वदृश्यरहितं निरामयम् ।
यत्परं विमलमद्वयं शिवं तत्सदाहमिति मौनमाश्रय ॥६॥
जन्ममृत्युसुखदुःखवर्जितं जातिनीतिकुलगोत्रदूरगम् ।
चिद्विवर्तजगतोऽस्य कारणं तत्सदाहमिति मौनमाश्रय ॥७॥
पूर्णमद्वयमखण्डचेतनं विश्वभेदकलनादिवर्जितम् ।
अद्वितीयपरसंविदंशकं तत्सदाहमिति मौनमाश्रय ॥८॥

satyaciddhanamakhaṇḍamadvayaṃ sarvadṛśyarahitaṃ nirāmayam
yatparaṃ vimalamadvayaṃ śivaṃ tatsadāhamiti maunamāśraya (6)
janmamṛttyusukhaduḥkhavarjitaṃ jātinītikulagotra-dūragam
cidvivartajagato'sya kāraṇaṃ tatsadāhamiti maunam-āśraya (7)
pūrṇamadvayamakhaṇḍacetanaṃ viśvabhedakalanādi-varjitam
advitīyaparasaṃvidaṃśakaṃ tatsadāhamiti maunam-āśraya (8)

Vocabulary

sadā: always; *āśraya*: practise; *mauna*: silence; *aham tat*: I am that; *yat-param*: which [is] supreme; *vimalam*: untainted; *advayam*: unique, non-dual; *akhaṇḍa*: indivisible; *cit-dhana*: permeating consciousness; *satya*: truth; *nirāmayam*: pure; *rahitam*: devoid of; *sarva-dṛśya*: whole visible; *cit*: consciousness; *kāraṇam*: cause; *vivarta*: illusory manifestation; *jagataḥ*: of the world; *varjitam*: devoid of; *janma-mṛtyu*: birth and death; *sukha-duḥkha*: happiness and suffering; *dūragam*: remote from; *jāti*: caste; *nīti*: law; *kula*: clan; *gotra*: lineage; *pūrṇam*: full; *advayam*: non-dual; *akhaṇḍa cetanam*: indivisible consciousness; *varjitam*:

without; *bheda-kalana-ādi*: divisions and other faults; *viśva*: universe; *aṃśakam*: forming part of; *advitīya*: unique; *para*: supreme.

Translation

Always practise silence 'I am that', which [is] the supreme, untainted, unique Śiva, the non-dual, indivisible, permeating consciousness of truth, pure, devoid of the whole visible [world]. Always practise silence 'I am that', consciousness the cause of the illusory manifestation of the world, devoid of birth and death, happiness and suffering, remote from caste, law, clan [and] lineage. Always practise silence 'I am that', the full, non-dual, indivisible consciousness, without divisions and other faults [existing in] the universe, forming part of the unique Supreme.

Commentary

Swami Sivananda describes the necessity of silence.

'Be silent. Enter silence. Silence is Atman. Silence is Brahman. Silence is centre. Silence is the *Hridaya-Guha* (heart-cave). When the mind runs from one object to another, that state in the interval wherein you become mindless for a very short time is Svarupasthiti [established in the Self]. That is Brahman. When the mind is controlled fully, Vrittis cease. When all the modifications subside, you enter into the silence then and then alone. Realise this, this very moment. Feel the divine glory and Brahmic splendour now by closing the eyes, by drawing the Indriyas, by stilling the mind, by silencing the thoughts, by sharpening the intellect, by purifying the Chitta, by meditating on Om, by chanting Om with Bhava (feeling). Keep up the continuity of Brahmic consciousness throughout the 24 hours. Have an unceasing flow of Atmic consciousness. This is very, very important.' [54]

Verses 9 to 10: Unimpeded Bliss

केनाप्यबाधितत्वेन त्रिकालेऽप्येकरूपतः ।

विद्यमानत्वमस्त्येतत्सद्रूपत्वं सदा मम ॥९॥

निरुपाधिकनित्यं यत्सुप्तौ सर्वसुखात्परम् ।

सुखरूपत्वमस्त्येतदानन्दत्वं सदा मम ॥१०॥

kenāpyabādhitatvena trikāle 'pyekarūpataḥ
vidyamānatvamastyetatsadrūpatvaṃ sadā mama (9)
nirupādhikanityaṃ yatsuptau sarvasukhātparam
sukharūpatvamastyetadānandatvaṃ sadā mama (10)

Vocabulary

etat: that; *asti vidyamānatvam*: exists; *eka-rūpataḥ*: composed of the one form; *tri-kāle*: throughout the three periods of time; *abādhitatvena*: unimpeded; *kenāpi*: by anything; *sadā*: always; *sat-rūpatvam*: form of my Second; *api*: even; *sukha-rūpatvam*: state of happiness; *yat*: which; *nityam*: eternal; *nirupādhika*: without limits; *param*: superior; *sarva-sukhāt*: to all the happiness; *suptau*: in sleep; *etat asti*: that is; *sadā*: always; *mama ānandatvam*: my bliss.

Translation

That [which] exists is composed of the one form throughout the three periods of time, unimpeded by anything, [and is] always the form of My existence. Even the state of happiness which [is] eternal without limits [and] superior to all the happiness in sleep, that is always My bliss.

Commentary

Viṣṇu remains changeless and unlimited throughout past, present and future. Happiness in sleep is not identifying with the individual personal self and it is bound by time. In deep sleep there is an absence of awareness and the darkness of ignorance, whereas Viṣṇu is always in the state of bliss and the light of knowledge.

Verses 11 to 13: Freedom From Darkness

दिनकरकिरणैर्हि शार्वतं तमो न निबिडतरं झटिति प्रणाशमेति ।

घनतरभवकारणं तमो यद्धरिदिनकृत्प्रभया न चान्तरेण॥११॥

मम चरणस्मरणेन पूजया च स्वकतमसः परिमुच्यते हि जन्तुः ।

नहि मरणप्रभवप्रणाशहेतुर्मम चरणस्मरणादृतेऽस्ति किंचित् ॥१२॥

आदरेण यथा स्तुति धनवन्तं धनेच्छया ।

तथा चेद्विश्वकर्तारं को न मुच्यते बन्धनात् ॥१३॥

dinakarakiraṇairhi śārvaraṃ tamo na nibiḍataraṃ jhaṭiti praṇāśameti
ghanatarabhavakāraṇaṃ tamo yaddharidinakṛtprabhayā na cāntareṇa (11)
mama caraṇasmaraṇena pūjayā ca svakatamasaḥ parimucyate hi jantuḥ
nahi maraṇaprabhavapraṇāśaheturmama caraṇasmaraṇadṛte'sti kiṃcit (12)
ādareṇa yathā stuti dhanavantaṃ dhanecchayā
tathā cedviśvakartāraṃ ko na mucyate bandhanāt (13)

Vocabulary

nahi iti: is it not so; *nibiḍa-taram*: very dense; *śārvaram*: gloom; *tamaḥ*: of darkness; *jhaṭiti*: immediately; *praṇāśama*: is banished; *kiraṇaiḥ*: by the rays; *dinakara*: sun; *kāraṇam*: cause; *bhava*: existence; *ghana-tara*: impassable crossing; *dinakṛt-prabhayā*: illumination of the sun; *ca na antareṇa*: and not by another; *jantuḥ*: person; *parimucyate*: is freed; *svaka-tamasaḥ*: from his own darkness; *smaraṇena*: by remembering; *ca pūjayā*: and worshipping; *mama caraṇa*: my feet; *ādṛte*: intent on; *asti*: there is; *na kiṃcit*: nothing;

hetuḥ: cause; *praṇāśa*: extinction; *prabhava*: origin; *maraṇa*: death; *yathā*: just as; *icchayā*: desires; *dhana*: wealth; *stuti*: praise; *dhanavantam*: rich man; *tathā*: so; *ced*: if; *ādareṇa*: with respect; *viśvakartāram*: creator of the universe; *kaḥ*: who; *na mucyate*: is not freed; *bandhanāt*: from bondage.

Translation

Is it not so [that] the very dense gloom of darkness is immediately banished by the rays [of] the sun? The darkness which [is] the cause of the existence of impassable crossing [is dispelled] by Hari, the illumination of the sun, and not by another. A person is freed from his own darkness by remembering and worshipping My feet. Intent on remembering My feet, there is nothing [which is] the cause [of] extinction [and] origin [of] death. Just as [one who] desires [to obtain] wealth [has] praise for a rich man, so if with respect [one praises] the creator of the universe, who is not freed from bondage?

Commentary

Viṣṇu exhorts Ṛbhu to worship his feet to attain the light and freedom of liberation, where there is no beginning or ending. Worshipping the feet of the guru or deity is a symbol of devotion, grace and detachment from the material world, and a sign of humility, respect and submissiveness. Such devotion frees one from the bondage of transitory attachments. The darkness of ignorance is due to attachment to the mundane world. The splendour of the Sun of Hari (another name for Viṣṇu, as well as Śiva, Indra and brahma) removes the darkness.

Verses 14 to 19: What is the World?

आदित्यसंनिधौ लोकश्चष्टते स्वयमेव तु ।
तथा मत्संनिधावेव समस्तं चेष्टते जगत् ।।१४।।
शुक्तिकाया यथा तारं कल्पितं मायया तथा ।
महदादि जगन्मायामयं मय्येव केवलम् ।।१५।।
चण्डालदेहे पश्वादिस्थावरे ब्रह्मविग्रहे
अन्येशु तारतम्येन स्थितेषु न तथा ह्यहम् ।।१६।।
विनष्टदिग्भ्रमस्यापि यथापूर्वं विभाति दिक् ।
तथा विज्ञानविध्वस्तं जगन्मे भाति तन्न हि ।।१७।।
न देहो नेन्द्रियप्राणो न मनोबुद्ध्यहंकृति ।
न चित्तं नैव माया च न च व्योमादिकं जगत् ।।१८।।
न कर्ता नैव भोक्ता च न च भोजयिता तथा ।
केवलं चित्सदानन्दब्रह्मैवाहं जनार्दनः ।।१९।।

ādityasaṃnidhau lokaścesṭate svayameva tu
tathā matsaṃnidhāveva samastaṃ ceṣṭate jagat (14)
śuktikāyā yathā tāraṃ kalpitaṃ māyayā tathā
mahadādi jaganmāyāmayaṃ mayyeva kevalam (15)
caṇḍāladehe paśvādisthāvare brahmavigrahe
anyeṣu tāratamyena sthiteṣu na tathā hyaham (16)
vinaṣṭadigbhramasyāpi yathāpūrvaṃ vibhāti dik
tathā vijñānavidhvastaṃ jaganme bhāti tanna hi (17)
na deho nendriyaprāṇo na manobuddhayahaṃkṛti
na cittaṃ naiva māyā ca na ca vyomādikaṃ jagat (18)
na kartā naiva bhoktā ca na ca bhojayitā tathā
kevalaṃ citsadānandabrahmaivāhaṃ janārdanaḥ (19)

Vocabulary

lokaḥ: world; *ceṣṭate*: is active; *svayam*: of its own accord; *eva*: only; *saṃnidhau*: in the presence of; *āditya*: sun; *tu tathā*: and thus; *mat-saṃnidhau-eva*: in my presence alone;

jagat: world; *ceṣṭate*: does act; *yathā*: just as; *śuktikāyā*: through mother-of-pearl; *taram*: silver; *kalpitam*: imagined; *māyayā*: through power of illusion; *tathā*: so; *mayi-eva*: in me alone; *jagat-māyā-mayam*: world consist of *māyā*, this power; *kevalam*: alone; *mahat-ādi*: from *mahat*, greater mind etc.

anyeṣu: while others; *sthiteṣu*: turn; *tāratamyena*: to differences; *dehe*: in the body; *caṇḍāla*: low-caste; *paśva-ādi*: animal etc; *sthāvare*: vegetable; *brahma-vigrahe*: body of a brahman; *aham na*: I am not; *tathā hi*: so; *yathā*: just as; *brahmasya*: to one who wanders; *vinaṣṭa-dik*: wrong direction; *vibhāti*: appears as; *pūrvam*: before; *tathā jagat*: so the world; *vidhvastam*: disappeared; *vijñāna*: spiritual wisdom; *na bhāti*: does not appear; *me*: to me; *hi*: thus.

jagat: world; *na*: not; *dehaḥ*: body; *prāṇaḥ*: vital energy; *indriya*: organs of sense and action; *ahaṃkṛti*: individual self; *manaḥ*: rational mind; *buddhi*: discerning mind; *māyā*: illusion; *vyoma-ādikam*: ether etc; *kartā*: creator; *bhoktā*: enjoyer; *bhojayitā*: cause of enjoyment; *tathā*: thus; *aham janārdanaḥ*: I am Janārdana; *brahma-eva*: Brahma alone; *kevalam*: nothing but; *cit-sat-ānanda*: consciousness existence bliss.

Translation

The world is only active of its own accord in the presence of the sun, and thus in My presence alone does the world act. Just as through mother-of-pearl [is] silver imagined through the power of illusion, so in Me alone [does] the world consist of this power alone, from *mahat* etc.

While others turn to differences in the body of a low-caste [person], an animal etc [and] a vegetable [and] the body of a brahman, I am not so. Just as to one who wanders in the wrong direction [and] the direction appears as before, so the world, disappeared through spiritual wisdom, does not appear to Me thus.

The world [is] not the body, nor the vital energy [of] the organs of sense and action, nor the individual self [with its] rational and discerning mind, nor the individual consciousness, nor illusion and nor ether etc. Neither the creator, nor the enjoyer, nor the cause of enjoyment, thus I am Janārdana, Brahman alone, nothing but consciousness, existence, bliss.

Commentary
Without the sun, the Supreme Consciousness, there is no life on Earth. Viṣṇu, who is the Supreme Consciousness, the unmanifest energy, is the cause of *prakṛti*, manifest energy, from which come *mahat*, the great principle, and its evolutes, viz. *ahaṃkāra*, individual identity; *ākāśa*, ether; *vāyu*, air; *agni*, fire; *apas*, water; and *pṛthvī*, earth.

Status, species, plants and bodies are superficial differences. One who has spiritual wisdom sees only pure consciousness, the spirit of Viṣṇu, pervading them all.

Janārdana is one of the twenty-four forms of Viṣṇu through which is Nārāyaṇa, the shelter (*ayaṇa*) for mankind (*nāra*).
Janārdana (Brahman) defines himself as nothing but *cit*, consciousness; *sat*, pure being or existence; *ānanda*, happiness, joy, bliss, which is the nature of the Ultimate Reality.

Verses 20 to 24: Root of the Mind

जलस्य चलनादेव चञ्चलत्वं तथा रवेः ।
तथाहं कारसंबन्धादेव संसार आत्मनः ॥२०॥
चित्तमूलं हि संसारस्तत्प्रयत्नेन शोधयेत् ।
हन्त चित्तमहत्तायां कैषा विश्वासता तव ॥२१॥
क्व धनानि महीपानां ब्राह्मणः क्व जगन्ति वा ।
प्राक्तनानि प्रयातानि गताः सर्गपरम्पराः ।
कोटयो ब्रह्मणां याता भूपा नष्टाः परागवत् ॥२२॥
स चाध्यात्माभिमानोऽपि विदुषोऽयासुरत्वतः ।
विदुषोऽप्यासुरश्चेत्स्यान्निष्फलं तत्त्वदर्षनम् ॥२३॥
उत्पाद्यमाना रागाद्या विवेकज्ञानवह्निना ।
यदा तदैव दह्यन्ते कुतस्तेषां प्ररोहणम् ॥२४॥

jalasya calanādeva cañcalatvaṃ tathā raveḥ
tathāhaṃkārasaṃbandhādeva saṃsāra ātmanaḥ (20)
cittamūlaṃ hi saṃsārastatprayatnena śodayet
hanta cittamahattāyāṃ kaiṣā viśvāsatā tava (21)
kva dhanāni mahīpānāṃ brāhmaṇaḥ kva jaganti vā
prāktanāni prayātāni gatāḥ sargaparamparāḥ
koṭayo brahmaṇāṃ yātā bhūpā naṣṭāḥ parāgavat (22)
sa cādhyātmābhimāno'pi viduṣo'yāsuratvataḥ
viduṣo'pyāsuraścetsyānniṣphalaṃ tattvadarṣanam (23)
utpādyamānā rāgādyā vivekajñānavahninā
yadā tadaiva dahyante kutasteṣāṃ prarohaṇam (24)

Vocabulary

calanāt: because of the movement; *jalasya*: of water; *cañcalatvam*: ripples; *raveḥ*: in the sun; *tathā*: so; *saṃsāra*: mundane existence; *saṃbandhāt*: because of the connection; *ahaṃkāra*: individual self; *citta-mūlam*: root of the mind; *śodayet*: should be purified; *prayatnena*: with effort; *hanta*:

alas; *ka-eṣā*: what is this; *viśvāsatā*: confidence; *tava*: of yours; *citta-mahattāyām*: in the greatness of the mind.

kva: where; *dhanāni*: wealth; *mahīpānām*: of kings; *brāhmaṇaḥ*: Brahmanas, priests; *jaganti*: worlds; *prāktanāni*: previous ones; *prayātāni*: have vanished; *gatāḥ*: gone; *paramparāḥ*: future; *sarga*: creations; *koṭayaḥ*: crores; *brahmaṇām*: of Brahmanas; *yātāḥ*: have gone; *bhūpāḥ*: kings; *naṣṭāḥ*: have disappeared; *parāgavat*: like dust.

yadā: when; *utpādyamānā*: generated; *rāga-ādyā*: desires and so on; *dahyante*: are burnt; *vahninā*: by the fire; *jñāna*: wisdom; *viveka*: discrimination; *tadā*: then; *kutaḥ*: how; *teṣām*: they; *prarohaṇam*: begin to grow.

Translation
Because of the movement of water, [there are] ripples in the [reflected] sun, so [is the appearance of] the ātman in mundane existence because of its connection [with] the individual self. The root of the mind, in mundane existence, should be purified with effort. Alas! What is this confidence of yours in the greatness of the mind?

Where is the wealth of the kings? Where are the Brahmanas and the worlds? The previous ones have vanished and gone to future creations. Crores of Brahmanas have gone. Kings have disappeared like dust.

When generated desires and so on are burnt by the fire [of] the wisdom [of] discrimination, then how [can] they begin to grow?

Commentary
The objects of the material world are a veil over the ātman, the innermost Self. It takes effort and discrimination to see through the veil.

Even the most admired beings and desired objects are transitory. Whoever realises this reduces worldly desires, until finally they no longer exist. Then there is no rebirth in the mundane world.

Verses 25 to 30: Ātman Alone

यथा सुनिपुनः सम्यक् परदोषेक्षने रतः ।
तथा चेन्निपुणः स्वेषु को न मुच्यते बन्धनात् ।।२५।।
अनात्मविदमुक्तोऽपि सिद्धिजालानि वाञ्छति ।
द्रव्यमन्त्रक्रियाकालयुक्त्याप्नोति मुनीश्वरः ।।२६।।
नात्यमञ्जस्यैष विषय आत्मज्ञो ह्यात्ममात्रदृक् ।
आत्मनात्मनि संतृप्तो नाविद्यामनुधावति ।।२७।।
ये केचन जगद्भावस्तानविद्यामयान्विदुः ।
कथं तेषु किलात्मज्ञस्त्यक्ताविद्यो निमज्जति ।।२८।।
द्रव्यमन्त्रक्रियाकालयुक्तयः साधुसिद्धिदाः ।
परमात्मपदप्राप्तौ नोपकुर्वन्ति काश्चन ।।२९।।
सर्वेच्छाकलनाशानतावात्मलाभोदयाभिधः ।
स पुनः सिद्धिवाञ्छायां कथमर्हत्यचित्ततः ।।३०।।

yathā sunipuṇaḥ samyak paradoṣekṣaṇe rataḥ
tathā cennipuṇaḥ sveṣu ko na mucyate bandhanāt (25)
anātmavidamukto'pi siddhijālāni vāñchati
dravyamantrakriyākālayuktyāpnoti munīśvaraḥ (26)
nātyamañjasyaiṣa viṣaya ātmajño hyātmamātradṛk
ātmanātmani saṃtṛpto nāvidyāmanudhāvati (27)
ye kecana jagadbhāvastānavidyāmayānviduḥ
kathaṃ teṣu kilātmajñastyaktāvidyo nimajjati (28)
dravyamantrakriyākālayuktayaḥ sādhusiddhidāḥ
paramātmapadaprāptau nopakurvanti kāścana (29)
sarvecchākalanāśāntāvātmalābhodayābhidhaḥ
sa punaḥ siddhivāñchāyāṃ kathamarhatyacittataḥ (30)

Vocabulary

yathā: just as; *sunipuṇaḥ*: very clever person; *rataḥ*: takes pleasure; *samyak paradoṣa-īkṣaṇe*: in seeing the exact faults;

tathā: thus; *cet*: if; *sveṣu*: of his own; *kaḥ*: who; *na mucyate*: will not be liberated; *bandhanāt*: from bondage.

munīśvaraḥ: lord of sages; *anātma-vid*: without knowledge of the ātman; *api*: also; *amuktaḥ*: not liberated; *vāñchati*: longs for; *siddhi-jālāni*: traps of *siddhis*; *āpnoti*: he attains; *dravya*: drugs; *kriya*: religious rites; *kāla*: time; *yukti*: through practice; *ātmajñaḥ*: one who knows the ātman; *eṣaḥ*: this; *viṣaya*: matter; *atyam*: absolute; *añjasya*; *dṛk*: sight; *ātma-mātra*: solely on the ātman; *saṃtṛptaḥ*: satisfied; with the ātman in his ātman; *na anudhāvati*: does not pursue; *āvidyām*: ignorance.

ye kecana: whoever; *bhāvaḥ*: exists; *jagat*: world; *viduḥ*: wise; *tān*: them; *avidyā-mayān*: nature of ignorance; *katham kila*: how then; *ātmajñaḥ*: knower of ātman; *tyaktā-avidyaḥ*: having abandoned ignorance; *nimajjati*: be immersed; *dāḥ*: can give; *sadhu-siddhi*: strong powers; *na-upakurvanti*: they do not lead; *kāścana*: in any way; *prāptau*: attainment; *pada*: seat; *paramātma*: supreme spirit; *katham*: how; *arhati saḥ*: can he; *acittataḥ*: beyond the mind; *śānta*: peace; *ātma-lābhodaya*: knowledge of existence; *abhidhaḥ*: burned; *sarva-icchā-kalanā*: all desires and actions; *punaḥ*: again; *siddhi-vāñchāyām*: crave powers.

Translation

Just as a very clever person takes pleasure in seeing the exact faults [of another], thus if he [is aware] of his own, who will not be liberated from bondage?

O Lord of sages, [whoever is] without knowledge of the ātman [and] also not liberated, longs for the traps of *siddhis*, [which] he attains through drugs, *mantra*, religious rites, time [and] practice. To one who knows the ātman this is a matter of absolute ignorance. [Whoever has] his sight solely on the ātman, satisfied with the ātman in his ātman, does not pursue ignorance.

Whoever exists [in] the world, the wise [know] them [to be] [of] the nature of ignorance. How then can the knower of ātman, having abandoned ignorance, be immersed [in it]? Drugs, *mantra*, religious rites, time [and] practice can give strong powers, [yet] they do not in any [way] lead to the attainment of the seat of the Supreme Spirit. How can he [who is] beyond the mind, in the peace of the knowledge of existence [where] all desires [and their] actions are burned, again crave powers?

Commentary
A person who thinks he is very clever by pointing out the faults of someone else, would be wiser reflecting on and removing his own faults, if he wants to be liberated from his limited ego self.

Swami Satyadharma comments on *siddhis* in Yoga Tattwa Upaniṣad. 'Although a worldly person may think of siddhis as most desireable and advantageous, the yogi looks upon them as obstacles to the spiritual path. The aim of a yogi is nothing less then enlightenment, while living in the physical body, in this material world. Delving into the powers of yoga may prove to be a great distraction to the yogi and prevent him or her from attaining his goal in this very lifetime. Therefore, the wise yogi, who has attained the level of siddhi, never takes pleasure in such powers or exhibits them to others, no matter who they may be. If asked whether or not the yogi has attained such powers, he or she will deny it.'[55]

चतुर्थोऽध्यायः

caturtho'dhyāyaḥ

Fourth Chapter

Verses 1 to 2: Definition of Jīvanmukti

अथ ह ऋभुं भगवन्तं निदाघः पप्रच्छ जीवन्मुक्तिलक्षणमनुब्रीति ।
तथेति स होवाच । सप्तभूमिषु जीवन्मुक्तश्चत्वारः ।
शुभेच्छा प्रथमा भुमिका भवति । विचारणा द्वितीया ।
तनुमानसी तृतीया । सत्त्वापत्तिस्तुरीया ।
असंसक्तिः पञ्चमी । पदर्थभावना षष्ठी । तुरीयगा सप्तमी ।
प्रणवात्मका भूमिका अकारोकारमकारार्धमात्रात्मिका ।
स्थूलसूक्ष्मबीजसाक्षिभेदेनाकारादयश्चतुर्विधाः ।

तदवस्था जाग्रत्स्वप्नसुषुप्तितुरीयाः ।
अकारस्थूलांशे जाग्रद्विश्वः । सुक्ष्मांशे तत्तैजसः ।
बीजांशे तत्प्राज्ञः । साक्ष्यंसे तत्तुरीयः ।
उकारस्थूलांशे स्वप्नविश्वः । सुक्ष्मांशे तत्तैजसः ।
बीजांशे तत्प्राज्ञः । साक्ष्यंसे तत्तुरीयः ।
मकारस्थूलांशे सुषुप्तविश्वः । सुक्ष्मांशे तत्तैजसः ।
बीजांशे तत्प्राज्ञः । साक्ष्यंशे तत्तुरीयः ।
अर्धमात्रास्थूलांशे तुरीयविश्वः । सुक्ष्मांशे तत्तैजसः ।
बीजांशे तत्प्राज्ञः । साक्ष्यंशे तुरीयतुरीयः ।

अकारतुरीयांशाः प्रथमद्वितीयतृतीयभूमिकाः ।
उकारतुरीयांशा चतुर्थी भूमिकाः ।
मकारतुरीयांशा पञ्चमी ।
अर्धमात्रातुरीयांशा षष्ठी । तदतीता सप्तमी ।
भूमित्रयेषु विहरन्मुमुक्षुर्भवति ।
तुरीयभूम्यां विहरन्ब्रह्मविद्भवति ।
पञ्चमभूम्यां विहरन्ब्रह्मविद्वरो भवति ।
षष्ठभूम्यां विहरन्ब्रह्मविद्वरीयान्भवति ।
सप्तभूम्यां विहरन्ब्रह्मविद्वरिष्ठो भवति ।
तत्रैते श्लोका भवन्ति ।
ज्ञानभूमिः शुभेच्छा स्यात्प्रथमा समुदीरिता ।
विचारणा द्वितीया तु तृतीया तनुमानसा ।।१।।
सत्त्वापत्तिश्चतुर्थी स्यात्ततोऽसंसक्तिनामिका ।
तदर्थभावना षष्थी सप्तमी तुरियगा स्मृता ।।२।।

atha ha ṛbhuṃ bhagavantaṃ nidāghaḥ papraccha
jīvanmuktilakṣaṇamanubrūhīti
tatheti sa hovāca; saptabhūmiṣu jīvanmuktaścatvāraḥ
śubhecchā prathamā bhumikā bhavati; vicāraṇā dvitīyā
tanumānasī tṛtīyā; sattvāpattisturīyā
asaṃsaktiḥ pañcamī; padarthabhāvanā ṣaṣṭhī
turīyagā saptamī
praṇavātmakā bhūmikā akārokāramakārārdhamātrātmikā
sthūlasūkṣmabījasākṣibhedenākārādayaścaturvidhāḥ

tadavasthā jāgratsvapnasuṣuptiturīyāḥ
akārasthūlāṃśe jāgradviśvaḥ; sukṣmāṃśe tattaijasaḥ
bījāṃśe tatprājñaḥ; sākṣyaṃśe tatturīyaḥ
ukārasthūlāṃśe svapnaviśvaḥ; sukṣmāṃśe tattaijasaḥ
bījāṃśe tatprājñaḥ; sākṣyaṃśe tatturīyaḥ

makārasthūlāṃśe suṣuptaviśvaḥ; sukṣmāṃśe tattaijasaḥ
bījāṃśe tatprājñaḥ; sākṣyaṃśe tatturīyaḥ
ardhamātrāsthūlāṃśe turīyaviśvaḥ; sukṣmāṃśe tattaijasaḥ
bījāṃśe tatprājñaḥ; sākṣyaṃśe turīyaturīyaḥ

akāraturīyāṃśāḥ prathamadvitīyatṛtīyabhūmikāḥ
ukāraturīyāṃśā caturthī bhūmikā
makāraturīyāṃśā pañcamī
ardhamātrāturīyāṃśā ṣaṣṭhī; tadatītā saptamī
bhūmitrayeṣu viharanmumukṣurbhavati
turīyabhūmyāṃ viharanbrahmavidbhavati
pañcamabhūmyāṃ viharanbrahmavidvaro bhavati
ṣaṣṭhabhūmyāṃ viharanbrahmavidvarīyānbhavati
saptabhūmyāṃ viharanbrahmavidvariṣṭho bhavati
tatraite ślokā bhavanti
jñānabhūmiḥ śubhecchā syātprathamā samudīritā
vicāraṇā dvitīyā tu tṛtīyā tanumānasā (1)
sattvāpattiścaturthī syāttato 'saṃsaktināmikā
tadarthabhāvanā ṣaṣṭhī saptamī turiyagā smṛtā (2)

Vocabulary

atha: then; *papraccha*: asked; *ṛbhum bhagavantam*: Lord Ṛbhu; *anubrūhi*: relate; *jīvanmukti-lakṣaṇam*: definition of *jīvanmukti*; *sa hovāca tatheti*: he answered in the affirmative; *catvāraḥ*: four; *sapta-bhūmiṣu*: in the seven stages; *prathamā bhumikā*: first stage; *bhavati*: is; *śubha-icchā*: desire for happiness; *vicāraṇā*: inquiry; *dvitīyā*: second; *tṛtīyā*: third; *tanu-mānasī*: fine-minded; *turīyā*: fourth; *sattva-āpattiḥ*: abundance of *sattwa*; *pañcamī*: fifth; *asaṃsaktiḥ*: non-attachment; *ṣaṣṭhī*: sixth; *padartha-bhāvanā*: right perception; *saptamī*: seventh; *turīya-gā*: entrance into the fourth state; *bhumikā*: stage; *praṇava-ātmakā*: in the form of *praṇava*; *ātmikā*: is based on; *akāra*: sound A; *ukāra*: sound U; *makara*: sound M; *ardha-mātra*: half-syllable; *akāra-ādayaḥ*: sound A and others; *caturvidhāḥ*: of four kinds; *bhedena*: because of the difference between; *sthūla*: gross; *sūkṣma*: subtle; *bīja*: causal; *sākṣi*: witness.

tat-avasthāḥ: these states; *jagrat*: waking; *svapna*: dreaming; *suṣupti*: sleeping; *turīya*: *turīya*, fourth state; *jāgrat-viśvaḥ*: waking *viśvaḥ*, pervading source; *akāra-sthūla-aṃśe*: in the gross part of A; *taijasaḥ*: seer of the dream state; *sukṣma-aṃśe*: in the subtle part; *prājñaḥ*: seer of the causal state; *bīja-aṃśe*: in the seed part; *sākṣi-aṃśe*: in the witness part.

akāra-turīya-aṃśāḥ: *turīya* part of A; *prathama*: first; *dvitīya*: second; *tṛtīya*: third; *bhūmikāḥ*: stages; *caturthī*: fourth; *pañcamī*: fifth; *ṣaṣṭhī*: sixth; *tat-atīta*: beyond this; *saptamī*: seventh; *viharan*: moving; *bhūmi-trayeṣu*: in the three stages; *bhavati*: one becomes; *mumukṣuḥ*: seeker of liberation; *turīya-bhūmyām*: in the fourth stage; *brahmavid*: knower of Brahman; *pañcama-bhūmyām*: in the fifth stage; *brahma-vidvaraḥ*: wise knower of Brahman; *ṣaṣṭha-bhūmyām*: in the sixth stage; *brahma-vidvarīyān*: exalted knower of Brahman; *sapta-bhūmyām*: in the seventh stage; *brahma-vidvariṣṭhaḥ*: most exalted knower of Brahman; *bhavanti*: there are; *ślokāḥ*: verses; *tatraite*: with reference to this; *prathamā jñāna-bhūmiḥ*: first stage of knowledge; *syāt samudīritā*: is said to be; *śubhecchā*: desire for happiness; *vicāraṇā*: inquiry; *tanumānasā*: fine-minded; *sattva-pattiḥ*: abundance of *sattwa*; *tataḥ syāt*: then there is; *asaṃsaktināmikā*: non-attachment; *smṛtā*: rememberance; *turiyagā*: entrance to *turīya*.

Translation

Then Nidāgha asked Lord Ṛbhu: "please relate [to me] the definition of *jīvanmukti*". He answered in the affirmative.

"[There are] four *jīvanmuktas* in the seven stages [of wisdom]. The first stage is desire for happiness. Inquiry [is] the second; the third fine-minded; the fourth abundance of *sattwa*; the fifth non-attachment; the sixth right perception; the seventh entrance into the fourth state. The stage in the form of *praṇava* is based on the sounds A, U, M [and] the half-syllable. The sound A and others [are] of four kinds because of the difference between gross, subtle, causal [and] witness.

These states [are] waking, dreaming, sleeping and *turīya*. The waking *viśva* is in the gross part of A. The *taijasa* is in the subtle part. The *prājña* is in the seed part. The *turīya* is in the witness part. The dreaming *viśva* is in the gross part of U. The *taijasa* is in the subtle part. The *prājña* is in the seed part. The *turīya* is in the witness part. The sleeping *viśva* is in the gross part of M. The *taijasa* is in the subtle part. The *prājña* is in the seed part. The *turīya* is in the witness part. The *turīya viśva* is in the gross part of the half-syllable. The *taijasa* is in the subtle part. The *prājña* is in the seed part. The *turīya* of the *turīya* is in the witness part.

The *turīya* part of A [includes] the first, second and third stages. The *turīya* part of U [includes] the fourth stage. The *turīya* part of M [includes] the fifth stage. The *turīya* part of the half-syllable [includes] the sixth stage. Beyond this [is] the seventh stage. Moving in the [first] three stages one becomes a seeker of liberation. Moving in the fourth stage, one becomes a knower of Brahman. Moving in the fifth stage, one becomes a wise knower of Brahman. Moving in the sixth stage, one becomes an exalted knower of Brahman. Moving in the seventh stage one becomes a most exalted knower of Brahman. There are verses with reference to this. The first stage of knowledge is said to be the desire for happiness, the second inquiry, the third fine-minded, the fourth abundance of *sattwa*; then there is [the fifth,] non-attachment, right perception, the sixth [and] rememberance of the entrance to *turīya* the seventh.

Commentary
Nidāgha was a devoted disciple of Ṛbhu.

Swami Sarvapriyananda says that 'jīvanmukti means full-blown enlightenment, applying it in life and being fully free in suffering while living in the body-mind in this *saṃsāra*. That's the goal. For that, a pure, focussed and controlled mind, and the ability to control the sensory system and to attain *samādhi*.'[56]

In Vedānta, a *jīvanmukta* is someone who has experienced all seven stages of wisdom.[57]

The first stage is desire for virtue; the second is inquiry into who we are; the third is working with a subtle mind; the fourth is the state of harmony and equanimity; the fifth non-attachment to the transitory world; the sixth right understanding of the reality of Brahman; the seventh entry into the fourth state, *turīya*.

Swami Satyananda, in his commentary on the Yoga Sutras of Patanjali, describes the seven stages of enlightenment thus: 'firstly, realization of what is to be avoided; secondly, awareness of the means for that removal; thirdly, awareness of spiritual evolution; fourthly, awareness of fulfilment and accomplishment; fifthly, awareness of the purpose of experience and liberation; sixthly, awareness of the fulfilment of the work of the gunas; lastly, awareness of one's own Self.'[58]

The remainder of this long verse is the topic of the Ultimate Reality in the Mandukyopanishad. *Praṇava* is Om, composed of the three sounds A, U and M which 'symbolize the gross, subtle and causal aspects of Brahman. Om is the means to know Brahman, and is inseparable from Him'.[59]

Each state has three parts, gross, subtle and seed. *Viśva* is the name of the gross part. *Taijasa* is the seer of the subtle dream state. *Prājña* is the causal state which contains the seed of life. It means the 'all-knowing', 'what is known'.

A is the objective waking state, the awareness of external things, which experiences the visible objects of the world. U is the subjective dreaming state, which experiences the invisible objects. M is the unconscious state of deep dreamless sleep, free from experience, desire and awareness of personal identity. When one chants Om, one passes from one state of consciousness to another phase. Each syllable has its own vibration, the combined sounds representing the superconscious state.

Swami Sarvapriyananda says that 'Turīya, meaning the fourth, is the underlying consciousness and witness of these three states. Turīya is ātman, the peace and bliss of pure awareness. The fourth is not the fourth; it is the one which appears as three with respect to the waking dreaming sleeping, it seems to be the fourth.'[60]

Verses 3 to 5: Virtuous Desire

स्थितः किं मूढ एवास्मि प्रेक्ष्योऽहं शास्त्रसज्जनैः ।
वैराग्यपूर्वमिच्छेति शुभेच्छेत्युच्यते बुधैः ॥३॥
शास्त्रसज्जनसंपर्कवैरग्याभ्यासपूर्वकम् ।
सदाचार प्रवृत्तिर्या प्रोच्यते सा विचारणा ॥४॥
विचारणाशुभेच्छामिन्द्रियार्थेषुरक्तता ।
यत्र सा तनुतामेति प्रोच्यते तनुमानसी ॥५॥

sthitaḥ kiṃ mūḍha evāsmi prekṣyo'haṃ śāstrasajjanaiḥ
vairāgyapūrvamiccheti śubhecchetyucyate budhaiḥ (3)
śāstrasajjanasaṃparkavairagyābhyāsapūrvakam
sadācāra pravṛttiryā procyate sā vicāraṇā (4)
vicāraṇāśubhecchāmindriyārtheṣuraktatā
yatra sā tanutāmeti procyate tanumānasī (5)

Vocabulary

iccha: desire; *pūrvam*: prior; *vairagya*: detachment; *kim*: why; *asmi sthitaḥ*: do I remain; *mūḍha*: ignorant; *aham prekṣyaḥ*: I am regarded; *śāstra-sajjanaiḥ*: by the teachings and the virtuous; *ucyate iti*: is said to be; *budhaiḥ*: by the wise; *śubheccha*: virtuous desire; *pravṛttiḥ*: leaning; *sadācāra*: good conduct; *pūrvakam*: previous; *abhyāsa*: constant practice; *vairagya*: detachment; *saṃparka*: contact; *sā procyate*: this is known as; *vicāraṇā*: inquiry; *yatra*: where; *raktatā*: passionate; *indriya-artheṣu*: sensual objects; *tanutāmeti*: is reduced by; *tanumānasī*: fine-minded.

Translation

The desire [which arises] from prior detachment, [namely] 'why do I remain ignorant? I am regarded by the teachings [and] the virtuous' is said by the wise to be virtuous desire. A leaning [towards] good conduct, previous constant practice of detachment, contact [with] the teachings [and] the virtuous, this is known as inquiry. Where passionate [attachment] to sensual objects is reduced by virtuous desire [and] inquiry, this is known as fine-minded.

Commentary

Who am I? This is the virtuous desire. Inquiry here means investigation into the Self.

Firstly, detachment from the worldly desires for name, fame and wealth and the sensory desires of sights, sounds, taste, touch and smell are necessary. Then there remains the one desire to know one's true Self. This is called *mumukshutva*, intense desire for liberation

Sri Krishna in the *Bhagavad Gīta* says 'while contemplating on the objects of the senses, one develops attachment to them. Attachment leads to desire, and from desire arises anger'.[61] The worldly person thinks desires will give satisfaction. When desire is satisfied, greed arises. When it is not satisfied, anger arises.

'That person, who gives up all material desires and lives free from a sense of greed, proprietorship, and egoism, attains perfect peace.'[62] Therefore the path to peace lies in reducing and finally eliminating all desires except for the One.

'But one who controls the mind, and is free from attachment and aversion, even while using the objects of the senses, attains the Grace of God.'[63] The objects of both attachment and its opposite, aversion, repeatedly come to mind, preventing the development of spiritual attachment and desire. The use of the five senses in daily life does not affect the mind which is free from material attachment and aversion.

Verses 6 to 9: Abundance of Sattwa

भूमिकात्रितयाभ्यासाच्चित्तेऽर्थविरतेर्वशात् ।
सत्वात्मनि स्थिते शुद्धे सत्त्वापत्तिरूदाहृयता ॥६॥
दशाचतुष्टयाभ्यासादसंसर्गफला तु या ।
रूढसत्वचमत्कारा प्रोक्ता असंसक्तिनामिका ॥७॥
भूमिकापञ्चकाभ्यासात्स्वात्मारामतया भृशम् ।
आभ्यन्तराणां बाहृयानां पदार्थनामभावनात् ॥८॥
परप्रयुक्तेन चिरं प्रत्ययेनावबोधनम् ।
पदर्थभावना नाम षष्ठी भवति भूमिका ॥९॥

bhūmikātritayābhyāsāccitte'rthaviratervaśāt
satvātmani sthite śuddhe sattvāpattirūdāhyatā (6)
daśācatuṣṭayābhyāsādasaṃsargaphalā tu yā
rūḍhasatvacamatkārā proktā asaṃsaktināmikā (7)
bhūmikāpañcakābhyāsātsvātmārāmatayā bhṛśam
ābhyantarāṇāṃ bāhyānāṃ padārthanāmabhāvanāt (8)
paraprayuktena ciraṃ pratyayenāvabodhanam
padarthabhāvanā nāma ṣaṣṭhī bhavati bhūmikā (9)

Vocabulary

citte: when the mind; *stithe*: is fixed; *śuddhe*: on the pure; *satvātmani*: nature of existence; *vaśāt*: because of; *abhyāsāt*: practice; *bhūmikā-tritaya*: three stages; *virateḥ*: cessation; *artha*: objects; *rūdāhyatā*: this is widely known; *sattva-pattiḥ*: abundance of *sattwa*; *satva-camatkārā*: manifestation of sattwa; *yāḥ*: which; *tu rūḍha*: has then risen; *asaṃsarga*: without attachment; *phalāḥ*: fruits; *abhyāsāt*: of the practice; *catuṣṭaya*: four; *daśāḥ*: stages; *proktā*: is known; *nāmikā*: by the name of; *asaṃsakti*: detachment; *bhūmikā-pañcaka*: five stages; *bhṛśam*: great; *svātmārāma-tayā*: through taking pleasure in the Self; *padārtha-nāma-bhāvanāt*: through correct perception; *ābhyantarāṇām*: of the internal; *bāhyānām*: of the external; *avabodhanam*: having been taught; *ciram*: for a long time; *paraprayuktena pratyayena*: through beneficial explanation; *ṣaṣṭhī bhūmikā*: sixth stage; *bhavati nāma*: is called; *padarthabhāvanā*: right perception.

Translation

When the mind is fixed on the pure nature of existence because of the practice of the three stages [and] the cessation [of desires] for [sensual] objects, this is widely known as abundance of *sattwa*. The manifestation of sattwa, which has then risen without attachment [to] the fruits [of actions] of the practice of the four stages is known by the name of detachment. [That stage where] due to practice of the five stages, through taking great pleasure in the Self [and] correct perception of the internal [and] external, [and] having been taught for a long time through beneficial explanation, the sixth stage is called right perception.

Commentary

Sri Krishna describes the three *guṇas* (the three qualities of nature which affect the human character), and in particular *sattva* in the following verses.

'O mighty-armed Arjun, the material energy consists of three *guṇas* (modes)—*sattva* (goodness), *rajas* (passion), and *tamas* (ignorance). These modes bind the eternal soul to the perishable body.

Amongst these, *sattva guṇa*, the mode of goodness, being purer than the others, is illuminating and full of well-being. O sinless one, it binds the soul by creating attachment for a sense of happiness and knowledge.' [64]

Swami Mukundunanda comments on *sattva guṇa*: 'While the mode of goodness creates an effect of serenity and happiness, attachment to them itself binds the soul to material nature. We must not get attached to it; instead, we must use it to step up to the transcendental platform.

Beyond these three, is *śuddha sattva,* the transcendental mode of goodness. It is the mode of the divine energy of God that is beyond material nature. When the soul becomes God-realized, by his grace, God bestows *śuddha sattva* upon the soul, making the senses, mind, and intellect divine.' [65]

Then, as stated in Verse 1 of this chapter, 'Moving in the sixth stage, one becomes an exalted knower of Brahman.'

Verses 10 to 13: Devotion to the Natural State

षड्भूमिकाचिराभ्यासाद्भेदस्यानुपलम्भनात् ।
यत्स्वभावैकनिष्ठत्वं सा ज्ञेया तुरयगा गतिः ॥१०॥
शुभेच्छादित्रयं भूमिभेदाभेदयुतं स्मृतम् ।
यथावद्वेद बुद्ध्येदं जगज्जाग्रति दृश्यते ॥११॥
अद्वैते स्थैर्यमायाते द्वैते च प्रशमं गते ।
पश्यन्ति स्वप्नवल्लोकं तुर्यभूमिसुयोगतः ॥१२॥
विच्छिन्नशरदभ्राम्शविलयं प्रविलीयते ।
सत्वावशेष एवास्ते हे निदाघ दृढीकुरु ॥१३॥

ṣadbhūmikācirābhyāsādbhedasyānupalambhanāt
yatsvabhāvaikaniṣṭhatvaṃ sā jñeyā turyagā gatiḥ (10)
śubhecchāditrayaṃ bhūmibhedābhedayutaṃ smṛtam
yathāvadveda buddhyedaṃ jagajjāgrati dṛśyate (11)
advaite sthairyamāyāte dvaite ca praśamaṃ gate
paśyanti svapnavallokaṃ turyabhūmisuyogataḥ (12)
vicchinnaśaradabhrāmśavilayaṃ pravilīyate
satvāvaśeṣa evāste he nidāgha dṛdhīkuru (13)

Vocabulary

sā jñeyā: that should be known as; *gatiḥ*: way; *turya-gā*: gone to the fourth; *yat*: which; *eka-niṣṭhatvam*: absolute devotion; *svabhāva*: one's natural state; *anupalambhanāt*: because of the non-perception; *bhedasya*: of difference; *abhyāsāt*: due to practice; *cira*: for a long time; *ṣad-bhūmikāḥ*: six stages; *trayam*: triad; *śubheccha-ādi*: beginning with virtuous desire; *smṛtam*: is known as; *bhūmi*: stages; *yutam bheda*: with differences; *abheda*: without differences; *yathāvat*: in which manner; *veda*: one perceives; *buddhyā*: through the intellect; *idam jagat*: this world; *dṛśyate*: is seen; *jāgrati*: in the waking state; *advaite*: when the non-dual; *āyāte*: becomes; *sthairyam*: fixed; *ca dvaite*: and the dual; *gate praśamam*: has gone to extinction; *paśyanti*: they see; *suyogataḥ*:

through union with; *turīya-bhūmi*: fourth stage; *lokam*: world; *svapnavat*: as a dream; *he nidāgha*: o Nidāgha; *dṛdhīkuru*: be convinced; *aste avaśeṣa*: there remains; *eva*: only; *satva*: True Reality.

Translation

That should be known as the way, having gone to the fourth, to absolute devotion to one's natural state, because of the non-perception of difference due to practice for a long time of the six stages. The triad [of stages], beginning with virtuous desire, is known as stages with and without differences. In which manner one perceives [the world] through the intellect, [so] this world is seen in the waking state. When the non-dual becomes fixed and the dual has gone to extinction, they see through union with the fourth stage the world as a dream. It vanishes [just as] the autumnal cloud, having dissipated, disappears. O Nidāgha, be convinced there remains only the True Reality.

Commentary

Turīya, the fourth, is 'the final superconscious state of existence, a state of complete absorption of the mind in Brahman in which the individual self or soul becomes one with the universal spirit'. [66]

Once one is established in the non-dual state, one sees only the True Reality, pure consciousness, which permeates everything in the material mundane world. The differences between the previous stages become irrelevant and disappear.

Verses 14 to 15: Seat of Deep Sleep

पञ्चभूमिं समारुह्य सुषुप्तिपदनामिकाम् ।
शान्ताशेषविशेषांशस्तिष्ठत्यद्वैतमात्रके ॥१४॥
अन्तर्मुखतया नित्यं बहिर्वृत्तिपरोऽपि सन् ।
परिश्रान्ततया नित्यं निद्रालुरिव लक्ष्यते ॥१५॥

pañcabhūmiṃ samāruhya suṣuptipadanāmikām
śāntāśeṣaviśeṣāṃśastiṣṭhatyadvaitamātrake (14)
antarmukhatayā nityaṃ bahirvṛttiparo'pi san
pariśrāntatayā nityaṃ nidrāluriva lakṣyate (15)

Vocabulary

samāruhya: having risen to; *pañca-bhūmim*: fifth stage; *nāmikam*: called; *suṣupti-pada*: seat of deep sleep; *śānta-aśeṣa*: peaceful; *tiṣṭhati*: one remains; *mātrake*: entirely; *advaita*: non-dual; *nityam*: always; *antarmukhatayā*: with [the mind] turned inwards; *api san*: although engaging in; *paraḥ*: other; *bahiḥ-vṛtti*: external activities; *lakṣyate*: one appears; *nidrāluḥ-iva*: like a sleeping person; *pariśrāntatayā*: when fatigued.

Translation

Having risen to the fifth stage called the seat of deep sleep, [which is] peaceful, one remains entirely in the non-dual state without special parts. With the [mind] always turned inwards, although engaging in other external activities, one always appears like a sleeping person when fatigued.

Commentary

The state of deep sleep, undisturbed by the senses, is peaceful because identity with the personal self is forgotten, as is the discriminating judgmental mind. In the state of turīya, which is ātman, there is also no personal identity and no discriminating mind. It differs from deep sleep, in that one lives actively in the mundane world with the peace and bliss of pure awareness, and therefore may appear to the ignorant as half asleep.

Verses 16 to 20: Non-dual State

कुर्वन्नभ्यासमेतस्यां भूम्यां सम्यग्विवासनः ।
साप्तमी गूढसुप्त्याख्या क्रमप्राप्ता पुरातनी ॥१६॥
यत्र नासन्न सद्रूपो नाहं नाप्यनहंकृतिः ।
केवलं क्षीणमनन स्तेऽद्वैऽतिनिर्भयः ॥१७॥
अन्तःशून्यो बहिःशून्यः शूनयाकुमगह इवाम्बरे ।
अन्तःपूर्णो बहिःपूर्णः पूर्णकुम्भ इवार्णवे ॥१८॥
मा भव ग्राह्यभावात्मा ग्राहकात्मा च मा भव ।
भावनामखिलां त्यक्त्वा यच्छिष्टं तन्मयो भव ॥१९॥
द्रष्टृदर्शनदृश्यानि त्यक्त्वा वासनया सह ।
दर्शनप्रथमाभासमात्मानं केवलं भज ॥२०॥

kurvannabhyāsametasyāṃ bhūmyāṃ samyag-vivāsanaḥ
saptamī guḍhasuptyākhyā kramaprāptā purātanī (16)
yatra nāsanna sadrūpo nāhaṃ nāpyanahaṃkṛtiḥ
kevalaṃ kṣīṇamanana āste'dvaite'tinirbhayaḥ (17)
antaḥśūnyo bahiḥśūnyaḥ śūnyakumbha ivāmbare
antaḥpūrṇo bahiḥpūrṇaḥ pūrṇakumbha ivārṇave (18)
mā bhava grāhyabhāvātmā grāhakātmā ca mā bhava
bhāvanāmakhilāṃ tyaktvā yacchiṣṭaṃ tanmayo bhava (19)
draṣṭṛdarśanadṛśyāni tyaktvā vāsanayā saha
darśanaprathamābhāsamātmānaṃ kevalaṃ bhaja (20)

Vocabulary

kurvan: doing; *abhyāsam*: practice; *etasyāṃ bhūmyāṃ*: in this stage; *samyak*: completely; *vivāsanaḥ*: eliminated; *saptamī*: seventh; *purātanī*: ancient; *ākhyā*: called; *gūḍha-supti*: secret sleep; *krama*: step by step; *prāptā*: attained; *yatra*: where; *kṛtiḥ*: there is; *na-asan*: neither non-existence; *na sadrūpa*: nor the form of existence; *na-aham*: neither the I; *na-api-anaham*: nor even the not-I; *āste*: one exists;

kevalam: alone; *advaite*: in non-duality; *manana*: thinking; *kṣīṇa*: diminished; *nirbhayaḥ*: without fear.

iva: like; *śūnya-kumbha*: empty pot; *ambare*: in the ether; *antaḥ-śūnyaḥ*: empty inside; *bahiḥ-śūnyaḥ*: empty outside; *antaḥ-pūrṇaḥ*: full inside; *iva pūrṇa-kumbha*: like a full pot; *arṇave*: in the ocean; *antaḥ-pūrṇaḥ*: full inside; *bahiḥ-pūrṇaḥ*: full outside; *mā bhava*: do not be; *ātmā*: one who; *grāhya-bhāva*: is grasped; *grāhaka-ātmā*: one who grasps; *tyaktvā*: having abandoned; *akhilām*: all; *bhāvanām*: concepts; *bhava tanmayaḥ*: be absorbed in; *yat-śiṣṭaṃ*: what remains; *tyaktvā*: disregarding; *draṣṭṛ-darśana-dṛśyāni*: seer sight seen; *saha vāsanayā*: with impressions; *bhaja ātmānam*: meditate on the ātman; *darśana*: seeing; *prathama-ābhāsam*: first light.

Translation
Doing the practice in this stage, [mental tendencies] completely eliminated, the seventh, [which is] ancient [and] called secret sleep, is step by step attained, where there is neither non-existence nor the form of existence, neither the I nor even the not-I. One exists alone in non-duality, thinking diminished [and] without fear.

Like an empty pot in the ether, empty inside [and] empty outside, like a full pot in the ocean, full inside [and] full outside, do not be one who is grasped and do not be one who grasps. Having abandoned all concepts, be absorbed in what remains. Disregarding the seer, sight and seen with their impressions, meditate on the ātman alone, seeing its first light.

Commentary
When the mind is free of mental impressions and conditioning, one reaches the seventh stage, which is the entrance into turīya, the fourth dimension of consciousness, ancient because it is pure primal consciousness, unmanifest

and therefore described as 'secret sleep'. This consciousness is steady, still and deep. It is beyond the duality of form and formless. The mind is clear and unfettered.

Just as an empty pot immersed in the ocean of infinite space is empty both inside and outside, and just as a pot immersed in the ocean of water is both full inside and outside, there is nothing to take and nothing to be taken. There is nothing to be understood by the intellectual mind. Give up all concepts such as full and empty, and remain absorbed in the ātman alone.

Verses 21 to 30: Who is a Jīvanmukta?

यथास्थतमिदं यस्य व्यवहारवतोऽपिच ।
अस्तंगतं स्थितं व्योम स जीवन्मुक्त उच्यते ।।२१।।
नोदेति नास्तमायाति सुखे दुःखे मनःप्रभा ।
यथाप्राप्तस्थितिर्यस्य स जीवन्मुक्त उच्यते ।।२२।।
यो जागर्ति सुषुप्तिस्थो यस्य जाग्रन्न विद्यते ।
यस्य निर्वासनो बोधः स जीवन्मुक्त उच्यते ।।२३।।
रागद्वेषभयादीनामनुरूपं चरन्नपि ।
योऽन्तर्व्योमवदच्छन्नः स जीवन्मुक्त उच्यते ।।२४।।
यस्य नाहंकृतो भावो बुद्धिर्यस्य न लिप्यते ।
कुर्वतोऽकुर्वतो वापि स जीवन्मुक्त उच्यते ।।२५।।
यस्मान्नोद्विजते लोको लोकान्नोद्विजते च यः ।
हर्षामर्षभयोन्मुक्तः स जीवन्मुक्त उच्यते ।।२६।।
यः समस्तार्थजालेषु व्यवहार्यपि शीतलः ।
परार्थेष्विव पूर्णात्मा स जीवन्मुक्त उच्यते ।।२७।।
प्रजहाति यदा कामान्सर्वांश्चित्तगतान्मुने ।
मयि सर्वात्मके तुष्टः स जीवन्मुक्त उच्यते ।।२८।।
चैत्यवर्जितचिन्मात्रे पदे परमपावने ।
अक्षुब्धचित्तो विश्रान्तः स जीवन्मुक्त उच्यते ।।२९।।
इदं जगदहं सोऽयं दृश्यजातमवास्तवम् ।
यस्य चित्ते न स्फुरति स जीवन्मुक्त उच्यते ।।३०।।

yathāsthatamidaṃ yasya vyavahāravato'pica
astaṃgataṃ sthitaṃ vyoma sa jīvanmukta ucyate (21)
nodeti nāstamāyāti sukhe duḥkhe manaḥprabhā
yathāprāptasthitiryasya sa jīvanmukta ucyate (22)
yo jāgarti suṣuptistho yasya jāgranna vidyate

yasya nirvāsano bodhaḥ sa jīvanmukta ucyate (23)
rāgadveṣabhayādinamanurūpaṃ carannapi
yo'ntarvyomavadacchannaḥ sa jīvanmukta ucyate (24)
yasya nāhaṃkṛto bhāvo buddhiryasya na lipyate
kurvato'kurvato vāpi sa jīvanmukta ucyate (25)
yasmānnodvijate loko lokānnodvijate ca yaḥ
harṣāmarṣabhayonmuktaḥ sa jīvanmukta ucyate (26)
yaḥ samastārthajāleṣu vyavahāryapi śītalaḥ
parārtheṣviva pūrṇātmā sa jīvanmukta ucyate (27)
prajahāti yadā kāmānsarvāṃścittagatānmune
mayi sarvātmake tuṣṭaḥ sa jīvanmukta ucyate (28)
caityavarjitacinmātre pade paramapāvane
akṣubdhacitto viśrāntaḥ sa jīvanmukta ucyate (29)
idaṃ jagadahaṃ so'yaṃ dṛśayajātamavāstavam
yasya citte na sphurati sa jīvanmukta ucyate (30)

Vocabulary

yasya: whoever; *āsthitam*: is occupied with; *vyavahāravataḥ*: daily life; *ca api*: and also; *gatam*: moves; *astham sthitam*: stays firm; *yathā vyoma*: like the ether; *sa ucyate jivanmukta*: he is said to be a *jivanmukta*; *yasya*: in whom; *prabhā*: light; *manaḥ*: mind; *na-udeti*: neither rises; *na-astamāyāti*: nor perishes; *sukhe*: in happiness; *duḥkhe*: in suffering; *sthitiḥ*: remains firm; *aprāpta*: not obtained; *yaḥ jāgarti*: whoever is awake; *suṣuptisthaḥ*: while in deep sleep; *yasya jāgrat*: whose waking state; *na vidyate*: is not known; *yasya bodhaḥ*: whose perception; *nirvāsanaḥ*: without impressions; *api caran*: although behaving; *anurūpam*: in accordance with; *raga*: desire; *dveṣa*: hatred; *bhaya-ādīnām*: fear and others; *accha*: pure; *antaḥ-vyomavat*: as the inner space; *yasya*: one whose; *bhāvaḥ*: state of mind; *na aham*: I am not; *kṛtaḥ*: doer; *yasya buddhiḥ*: whose intellect; *na lipyate*: is not attached to; *kurvataḥ*: doing; *vā akurvataḥ*: not doing.

yasmāt: one from whom; *lokaḥ*: world; *na udvijate*: does not shrink; *ca yaḥ*: and who; *lokāt*: from the world; *unmukta*: unfettered by; *harṣa*: pleasure; *amarṣa*: anger; *bhaya*: fear;

api: although; *vyavahāri*: engaging; *samasta*: all; *jāleṣu*: in trap-like; *artha*: matters; *śītalaḥ*: cool; *para-artheṣu*: in the highest attainment; *pūrṇa-ātmā*: Absolute Consciousness; *yadā*: when; *sarva*: always; *tuṣṭaḥ*: content; *mayi ātmake*: in my true nature; *prajahāti*: renouncing; *sarvām*: all; *gatān*: past; *kāmān*: desires; *citta*: heart; *mune*: o Sage; *akṣubdha-citta*: serene mind; *viśrāntaḥ*: resting; *parama-pāvane*: in the most pure; *pade*: state; *cinmātre*: consciousness; *varjita*: devoid of; *caitya*: thought; *yasya cite*: in whose mind; *na sphurati*: does not spring; *idam jagat*: this world; *ajātam*: having no; *aham*: I; *saḥ*: he; *ayam*: this one; *dṛśa*: visible; *avāstavam*: unreal.

Translation

Whoever is occupied with this daily life, and also moves [or] stays firm like the ether, is said to be a *jīvanmukta*. In whom the light [of] the mind neither rises nor perishes in happiness [and] suffering [and] remains firm when [one's desire] is not obtained, is said to be a jīvanmukta. Whoever is awake while in deep sleep, whose waking state is not known [and] whose perception is without impressions, is said to be a jīvanmukta. Whoever, although behaving in accordance with desire, hatred, fear and others, is as pure as the inner space, is said to be a jīvanmukta. One whose state of mind is 'I am not the doer' and whose intellect is not attached to doing or not doing, is said to be a jīvanmukta.

One from whom the world does not shrink and who, unfettered by pleasure, anger [and] fear, does not shrink from the world, is said to be a jīvanmukta. One who, although engaging in all trap-like matters, [remains] cool, while [engrossed] in the highest attainment, the Absolute Consciousness, is said to be a jīvanmukta. When, always content in My True Nature, renouncing all past desires [of] the heart, o Sage, that person is said to be a jīvanmukta. [One whose] mind [is] serene, resting in the most pure state of consciousness, devoid of thought, is said to be a jīvanmukta.

In whose mind does not spring this world having no I, he, this one, [and what is] visible [and] unreal, that person is said to be a jīvanmukta.

Commentary

Georg Feuerstein defines a jīvanmukta as 'an adept (a master of one's own self-body-mind) who is liberated, or enlightened, while still embodied'. [67]

The jīvanmukta does not hide or escape from the world. Śri Krishna describes in the *Bhagavad Gīta* how the jīvanmukta lives in the world. Swami Mukundananda has translated and commented on the following verses of the *Bhagavad Gīta.*

'One whose mind remains undisturbed amidst misery, who does not crave for pleasure, and who is free from attachment, fear, and anger, is called a sage of steady wisdom.' Vs.2.56

Commentary

'Śrī Krishna describes sages of steady wisdom as: 1) *Vīta rāga*—they give up craving for pleasure, 2) *Vīta bhaya*—they remain free from fear, 3) *Vīta krodha*—they are devoid of anger. Only then can the mind steadily contemplate on transcendence and be fixed in the divine.'

'One who remains unattached under all conditions, and is neither delighted by good fortune nor dejected by tribulation, he is a sage with perfect knowledge.' Vs.2.57

Commentary

'The urge for enlightenment is the intrinsic nature of the soul. Hence, knowingly or unknowingly, everyone craves for it, in all cultures around the world. Śrī Krishna is describing it here, in response to Arjun's question.'

2.59: 'Aspirants may restrain the senses from their objects of enjoyment, but the taste for the sense objects remains. However, even this taste ceases for those who realizes the Supreme.' Vs.2.59

Commentary
'When the soul engages in devotion toward God, and gets divine bliss, it experiences the higher taste for which it had been craving since infinite lifetimes. The Taittirīya Upaniṣhad states:
raso vai saḥ rasaṁ hyevāyaṁ labdhvā 'nandī bhavati (2.7.2) [v50]
"God is all-bliss. When the soul attains God, it becomes satiated in bliss." Then, one naturally develops dispassion toward the lower sensual pleasures. This detachment that comes through devotion is firm and unshakeable.' [68]

Here are Georg Feuerstein's translation and commentary on verses 12.13-14.

'[He who feels] no hatred toward any being, [who is] friendly and compassionate . . . [that] yogin who is ever content, self-controlled, of firm resolve, with mind and wisdom (*buddhi*) offered up in Me, who is My devotee – he is dear to Me. He from whom the world does not shrink and who does not shrink from the world and who is free from exultation, anger, fear and exultation, is dear to Me.'
Commentary
'The jīvanmukta's continual immersion in the Self allows him to recognize the same (*sama*) in all things. His equanimity has positive outgoing characteristics. He is, above all, a compassionate being.' [69]

The *Yoga Vaśiṣṭha*, composed some time between the 6th CE and 15th CE, describes the jīvanmukta as one who does not abide in the past, present or future, nor in the waking or sleeping state, but always equanimous, does what is necessary, knowing he is not the doer. He is wise, a good friend, radiates peace, and is undisturbed by changing events. '[He behaves] as a boy among boys; and elder among elders; a sage among sages; a youth among youths; and as a sympathizer among the well-behaved afflicted.' [70]

Verses 31 to 33: Śiva

सद्ब्रह्माणि स्थिरे स्फारे पूर्णे विषयवर्जिते ।
आचार्यशास्त्रमार्गेण प्रविश्याशु स्थिरे भव ॥३१॥
शिवो गुरुः शिवो वेदः शिव देवः शिवः प्रभुः ।
शिवोऽस्म्यहं शिवः सर्वं शिवादन्यन्न किंचनन ॥३२॥
तमेव धीरो विज्ञाय प्रज्ञां कुर्वीत ब्राह्मणः
नानुध्यायाद्वहुञ्छब्दान्वाचो विग्लापनं हि तत् ॥३३॥
sadbrahmāṇi sthire sphāre pūrṇe viṣayavarjite
ācāryaśāstramārgena praviśyāśu sthire bhava (31)
śivo guruḥ śivo vedaḥ śiva devaḥ śivaḥ prabhuḥ
śivo'smyahaṃ śivaḥ sarvaṃ śivādanyanna kiṃcana (32)
tameva dhīro vijñāya prajñāṃ kurvīta brāhmaṇaḥ
nānudhyāyādvahūñchabdānvāco viglāpanaṃ hi tat (33)

Vocabulary

mārgena: through the path; *ācārya*: spiritual masters; *śāstra*: sacred teachings; *āsu*: immediately; *praviśya*: enter; *sthire*: changeless; *sphāre*: abundant; *pūrṇe*: full; *varjite*: free of; *viṣaya*: sense objects; *bhava sthire*: remain fixed; *aham asmi*: I am; *devaḥ*: God; *prabhuḥ*: Lord; *sarvam*: all; *anya-na kiṃcana*: none other; *śivāt*: than Śiva; *dhīraḥ*: courageous; *vijñāya*: having known; *tam-eva*: him alone; *kurvīta prajñām*: attains wisdom; *na-anudhyāyāt*: without remembering; *bahūn-śabdān*: many words; *tat viglāpanaṃ*: which fatigue; *vācaḥ*: speech organs.

Translation

Through the path of the spiritual masters and sacred teachings immediately enter the *sat*, the Brahman [which is] changeless, abundant, full [and] free of sense objects, [and] remain fixed [there]. Śiva is *guru*; Śiva is the *veda*; Śiva is God; Śiva is the Lord; I am Śiva; Śiva is all. There is none other than Śiva. The courageous *brāhmaṇa*, having known him alone, attains wisdom, without remembering many words which fatigue the speech organs.

Commentary

Ṛbhu now instructs Nidāgha to embark on the path of the spiritual masters and sacred teachings, thereby entering Brahman, that state of existence which is permanent, abundant, both full and devoid of sense objects.

Here resides Śiva, whose literal meaning is 'auspicious'. He is the destroyer, in the sense of transformer. Through his power the ego personality is destroyed, and the yogin enters the divine light of wisdom. This process is not easy, as it takes courage to let go of one's personal identity. The *brāhmaṇa* is the 'priest who is dedicated to the study of the Vedas and dispensation of the knowledge of Brahman'. [71] In the silent presence of Śiva, he will attain wisdom.

Not only does too much talk tire the speech organs, but deep silence, *mauna*, is where wisdom is attained. The jīvanmukta has the quality of a *muni*. Ramana Maharishi taught more by silence than by word of mouth. In his presence the questioner either realised that the question needed no answer, or found the answer in themselves. He said 'silence is the language of the Self, and it is the most important teaching. Language is like the glow of the filament in the electric lamp; but Silence is like the current in the wire'. [72]

Verses 34 to 42a: The Two Paths

शुको मुक्तो वामादेवोऽपि मुक्तस्ताभ्यां विना मुक्तिभाजो न सन्तिः ।
शुकमार्गं येऽनुसरन्ति धीराः सद्यो मुक्तास्ते भवन्तीह लोके ।।३४।।
वामदेवं येऽनुसरन्ति नित्यं मृत्वा जनित्वा च पुनःपुनस्तत ते वै लोके क्रममुक्ता भवन्ति योगैः सांख्यैः कर्मभिः सत्त्वयुक्तैः ।।३५।।
शुकश्च वामदेवश्च देव सृती देवनिर्मिते ।
शुको विहङ्गमः प्रोक्तो वामदेवः पिपीलिका ।।३६।।
अतद्व्यावृत्तिरूपेण साक्षाद्विधिमुखेन वा ।
महावाक्यविचारेण सांख्ययोगसमाधिना ।।३७।।
विदित्वा स्वात्मनो रूपं संप्रज्ञातसमाधितः ।
शुकमार्गेण विरजाः प्रयान्ति परमं पदम् ।।३८।।
यमाद्यासनजायासहठाभ्यासात्पुनःपुनः
विघ्नबाहुल्यसंजात अणिमादिवशादिह ।।३९।।
अलब्ध्वापि फलं सम्यक्पुनर्भूत्वा महाकुले ।
पुनर्वास्न्यैवायं योगाभ्यासं पेनश्चरन् ।।४०।।
अनेकजन्माभ्यासेन वामदेवेन वे पक्ष ।
सोऽपि मुक्तिं समाप्नोति तद्विष्णो परं पदम् ।।४१।।
द्वाविमावपि पन्थानौ ब्रह्मप्राप्तिकरौ शिवौ ।
सद्यौ मुक्तिप्रदश्चैकः क्रममुक्तिप्रदः परः ।४२।

śuko mukto vāmadevo'pi muktastābhyāṃ vinā mukti-bhājo na santiḥ
śukamārgaṃ ye'nusaranti dhīrāḥ sadyo muktāste

bhavantīha loke (34)
vāmadevaṃ ye'nusaranti nityaṃ mṛtvā janitvā ca punaḥ-punastat
te vai loke kramamuktā bhavanti yogaiḥ sāṃkhyaiḥ karmabhiḥ sattvayuktaiḥ (35)
śukaśca vāmadevaśca deva sṛtī devanirmite
śuko vihaṅgamaḥ prokto vāmadevaḥ pipīlikā (36)
atadvyāvṛttirūpeṇa sākṣādvidhimukhena vā
mahāvākyavicāreṇa sāṃkhyayogasamādhinā (37)
viditvā svātmano rūpaṃ samprajñātasamādhitaḥ
śukamārgeṇa virajāḥ prayānti paramaṃ padam (38)
yamādyāsanajāyāsahaṭhābhyāsātpunaḥpuṇaḥ
vighnabāhulyasaṃjāta aṇimādivaśādiha (39)
alabdhvāpi phalaṃ samyakpunarbhūtvā mahākule
punarvāsnyaivāyaṃ yogābhyāsaṃ punaścaran (40)
anekajanmābhyāsena vāmadevena ve pakśa
so'pi muktiṃ samāpnoti tadviṣṇo paraṃ padam (41)
dvāvimāvapi panthānau brahmaprāptikarau śivau
sadyau muktipradaścaikaḥ kramamuktipradaḥ paraḥ (42a)

Vocabulary

muktaḥ: liberated; *api*: too; *na santiḥ*: there are no; *vinā*: apart from; *tābhyām*: from these two; *mukti-bhājaḥ*: attained liberation; *dhīrāḥ*: courageous; *ye anusaranti*: who follow; *śuka-mārgam*: path of Śuka; *bhavanti*: become; *iha*: here; *te loke*: in this world; *nityam*: always; *mṛtvā*: dying; *ca janitvā*: and born; *punaḥpunaḥ*: again and again; *krama*: gradually; *yogaiḥ sāṃkhyaiḥ karmabhiḥ*: through yoga, *sāṃkhya* [and] actions; *sattva-yuktaiḥ*: devoted to goodness; *sṛtī*: two paths; *nirmite*: created by; *deva deva*: Lord of the *devas*; *proktaḥ*: is called; *vihaṅgamaḥ*: bird; *pipīlikā*: ant; *virajāḥ*: purified; *prayānti*: enter; *paramam padam*: highest state; *śuka-mārgeṇa*: through the path of Śuka; *viditvā*: having perceived; *rūpam*: nature; *sva-ātmanaḥ*: their own ātman; *saṃprajñāta*: discerning; *samādhitaḥ*: *samādhi* state; *samādhinā*: through the samādhi; *vicāreṇa*: through investigation; *mahāvākya*: sacred words; *sākṣāt*: straight;

mukhena: through the mouth; *vidhi*: creator; *rūpeṇa*: by the way; *vyāvṛtti*: distinction; *atat*: not that.

haṭha-abhyāsāt: through the practice of *haṭha*; *punaḥpuṇaḥ*: regular; *āyāsa*: strain; *jā*: caused by; *āsana*: postures; *yama-ādi*: restraints and others; *saṃjāta*: having produced; *bāhulya*: multiple; *vighna*: obstacles; *vaśāt*: caused by; *iha*: in this world; *api*: as well as; *alabdhva*: having not obtained; *phalam*: rewards; *samyak bhūtvā*: well-born; *punaḥ*: again; *mahākule*: in a noble family; *punaḥ-caran*: again practising; *yoga-abhyāsam*: yoga; *vāyam*: in relation to; *punaḥ-vāsanaiḥ*: previous tendencies; *abhyāsena*: through the practice of yoga; *aneka-janma*: in many births; *saḥ samāpnoti*: one attains; *muktim*: liberation; *param padam*: supreme seat; *vāmadevena*: through the Vāmadeva; *ve-pakśa*: bird; *dvāvimā panthānau*: two paths; *brahma-prāpti-karau*: leading to the attainment of Brahman; *śivau*: auspicious; *ekaḥ pradaḥ*: one bestows; *sadyau mukti*: immediate liberation; *paraḥ*: the other; *pradaḥ*: gives; *karma-mukti*: gradual liberation.

Translation

The *Śuka* is liberated; the *Vāmadeva* is liberated too. There are no [others] apart from these two [who have] attained liberation. The courageous [ones] who follow the path of Śuka quickly become liberated here in this world. Those who always follow [the path of] Vāmadeva, dying and born again and again in this world, gradually become liberated through yoga, *sāṃkhya* [and] actions devoted to *sattva*. Śuka and Vāmadeva are the two paths created by the Lord of the *devas*. Śuka is called the bird [path and] Vāmadeva the ant. The purified [ones] enter the highest state through the path of Śuka, having perceived the nature of their own ātman by discerning the *samādhi* state, through the samādhi [of] *sāṃkhyayoga* [or] through investigation of the sacred words, or straight through the mouth of the creator [or] by the way of distinction 'not that'.

Having, through the regular practice of *haṭha* [yoga] its strain caused by postures, restraints and others, become vulnerable to multiple obstacles caused by *aṇima* and other [siddhis] in this world, as well as having not obtained rewards, one is well-born again in a noble family, again practising yoga in relation to one's previous tendencies. Through the practice of yoga in many births one attains liberation, the supreme seat of Viṣṇu, through the Vāmadeva or bird [path]. These two paths leading to the attainment of Brahman [are] auspicious. One bestows immediate liberation; the other gives gradual liberation.

Commentary
There are two certain paths to final liberation. The bird path is the quickest and most direct. It is named after Śuka, meaning 'parrot' in Sanskrit, whose mother was the beautiful Apsaras Ghṛtācī in the form of a parrot and whose father was Vyāsa[73], the sage who wrote the *Brahma Sutra* and the *Mahābhārata*[74] and, according to the *Mahābhārata*[75], was able to fly through the air like a bird directly to his destination. Followers of the bird path are courageous because they have already done the long difficult *sādhana* of purification of the mind and release of all attachments. They are able to enter and maintain higher states of consciousness, unwavering wisdom, adopting the method of exclusion 'not this not that' and having meditated deeply or through direct realisation on these four *mantras*, 'Consciousness is Brahman; I am Brahman; You are That; Ātman is Brahman'. Only then, perceiving their own true nature, can they enter the Śuka path.

Vāmadeva was a sage and poet who is said to have composed Maṇḍala 4 of the Rigveda.[76] The word 'vāma' means 'left' and 'deva' deity, so in this context the name might refer to the left, and therefore longer, way to liberation. Thus this is also called the ant's path. Those who only follow the

Vāmadeva path will, after many lifetimes, become liberated through spiritual knowledge, yoga practices, and burning of their karmas through virtuous and unselfish actions.

Yoga practices, siddhis and a good family can keep one attached to *saṃsāra* through both pain and pleasure. The aspirant must have one-pointed concentration on and intense desire for the goal of enlightenment to succeed.

Verses 42b to 44: Knower of Brahman

अत्र को मोहः कः शोक एकत्वमनुपश्यतः ॥४२॥
यस्यानुभवपर्यन्ता बुद्धिस्तत्त्वे प्रवर्तते ।
तद्दृष्टिगोचराः सर्वे मुच्यन्ते सर्वपातकैः ॥४३॥
खेचरा भूचराः सर्वे ब्रह्मविद्दृष्टिगोचराः
सद्य एव विमुच्यन्ते कोटिजन्मार्जितैरदैः ॥४४॥

atra ko mohaḥ kaḥ śoka ekatvamanupaśyataḥ (42b)
yasyānubhavaparyantā buddhistattve pravartate
taddṛṣṭigocarāḥ sarve mucyante sarvapātakaiḥ (43)
khecarā bhūcarāḥ sarve brahmaviddṛṣṭigocarāḥ
sadya eva vimucyante koṭijanmārjitairadaiḥ (44)

Vocabulary
kaḥ: what; *mohaḥ*: delusion; *śokaḥ*: sorrow; *anupaśyataḥ*: one who sees; *ekatvam*: oneness; *atra*: here; *yasya*: whose; *buddhi*: intellect; *paryantā*: at the end of; *anubhava*: experience; *pravartate*: is intent; *tattve*: on the Truth; *sarva-pātakaiḥ*: all who fall; *gocarāḥ*: range; *tat-dṛṣṭi*: this vision; *mucyante*: are freed from; *sarve*: all; *kecarāḥ*: move in the ether; *bhūcarāḥ*: move on the earth; *dṛṣṭi brahmavid*: vision of the knower of Brahman; *sadya vimucyante*: are immediately released from; *arjitaiḥ*: accumulated; *koṭi-janma*: crores of births.

Translation
What [is] delusion [and] what [is] sorrow [to] one who sees oneness here, whose intellect, at the end of experience, is intent on the Truth. All who fall [within] the range [of] this vision are freed from all [sins]. All who move in the ether and on the earth within the range of the vision of the knower of Brahman are immediately released from [sins] accumulated through crores of births.

Commentary
This description of one who knows Brahman is emphasised in the following verses of the *Bhagavad Gīta*, here translated by Swami Mukundananda.[77]

'Following this path and having achieved enlightenment from a Guru, O Arjun, you will no longer fall into delusion. In the light of that knowledge, you will see that all living beings are but parts of the Supreme, and are within Me.' Vs.4.35

'Those who are free from vanity and delusion, who have overcome the evil of attachment, who dwell constantly on the Self and on God, who are free from the desire to enjoy the senses, and are beyond the dualities of pleasure and pain, such liberated personalities attain My eternal Abode.' Vs.15.5

'In that joyous state of Yoga, called samādhi, one experiences supreme boundless divine bliss, and thus situated, one never deviates from the Eternal Truth.' Vs.6.21

Verses 9 and 10 in *Yoga Darshana Upanishad* define *satyam*, truth, thus:

'Truth: O great Sage, that which is seen, heard and smelt through the sense organs of the eyes etc is said to be *satyam,* as *Brahman* is no different from that. The highest truth is that *Brahman* is everywhere and not elsewhere. This understanding leads to the highest truth as declared by those who have absorbed the wisdom of *Vedānta.*'[78]

पञ्चमोऽध्यायः

pañcamo'dhyāyaḥ

Fifth Chapter

Verses 1 to 3: Knowledge of the Body

अथ इमं ऋभुं भगवन्तं निदाघः पप्रच्छ योगाभ्यास-

विधिमनुब्रूब्रूहीति ।

तथेति स होवाच ।

पञ्चभूतात्मको देहः पञ्चमण्डलपूरितः ।

काठिन्यं पृथिवीमेका पानीयं तद्द्रवाकृति ॥१॥

दीपनं च भवेत्तेजः प्रचारो वायुलक्षणम ।

आकाशः सत्वतः सर्वं ज्ञातव्यं योगमिच्छता ॥२॥

षट्शतान्यधिकान्यत्र सहस्त्राण्येकविंशतिः ।

अहोरात्रवहैः श्वासैर्वायुमण्डलघाततः ॥३॥

atha imaṃ ṛbhuṃ bhagavantaṃ nidāghaḥ papraccha
yogābhyāsavidhimanubrūhīti
tatheti sa hovāca
pañcabhūtātmako dehaḥ pañcamaṇḍalapūritaḥ
kāthinyaṃ pṛthivīmekā pānīyaṃ taddravākṛti (1)
dīpanaṃ ca bhavettejaḥ pracāro vāyulakṣaṇam
ākāśaḥ sattvataḥ sarvaṃ jñātavyaṃ yogamicchatā (2)
ṣaṭśatānyadhikānyatra sahastrāṇyekaviṃśatiḥ
ahorātravahaiḥ śvāsairvāyumaṇḍalabhātataḥ (3)

Vocabulary

atha: then; *papraccha*: asked; *imam*: this; *bhagavantam ṛbhum*: Lord Ṛbhu; *anubrūhi*: please tell; *vidhim*: rule; *yoga-abhyāsa*: practice of yoga; *tatheti*: so be it; *sa hovāca*: he said; *dehaḥ*: body; *ātmakaḥ*: is composed of; *pañca-bhūta*: five elements; *pūritaḥ*: filled with; *pañca-maṇḍala*: five regions; *ekā*: one; *yam*: which; *kaṭhin*: hard; *pṛthivīm*: earth; *tat*: that; *dravākṛti*: has a fluid nature; *pānīyam*: water; *dīpanam*: inflames; *bhavet*: is; *tejas*: fire; *pracāraḥ*: movement; *lakṣaṇam*: characteristic; *vāyu*: air; *sattvataḥ*: essence; *ākāśaḥ*: ether; *sarvaṃ*: everywhere; *jñātavyam*: should be known; *yogam-icchatā*: one who desires yoga.

vahaiḥ: through the cause; *ghātataḥ*: blowing; *vāyu-maṇḍala*: region of air; *ahorātra*: day and night; *eka-viṃśatiḥ*: twenty-one; *sahastrāṇi*: thousand; *ṣaṭ-śatāni*: six hundred; *śvāsaiḥ*: breaths; *adhika*: more; *anyatra*: elsewhere.

Translation

Then Nidāgha asked this Lord Ṛbhu: 'Please tell me the rule for the practice of yoga'.

'So be it', he said. 'The body is composed of the five elements, [and] filled with five regions. One, which is hard, is earth. That [which] has a fluid nature is water. [That which] inflames is fire. Movement is the characteristic of air. The essence of ether is everywhere. This should be known by one who desires yoga.

Through the cause of the blowing of the region of air day and night, [there are] twenty-one thousand six hundred breaths [and] more elsewhere.

Commentary

The theme of the fifth chapter is Yoga, presented as a discussion between Ṛbhu and his student Nidāgha. As Viṣṇu in the first chapter has stressed the importance of understanding the body by describing in length its composition, now Ṛbhu passes this knowledge in brief to his student Nidāgha. The five elements are earth which has the quality of weight, water whose quality is fluidity, fire with the quality of heat, air which has the quality of movement and ether which is unlimited space.

The tattwas are not physical or chemical elements. They are creations of vibrations of energy or prāṇa, which pervade the whole body and mind. All our actions and thoughts are constantly influenced by them. Therefore the yogin must have a complete understanding of the tattwas, their functions and influences, so that they can be well managed. Although everyone has the same five elements, their proportions are different. That is why some people are more fiery, others are more earthy and so on.

The verse states that each person takes twenty-one thousand six hundred breaths every twenty-four hours. But what is the breath? Paramahamsa Niranjananda defines the breath as 'a medium through which there is an awareness of the pranic movement, or the pranic expansion and relaxation'.[79]

Georg Feuerstein says that we are usually unaware of breathing until we start to meditate. Then we become aware of the sound produced by the two bellows in the chest. In yoga the breath is regarded as 'a manifestation of the transcendental Self, also referred to as *ham-sa* (swan), the two syllables of which stand for the ingoing and outgoing breaths, as well as the ascending and descending currents of the life force.' The continuous sound of *ham-sa*, meaning 'I am that', is a reminder that we are identical with the *mahā prāṇa*, the cosmic energy of the transcendental Self. [80]

Verses 4 to 6a: Aging of the Body

तत्पृथ्वीमण्डले क्षीणे वलिरायाति देहिनाम् ।
तद्वदाहो गणापाये केशाः स्युः पाण्डुराः क्रमात् ।।४।।
तेजःक्क्षये क्षुधा कान्तिर्नश्यते मारुतक्षये ।
वेपशुः संभवेन्नित्यं नाम्भसेनैव जीवति ।।५।।
इत्थंभूतं क्षयान्नित्यं जीवितं भूतधारणम् ।६।

tatpṛthvīmaṇḍale kṣīṇe valirāyāti dehinām
tadvadāho gaṇāpāye keśāḥ syuḥ pāṇḍurāḥ kramāt (4)
tejaḥkṣaye kṣudhā kāntirnaśyate mārutakṣaye
vepaśuḥ saṃbhavennityaṃ nāmbhasenaiva jīvati (5)
itthaṃbhūtaṃ kṣayānnityaṃ jīvitaṃ bhūtadhāraṇam (6a)

Vocabulary

tat-pṛthvī-maṇḍale: when the earth region; *kṣīṇe*: worn away; *valiḥ*: wrinkles; *āyāti*: appear; *dehinām*: in the body; *āhaḥ*: indeed; *tadvat*: just as; *gaṇa-apāye*: in the water region; *keśāḥ*: hair; *syuḥ*: becomes; *kramāt*: gradually; *pāṇḍurāḥ*: pale white; *tejaḥ-kṣaye*: when the fire element is weakened; *kṣudhā*: hunger; *kāntiḥ*: radiance; *naśyate*: disappear; *saṃbhavet*: there is; *nityam*: constant; *vepaśuḥ*: tremor; *āmbhasena*: ether; *na jīvati eva*: no life at all; *kṣayāt*: because of weakness; *bhūta*: elements; *dhāraṇam*: maintained; *itthaṃbhūtam*: in such a way; *nityam jīvitam*: constant life.

Translation

When the earth region is worn away, wrinkles appear in the body, indeed just as in the water region the hair becomes gradually pale white. When the fire element is weakened, hunger [and] radiance disappear. When the air element is weakened, there is constant tremor [and when] the ether [is weakened] there is no life at all. Because of [this] weakness, the elements [must be] maintained in such a way [that there is] constant life.

Commentary
As the body ages, vibrations of energy or prāṇa weaken. This verse describes the effects of the weakening of the elements in the aging body. When the essence of the earth element weakens, wrinkles appear. When the essence of the water element weakens, the hair fades to grey and then white. When the essence of the fire element weakens, there is loss of appetite and the body loses its glow. When the essence of the air element weakens, there is incessant shaking and trembling. When the essence of the ether element weakens, life fades away.

The last sentence suggests that it is possible to maintain the strength of the elements.

Verses 6b to 9: Uḍḍiyāṇa Bandha

उड्याणं कुरुते यस्मादविश्रान्तं महाखगः ॥६॥
उड्डियाणं तदेव स्यात्तत्र बन्धोऽमिधीयते ।
उड्डियाणे ह्यसै बन्धो मृत्युमातङ्गकेशरी ॥७॥
तस्य मुक्तिस्तनोः कायात्तस्य बन्धो हि दुष्करः ।
अग्नै तु चलिते कुक्षै वेदना जायते भृशम् ॥८॥
न कार्या क्षुधि तेनापि नापि विण्मूत्रवेगिना
हितं मितं च भोक्तव्यं स्तोकं स्तोकमनेकधा ॥९॥

uḍyāṇāṃ kurute yasmādaviśrāntaṃ mahākhagaḥ (6b)
uḍḍiyāṇaṃ tadeva syāttatra bandho'midhīyate
uḍḍiyāṇe hyasai bandho mṛtyumātaṅgakeśarī (7)
tasya muktistanoḥ kāyāttasya bandho hi duṣkaraḥ
agnai tu calite kukṣai vedanā jāyate bhṛśam (8)
na kāryā kṣudhi tenāpi nāpi viṇmūtraveginā
hitaṃ mitaṃ ca bhoktavyaṃ stokaṃ stokamanekadhā (9)

Vocabulary

yasmāt: as; *mahā-khagaḥ*: great bird; *kurute uḍyāṇām*: can soar; *aviśrāntam*: incessantly; *tadeva*: that is; *syāt*: one should practise; *dhīyate tatra*: is reflected there; *hi*: definitely; *keśarī*: lion; *mātaṅga*: elephant; *mṛtyu*: death; *mukti*: release; *tasya*: from that; *kāyāt*: from the body; *tasya bandhaḥ*: this bandha; *duṣkaraḥ*: arduous; *tu*: then; *agnai*: when the fire; *kukṣai*: in the belly; *calite*: has gone; *bhṛśam*: severe; *vedanā*: pain; *jāyate*: is produced; *na kāryā*: it should not be done; *tena* by one; *kṣudhi*: hungry; *na-api*: nor; *veginā*: rapid; *viṇmūtra*: faeces and urine; *hitam*: beneficial; *ca mitam*: moderate; *bhoktavyam*: should be eaten; *anekadhā*: often; *stokam stokam*: little by little.

Translation

As the great bird can soar incessantly, that is [why] one

should practise *uḍḍiyāṇa*. The *bandha* is reflected there [in the name]. The *uḍḍiyāṇa bandha* is definitely the lion of the elephant of death. The release from that [depends on power] from the body [as] this bandha is arduous. Then when the fire in the belly has gone, severe pain is produced. It should not be done by one [who is] hungry nor [by one who has] rapid faeces and urine. Beneficial and moderate [food] should be eaten often little by little.

Commentary

The 'great bird' is a symbol of *śakti,* the spiritual energy which, when activated, moves up *brahma nāḍī*, the innermost channel of *suṣumnā nāḍī*, to *sahasrāra cakra*, at the crown of the head opening the way to spiritual freedom. '*Uḍḍiyāṇa*' means 'soaring, flying up' and a bandha is a concentration of energy at one point. This bandha has the strength and power to delay death, if the practioner is well-endowed with vitality and energy.

Swami Satyadharma says in *Yoga Chudamani Upanishad*: 'The bird which flies in the air is a symbol of prana, so the movement of prana shakti in the physical body is described as a bird. It is the great bird, which implies that *uḍḍīyaṇa* is a powerful practice able to raise a substantial force to the highest point. After resting, the great bird takes to flight; similarly, the practitioner rests before drawing in the abdomen, enabling the prana vayu to fly up the sushumna. Rest is required before each round because *uḍḍiyāṇa bandha* is a strenuous practice.'[81]

Uḍḍiyāṇa bandha is described in *Haṭha Yoga Pradīpikā* in the following two verses:

'*Uḍḍiyāṇa bandha* is so-called by the yogis because through its practice the *prāṇa* (is concentrated at one point and) rises through *suṣumnā*. Vs.3.55

The bandha described is called the rising or flying bandha, because through its practice the great bird (*śakti*) flies upward with ease. Vs.3.56'

Swami Muktibodhananda says in her commentary on these verses: '*uḍḍīyaṇa* means to rise up or fly. In the practice of *uḍḍiyāṇa bandha*, the abdominal organs are pulled up and in, creating a natural upward flow of energy, therefore it is often translated as the stomach lift.' [82]

These verses compare the rising of *śakti* in the body to a bird freed from its perch. The practice can slow down and even reverse the aging process.

Only one who is guided by the *guru* and who has a light, healthy, regular diet and a strong digestive system should practise this bandha or lock.

Verses 10 to 12a: The Three Yogas

मृदुमध्यममन्त्रेषु क्रमानमन्त्रं लयं हठम् ।

लयमन्त्रहठा योगा योगो ह्यष्टाङ्न्गसंयुतः ॥१०॥

यमश्च तथा चासनमेव च ।

प्राणायामस्तथा पश्चात्याहारस्तथा परं ॥११॥

धारणा च तथा ध्यानं समाधिश्चाष्टमो भवेत् ।१२।

mṛdumadhyamamantreṣu kramānmantraṃ layaṃ haṭham
layamantrahaṭhā yoga yogo hyaṣṭāṅgasaṃyutaḥ (10)
yamaśca tathā cāsanameva
prāṇāyāmastathā paścātpratyāhārastathā paraṃ (11)
dhāraṇā ca tathā dhyānaṃ samādhiścāṣṭamo bhavet (12a)

Vocabulary

mṛdu: gentle; *madhyama*: moderate; *mantreṣu*: subtle; *kramāt*: respectively; *saṃyutaḥ*: include; *hi-aṣṭāṅga*: these eight limbs; *tathā*: then; *paraṃ*: henceforth; *bhavet aṣṭamaḥ*: is the eighth.

Translation

[One should practise] gentle, moderate [and] subtle [yogas which are] respectively *laya, haṭha* [and] *mantra.* Laya, haṭha [and] mantra yogas include these eight limbs: thus *yama, niyama, āsana, prāṇāyama,* then henceforth *pratyāhāra, dhāraṇā, dhyāna* [and] *samādhi* is the eighth.

Commentary

Mantra Yoga is 'the path of yoga which liberates the mind through sound vibration'.[83] Its literal meaning is 'the force which liberates the mind from bondage'. Swami Niranjanananda explains why the mind is in bondage and needs to be liberated. 'According to yoga, the gross mind or mental nature has two attributes which hold it in bondage.

The first is *mala* which means 'impurities', and the second is *vikṣepa* meaning 'dissipation'. So the manifest mind contains impurities and it is dissipated.' The impurities are the selfish desires and ambitions. The dissipation of the mind is caused by constant searching for distractions and amusement. [84]

Georg Feuerstein defines Mantra-Yoga as 'the yoga of potent sound, aiming at liberation through the recitation (aloud or mental) of empowered sounds (such as *om, hum, ram, hare krishna,* etc), which is often considered an aspect of Tantra-Yoga'.[85]

Swami Niranjanananda describes *Haṭha Yoga* as the 'yoga of attaining physical and mental purity, and channelling of the prāṇas in the body'.[86]

Georg Feuerstein says that although the literal meaning of *haṭha* is 'force', 'esoterically the syllables *ha* and *tha* are said to symbolise 'sun' and 'moon' respectively. Specifically, they refer to the inner luminaries: the 'sun' or solar energy coursing through the right energetic pathway (*piṅgalā-nāḍī*) and the 'moon' or lunar energy travelling through the left pathway (*iḍā-nāḍī*). Haṭha Yoga utilises these two currents – corresponding to the sympathetic and parasympathetic nervous systems respectively – in order to achieve a psychoenergetic balance and mental tranquillity.' [87]

Laya Yoga is the 'yoga of conscious dissolution of individuality'.[88] Literally it means the 'Yoga of [Meditative] Absorption'. It can be 'any of various Tantric meditation approaches that seek to dissolve the conditional mind, often through such means as breath control (*prāṇāyāma*) and seals (*mudrā*) of *Haṭha Yoga*'.[89]

Dissolution of the mind can be achieved through the practices of *kriya* and *kuṇḍalinī yoga*. These practices aim to awaken the energy centres (*cakras*) and currents (*nāḍīs*), thus giving experiences of the psychic body. 'In laya yoga, consciousness is observed more intensely and energy simply becomes the tool, or the medium, through which changes within the consciousness take place.' [90]

The *Haṭha Yoga Pradīpikā* defines *laya* as 'the non-recollection of the objects of the senses when the previous deep-rooted desires (and impresssions) are non-recurrent'. [91]

All three yogas include eight limbs which are (i) *yama*, moral code, (ii) *niyama*, internal disciplines, (iii) *āsana*, postures, (iv) *prāṇāyāma*, breath control, (v) *pratyāhāra*, introversion of the senses, (vi) *dhāraṇā*, concentration, (vii) *dhyāna*, meditation, and (viii) *samādhi*, transcendental consciousness.

Verses 12b to 14: Yamas and Niyamas

अहिंसा सत्यमस्तेयं ब्रह्मचर्यं दयार्जवम् ।।१२।।
क्षमा धृतिर्मिताहारः शौचं चेति यमा दश ।
तपः सन्तोषमस्तिक्यं दानमीश्वरपूजनम् ।।१३।।
सिद्धान्तश्रवणं चैव ह्रीर्मतिश्च जपो व्रतम् ।
एवे हि नियमाः प्रोक्ता दशधैव महामते ।।१४।।

ahiṃsā satyamasteyaṃ brahmacaryaṃ dayārjavam (12b)
kṣamā dhṛtirmitāhāraḥ śaucaṃ ceti yamā daśa
tapaḥ santoṣamastikyaṃ dānamīśvarapūjanam (13)
siddhāntaśravaṇaṃ caiva hrīrmatiśca japo vratam
eve hi niyamāḥ proktā daśadhaiva mahāmate (14)

Vocabulary
daśa yamāḥ: ten rules of conduct; *ahiṃsā*: non-violence; *satya*: truth; *asteya*: honesty; *brahmacarya*: celibacy; *daya*: kindness; *ārjava*: straightforwardness; *kṣamā*: patience; *dhṛti*: equanimity; *mitāhāra*: moderate diet; *śauca*, cleanliness.

mahāmate: o Wise One; *daśadhā*: tenfold; *niyamāḥ*: rules of personal discipline; *proktāḥ*: are said to be; *tapas*: austerity; *santoṣa*: contentment; *āstikya*: faith in the highest consciousness; *dāna*: giving to others; *īśvara puja*: worship of the highest consciousness; *siddhānta śravaṇa*: listening to the scriptures; *hrī*: remorse; *mati*: conviction; *japa*, repetition of *mantra*; *vrata*: vow.

Translation
The ten yamas are *ahiṃsā*, non-violence; *satya*, truthfulness in speech; *asteya*, honesty in action; *brahmacarya*, abstinence or moderation in sexual conduct; *daya*, kindness or compassion; *ārjava*, straightforwardness; *kṣamā*, patience;

dhṛti, equanimity; *mitāhāra*, moderate and balanced diet; and *śauca*, cleanliness of body and mind.

O Wise One, the tenfold niyamas are said to be *tapas* (austerity, endurance) *santoṣa* (contentment) *āstikya* (faith in the highest consciousness) *dāna* (charity, giving to others) *īśvara pūja* (worship of the highest consciousness) *siddhānta śravaṇa* (listening to the scriptures) *hrī* (shame or remorse) *mati* (desire for humility) *japa* (repetition of mantra, syllables or words of power) and *vrata* (vow or commitment).

Commentary

Swami Satyadharma emphasises the importance of the practice of the ten *yamas*: 'The practice of *yama* is considered to be an important requisite for the higher stages of meditation, because it removes mental disturbance and dissipation, caused by negative interactions within the world. In order to progress in meditation, the mind must be free from these impurities and at peace within itself.'[92]

She says the ten *niyamas* are qualities, 'more internal disciplines, which allow the practitioner to gain control over the senses and manage the mind at a deeper level'.[93]

Verses 15 to 17: Eleven Āsanas

एकदशासनानि स्युश्चक्रादि मुनिसत्तम ।
चक्रं पद्मासनं कूर्मं कुक्कुटं तथा ॥१५॥
वीरासनं स्वास्तिकं च भद्रं सिंहासनं तथा ।
मुक्तासनं गोमुखं च कीर्तितं योगवित्तमैः ॥१६॥
सव्योरु दक्षिणे गुल्पे दक्षिणं दक्षिणेतरे ।
निदध्यादृजुकायस्तु चक्रासनमिदं मतम् ॥१७॥

ekadaśāsanāni syuścakrādi munisattam
cakraṃ padmāsanaṃ kūrmaṃ kukkuṭaṃ tathā (15)
vīrāsanaṃ svāstikaṃ ca bhadraṃ siṃhāsanaṃ tathā
muktāsanaṃ gomukhaṃ ca kīrtitaṃ yogavittamaiḥ (16)
savyoru dakṣiṇe gulpe dakṣiṇaṃ dakṣiṇetare
nidadhyādṛjukāyastu cakrāsanamidaṃ matam (17)

Vocabulary

cakra-ādi: beginning with *cakra*; *syuḥ*: there are; *ekadaśa-āsanāni*: eleven postures; *muni-sattam*: excellent sage; *tathā*: thus, similarly; *kīrtitam*: are named; *yoga-vittamaiḥ*: by well-known yogins; *nidadhyāt*: by placing; *savya-ūru*: left thigh; *dakṣiṇe gulpe*: on the right ankle; *dakṣiṇaṃ*: right; *dakṣiṇetare*: on the left; *kāyaḥ*: body; *ṛju*: upright; *tu*: then; *idam*: this; *matam*: is regarded.

Translation

Beginning with *cakra*, there are eleven postures, o Excellent Sage! Thus *cakra, padmāsana, kūrma, kukkuṭa* and similarly *vīrāsana, svāstika, bhadra, siṃhāsana, muktāsana* and *gomukha* are named by well-known yogins. Placing the left thigh on the right ankle [and] the right [thigh] on the left [ankle], the body upright, then this [is] regarded as the cakra posture.

Commentary

Advanced yogins name these eleven postures as the most important: *cakra*, wheel; *padmāsana*, lotus pose; *kūrma*, tortoise; *kukkuṭa*, cockerel; *vīrāsana*; hero pose; *svāstika*, auspicious; *bhadra*, gracious; *siṃhāsana*, lion pose; *muktāsana*, liberated pose; and *gomukha*, cow.

Seated comfortably on the ground, head, neck and spine in a straight line, shoulders back and relaxed, placing the left thigh on the right ankle, and the right thigh on the left ankle, hands in *chin* or *gyana mudra*, this is *cakrāsana*.

Verse 18: Prāṇāyāma

पूरकः कुम्भकस्तद्वद्रेचकः पूरकः पुनः ।
प्राणायामः स्वनाडीभिस्तस्मान्नाडीः प्रचक्षते ।।१८।।

pūrakaḥ kumbhakastadvadrecakaḥ pūrakaḥ punaḥ
prāṇāyāmaḥ svanāḍībhistasmātnāḍīḥ pracakṣate (18)

Vocabulary

pūrakaḥ: inhaling; *kumbhakaḥ*: retaining; *tadvat*: thus; *recakaḥ*: exhaling; *punaḥ*: again; *sva-nāḍībhiḥ*: through one's own *nāḍīs*; *tasmāt*: thus; *pracakṣate*: it is regarded as.

Translation

Inhaling, retaining, thus exhaling, inhaling again through one's own *nāḍīs* [is] *prāṇāyāma*. Thus it is regarded as the *nāḍīs*.

Commentary

Swami Satyadharma explains *prāṇayāma* thus: 'The three components of prāṇayāma are the three stages of the breathing process. *Pūraka* is inhalation. *Kumbhaka* is breath retention, as if holding the breath inside a pot. *Recaka* is exhalation. In normal breathing these three stages of breath go on automatically, day and night, throughout life. The main difference between prāṇayāma and normal breathing is the awareness of the breath and the ratios or counts. It is said that our lives, from birth to death, are measured by breaths. Every automatic or normal breath is counted in the duration of life. However, when we switch over to breathing with awareness and ratio, as in prāṇayāma, this type of breath is not counted. Therefore, yogis who mastered the three components of prāṇayāma, were often very long lived, while others were not.'

Swami Satyananda in *Kundalini Tantra* says: 'Pranayama is not only a breathing exercise or a means to increase prana in the body; it is a powerful method of creating yogic fire to heat the kundalini and awaken it. However, if it is practised without sufficient preparation, this will not occur because the generated heat will not be directed to the proper centres. Therefore Jalandhara, uddiyana and mula bandhas are practiced to lock the prana in and force it up to the frontal brain.'[95] Jālandhara Banda is the throat lock, and Mūla Bandha is the perineal lock. Swami Satyananda advises the aspirant to have a minimal diet before practising intense prāṇāyāma in a calm, cool and quiet environment, preferably at a high altitude. He emphasizes that this method can give experiences which are painful physically, mentally and emotionally, and are difficult to manage.

Verses 19 to 21: The Subtle Body

शरीरं सर्वजन्तूनां षण्णवत्यङ्गुलात्मकम् ।
तन्मध्ये पायुदेशात्तु द्व्यङ्गुलात्परतः परम् ॥१९॥
मेढ्रदेशादधस्तात्तु द्व्यङ्गुलान्मध्यमुच्यते ।
मेढ्रान्नवाङ्गुलादूर्ध्वं नाडीनां कन्दमुच्यते ॥२०॥
चतुरङ्गुलमुत्सेधं चतुरङ्गुलमायतम् ।
अण्डाकारं परिवृतं मेदोमज्जास्थिशोणितैः ॥२१॥

śarīraṃ sarvajantūnāṃ ṣaṇṇavatyaṅgulātmakam
tanmadhye pāyudeśāttu dvyaṅgulātparataḥ param (19)
meḍhradeśādadhastāttu dvyaṅgulānmadhyamucyate
medhrānnavāṅgulādūrdhvaṃ nāḍīnāṃ kandamucyate (20)
caturaṅgulamutsedhaṃ caturaṅgulamāyatam
aṇḍākāraṃ parivṛtaṃ medomajjāsthiśoṇitaiḥ (21)

Vocabulary

śarīram: body; *sarva-jantūnām*: of all people; *ātmakam*: consists of; *ṣaṇṇavati*: ninety-six; *aṅgula*: digits; *tat-madhye*: in its middle; *dvi-aṅgulāt*: two digits; *deśāt*: from the place; *pāyu*: anus; *tu*: then; *adhaḥ*: below; *meḍhra*: genitals; *ucyate*: is said to be; *madhyam*: centre; *nava-aṅgulāt*: nine digits; *ūrdhvam*: above; *kandam*: knot; *nāḍīnām*: of the nāḍīs; *catuḥ-aṅgulam*: four digits; *utsedham*: height; *āyatam*: length; *aṇḍa-ākāram*: shape of an egg; *parivṛtam*: surrounded; *śoṇitaiḥ*: by blood; *meda*: fat; *majja*: marrow; *asthi*: bone.

Translation

The body of all people consists of ninety-six digits in length. In its middle, two digits from the place of the anus, then two digits below the place of the genitals is said to be the centre. Nine digits above the genitals is said to be the knot of the nāḍīs, four digits in height, four digits in length, the shape of an egg [and] surrounded by fat, marrow, bone [and] blood.

Commentary

The subtle body, also known as the pranic body, gives energy, life and movement to the physical body including its organs and systems. Its length is 96 finger widths. *Yoga Darshana Upanishad* describes the centre of the body as 'the site of *agni*, whose light glows like gold from the Jambū River'. This may be compared to the reflection of the sun, as it rises and sets over the Jambū River. [96]

'The location of *kanda*, the root of the *nāḍīs*, or energy channels, is nine finger widths above mūlādhāra cakra, and just below the manipura cakra. It is four finger widths long and oval-shaped, like an egg. It is covered with a subtle membrane. The wise, who are able to see this phenomenon with their inner vision, have said that the navel lies within it. The navel is also the centre of the solar plexus and many nerves and nāḍīs are connected with it.' [97]

Verses 22 to 27: The Nāḍīs

तत्रैव नाडीचक्रं तु द्वादशारं प्रतिषठितम् ।
शरीरं धृयते येन वर्तते तत्र कुण्डली ।।२२।।
ब्रह्मरन्ध्रं सुषुम्णा या वदनेन पिधाय सा ।
अलम्बुसा सुषुम्नायाः कुरूर्नाडी वसत्यसौ ।।२३।।
अनन्तरारयुग्मे तु वारूणा च यशस्विनी ।
दक्षिणारे सुषुम्नायाः पिङ्गला वर्तते क्रमात् ।।२४।।
तदन्तरारयोः पूषा वर्तते च पयस्विनी ।
सुषुम्ना पश्चिमे चारे स्थिता नाडी सरस्वती ।।२५।।
शङ्खिनी चैव गान्धारी तदनन्तरयोः स्थिते ।
उत्तरे तु सुषुम्नाया इडाख्या निवसत्यसै ।।२६।।
अनन्तरं हस्तिजीह्वा ततो विश्वोदरी स्थिता ।
प्रदक्षिणक्रमेणैव चक्रस्यारेषु नाड्यः ।।२७।।

tatraiva nāḍīcakraṃ tu dvādaśāraṃ pratiṣṭhitam
śarīraṃ dhṛyate yena vartate tatra kuṇḍalī (22)
brahmarandhraṃ suṣumṇā yā vadanena pidhāya sā
alambusā suṣumnāyāḥ kurūrnāḍī vasatyasau (23)
anantarārayugme tu vārūṇā ca yaśasvinī
dakṣiṇāre suṣumnāyāḥ piṅgalā vartate kramāt (24)
tadantarārayoḥ pūṣā vartate ca payasvinī
suṣumnā paścime care sthitā nāḍī sarasvatī (25)
śaṅkhinī caiva gāndhārī tadanantarayoḥ sthite
uttare tu suṣumnāyā iḍākhyā nivasatyasai (26)
anantaraṃ hastijīhvā tato viśvodarī sthitā
pradakṣiṇakrameṇaiva cakrasyāreṣu nāḍyaḥ (27)

Vocabulary
dvādaśāram: twelve-spoked; *nāḍī-cakram*: wheel of nāḍīs; *pratiṣṭhitam*: is situated; *tatra*: there; *yena*: through which; *śarīram*: body; *dhṛyate*: is supported; *vartate*: is; *sā pidhāya*:

she covers; *vadanena*: with her face; *suṣumnāyāḥ*: from/of *suṣumṇā*; *vasati*: dwells; *asau*: that; *tu*: then; *anantarāra-yugme*: in another pair; *kramāt*: continuously; *dakṣiṇāre*: on the right; *tat-antarārayoḥ*: between them; *care*: on the spoke; *paścime*: behind; *sthitā*: is; *uttare*: north; *nivasati*: lives; *khyā*: called; *anantaram*: next; *tataḥ*: then; *cakrasyāreṣu*: in the spokes; *pradakṣiṇa-krameṇa*: in the clockwise order.

Translation

The twelve-spoked wheel of nāḍīs is situated there. The *kuṇḍalī* through which the body is supported is there. She covers with her face the *brahmarandhra* of *suṣumṇā.* From suṣumṇā dwells that [spoke of] *alambusā* [and] *kurūḥ* nāḍī. Then in another pair [of spokes are] *vārūṇī* and *yaśasvinī. Piṅgalā* is continuously on the right of suṣumṇā. Between them are *pūṣā* and *payasvinī.* On the spoke behind suṣumṇā is *sarasvatī* nāḍī. *Śaṅkhinī* and *gāndhārī* are between the two. North of suṣumṇā lives [the nāḍī] known as *iḍā.* Next is *hastijīhvā*, then *viśvodarī* [and] the nāḍīs in the spokes in the clock-wise order.

Commentary

In the knot is situated the *nāḍī-cakra* (wheel of nerves), which has twelve spokes. The 72,000 nāḍīs originate from the *medhrā*, or plexus of the prānic body, situated in the region between *mūlādhāra* and *svādiṣṭhāna*, a few centimetres below the navel. The *kuṇḍalī* remains there, covering with her face the opening of the door to Brahman. The verses then give the location of the major nāḍīs in clockwise order.

Although *kuṇḍalī*, also known as the 'serpent power', starts to uncoil and rise from the base cakra (*mūlādhāra*), the actual awakening takes place at maṇipura. *Maṇipura cakra*, literally 'city of jewels', is associated with vitality, energy and willpower, and has twelve petals which 'represent the rays of energy or number of pranic channels leading in and out of it'.[98]

Verses 28 to 31a: Carriers of Vital Airs

वर्न्ते द्वादश ह्येता द्वादशानिलवाहकाः ।
पटवत्संस्थिता नाड्यो नानावर्णाः समीरिताः ।।२८।।
पटमध्यं तु यत्स्थानं नाभिचक्रं चदुच्यते ।
नादाधारा समाख्याता ज्वलन्ती नादरूपिणी ।।२९।।
पररन्ध्रा सुषुम्ना च चत्वारो रत्नपूरिताः ।
कुण्डल्या पिहितं शश्वद्ब्रह्मरन्ध्रस्य मध्यमम् ।।३०।।
एवमेतासु नाडीषु धरन्ति दश वायवः ।३१।

vartante dvādaśa hyetā dvādaśānilavāhakāḥ
paṭavatsaṃsthitā nāḍyo nānāvarṇāḥ samīritāḥ (28)
paṭamadhyaṃ tu yatsthānaṃ nābhicakraṃ caducyate
nādādhārā samākhyātā jvalantī nādarūpiṇī (29)
pararandhrā suṣumṇā ca catvāro ratnapūritāḥ
kuṇḍalyā pihitaṃ śaśvadbrahmarandhrasya madhyamam (30)
evametāsu nāḍīṣu dharanti daśa vāyavaḥ (31a)

Vocabulary
etāḥ: these; *dvādaśa*: twelve; *nāḍyāḥ*: nāḍīs; *vartante*: are; *hi*: indeed; *vāhakāḥ*: carriers; *anila*: vital airs; *samīritāḥ*: they are said to be; *saṃsthitāḥ*: shaped; *paṭavat*: like woven cloth; *nānā-varṇāḥ*: different colours; *madhyam*: middle; *sthānam*: part; *yat paṭa*: this cloth; *ucyate*: is called; *nābhi-cakram*: navel plexus; *samākhyātāḥ*: are called; *ādhārā*: support; *ca catvāraḥ*: and the four; *pūritāḥ*: are filled with; *ratna*: gems; *madhyamam*: centre; *brahmarandhrasya*: of the *brahma-randhra*; *śaśvat*: always; *pihitam*: covered; *kuṇḍalyā*: by the *kuṇḍalī*; *evam*: thus; *daśa vāyavaḥ*: ten vital airs; *dharanti*: flow; *etāsu nāḍīṣu*: in these nāḍīs.

Translation
These twelve nāḍīs are indeed the twelve carriers of vital

airs. They are said to be shaped like woven cloth [of] different colours. The middle part [of] this cloth is called the navel plexus. *Jvalantī*, *nādarūpiṇī*, *pararandhrā* and *suṣumṇā* are called the support of the *nāda*, and the four are filled with gems. The centre of the *brahmarandhra* is always covered by the *kuṇḍalī*. Thus the ten vital airs flow in these nāḍīs.

Commentary

Of the 72,000 nāḍīs, only 72 are considered important and ten considered to be major. They are situated in the spinal cord and pass through each *cakra*. Each one carries different manifestations of *prāṇa* in the subtle body.

The word 'nāḍī' means 'flow', so the nāḍīs are the channels through which the energy or prāṇa flows. The nāḍīs which emanate from the *medhrā*, or plexus, are conductors of the pranic force which is distributed throughout the various parts of the body.

So that the yogin can develop an inner vision of the nāḍīs, their location is given in the previous verses, and here they are described as 'shaped like woven cloth [of] different colours' and having jewels.

'There are five major and five minor vital airs. The five major prāṇas are: prāṇa, apāna, vyāna, samāna, and udāna. These five prāṇas continuously sustain the physical body with vitality and life. Of these five, prāṇa is considered to be the most important. It flows upward from the navel to the heart and in the nostrils. It supports the lungs and heart. Vyāna flows in the region of the shoulders, neck and head, sustaining the sensory organs, such as ears, eyes, nose, tongue, as well as the nervous system and the brain. Apāna flows downward from the navel to the anus, hips, thighs and knees. It sustains the reproductive and excretory organs.

Udāna flows in the hands and feet. Samāna flows throughout the whole body.

The five minor prāṇas are said to be located in the skin and bones. Of the five minor prāṇas, *nāga* is responsible for belching, vomiting and hiccuping. *Dhanaṃjaya* gives lustre to the skin. *Kūrma* causes blinking and shutting of the eyes. *Kṛkara* causes hunger and *devadatta* is the cause of sleep.' [99]

Verses 31b to 33a: Flow of Nectar

एवं नाडीगतिं वायुगतिं ज्ञात्वा विचक्षणः ।।३१।।
समग्रीवशिरःकायः संवृतास्यः सुनिश्चलः ।
नासाग्रे चैव हृन्मध्ये बिन्दुमध्ये तुरीयकम् ।।३२।।
स्रवन्तममृतं पश्येन्नेत्राभ्यां सुसमाहितः ।३३।

evaṃ nāḍīgatiṃ vāyugatiṃ jñātvā vicakṣaṇaḥ (31b)
samagrīvaśiraḥkāyaḥ saṃvṛtāsyaḥ suniścalaḥ
nāsāgre caiva hṛnmadhye bindumadhye turīyakam (32)
sravantamamṛtaṃ paśyennetrābhyāṃ susamāhitaḥ (33a)

Vocabulary
vicakṣaṇaḥ: wise; *jñātvā*: having understood; *gatim*: movement; *vāyu*: vital airs; *grīva*: neck; *śiraḥ*: head; *kāyaḥ*: body; *sama*: aligned; *āsyaḥ*: mouth; *saṃvṛta*: closed; *suniścalaḥ*: motionless; *paśyet*: should contemplate; *turīyakam*: form of *turīya*; *nāsāgre*: at the nosetip; *hṛt-madhye*: in the centre of the heart; *ca*: and;. *bindu-madhye*: in the middle of the *bindu*; *netrābhyām*: with the eyes; *susamāhitaḥ*: intent; *amṛtam*: nectar; *sravantam*: flowing.

Translation
The wise one, having understood the movement of the nāḍīs and vital airs, [with] neck, head and body aligned, mouth closed, motionless, should contemplate the form of *turīya*, at the nosetip, in the centre of the heart and the middle of the *bindu*, with the eyes intent on the nectar flowing [from there].

Commentary
The vital airs (prāṇa, vāyu, life force) flow through the nāḍīs (channels, tubes), which go from the soles of the feet up to the crown of the head. Once the yogin knows and is aware of the passage of the nāḍīs and vital airs, he should meditate on *turīya*, the ātman, at the nosetip (a trigger point for *mūlādhāra cakra*), in the centre of the heart (the location of

amrita nāḍī), and the middle of the *bindu,* the source of the nectar.

Here *amrita* refers to the nectar of immortality that trickles down from a point in the head.

'According to the *Shiva-Samhitā* (2.7f.), the nectar of immortality has two forms: one flows through the left conduit (*iḍā-nāḍī*) and nourishes the body; the other flows along the central pathway (*suṣumnā- nāḍī*) and creates the 'moon' (*candra*). The nectar's flow increases when the 'serpent power' (*kuṇḍalinī-śakti*) has ascended from the base centre to the psychoenergetic centre at the throat.' [100]

Here the moon (*candra*) refers to 'an esoteric structure in the human body from which oozes the nectar of immortality (*amrita, soma*). The moon showers its ambrosia continuously, but in the ordinary mortal this precious liquid is wasted. The yogin, however, learns to check its flow and employ it in the quest for the transubstantiation of the body.' [101]

The *Haṭha Yoga Pradīpikā* emphasises the importance of the nectar. 'The whole body from the soles of the feet to the head should become filled with nectar. Thus, the one who perfects this has a superior body, superior strength and immense valour.'[102]

Verses 33b to 36: Illusion of Time

अपानं मुकुलीकृत्य पायुमाकृष्य चैन्मुखम् ॥३३॥
प्रणवेन समुत्थाप्य श्रीबीजेन निवर्तयेत् ।
स्वात्मानं च श्रियं ध्यायेदमृतप्लावनं ततः ॥३४॥
कालवञ्चनमेतद्धि सर्वमुख्यं प्रचक्षते ।
मनसा चिन्तितं कार्यं मनसा येन सिध्यति ॥३५॥
जलेऽग्निज्वलनाच्छाखापल्लवानि भवन्ति हि ।
नाधन्यं जागतं वाक्यं विपरीता भवेत्क्रिया ॥३६॥

apānaṃ mukulīkṛtya pāyumākṛṣya cainmukham (33b)
praṇavena samutthāpya śrībījena nivartayet
svātmānaṃ ca śriyaṃ dhyāyedamṛtaplāvanaṃ tataḥ (34)
kālavañcanametaddhi sarvamukhyaṃ pracakṣate
manasā cintitaṃ kāryaṃ manasā yena sidhyati (35)
jale'gnijvalanācchākhāpallavāni bhavanti hi
nādhanyaṃ jāgataṃ vākyaṃ viparītā bhavetkriyā (36)

Vocabulary

ākṛṣya: having contracted; *mukham*: entrance; *pāyu*: anus; *mukulīkṛtya*: closing off; *apāna*: downward vital air; *samutthāpya*: raising; *praṇavena*: through the *praṇava*, om; *nivartayet*: one should expel; *śrībījena*: through the fire element; *tataḥ*: then; *dhyāyet*: one should meditate on; *sva-ātmānam*: one's own ātman; *plāvanam*: be immersed; *amṛta*: nectar; *etad*: this; *kālavañcana*: illusion of time; *pracakṣate*: it radiates; *sarva-mukhyam*: all-important; *yena*: whatever; *cintitam*: thought; *sidhyati*: originates; *manasā*: through the mind; *kāryam*: is accomplished; *manasā*: by the mind; *agni-jvalanāt*: by the flame of fire; *jale*: in water; *bhavanti*: there are; *pallavāni*: sprouts; *śākhā*: branches; *bhavet*: should there be; *vākyam*: speech; *kriya*: actions; *hi*: surely; *na viparītā adhanyam*: no adverse results.

Translation

Having contracted the entrance to the anus, closing it off, causing *apāna vāyu* to rise through [repetition of] the *praṇava*, one should expel [the *prāṇa*] by means of the *śrī-bīja*. Then one should meditate on one's own ātman as *śri* [and] be immersed in the nectar. This is *kāla-vañcana*, the illusion of time. It radiates as far-reaching. Whatever thought originates through the mind is accomplished by the mind. By the flame of fire in water, there are sprouts and branches. Should there be speech [or] actions in the *jāgati* metre, [there are] surely no adverse results.

Commentary

Having closed the anus and repeating the mantra *Om*, the yogin causes the *apāna vāyu* to rise. Then through the repetition of the mantra *Śrīṃ* the *prāṇa* is pulled downwards. The *śrī-bīja,* the seed mantra of *śrī* containing the essence of the deity Lakṣmī, the wife of Viṣṇu, is associated with the element of fire. The *apāna vāyu* is raised to the *maṇipura cakra*, the seat of fire.

Time is described as an illusion because, although it seems to go on forever, our identities and roles in this life are not permanent. The definition of *kāla* is both time and death. Georg Feuerstein says: 'Yet the transcendence of time is precisely the objective of all spiritual traditions. Hence the yogin seeks to cheat time and death by realizing the transcendental Reality, which is immortal. The perfected adept is also called *kāla-atīta* (*kālātīta*), one who has transcended time.' [103]

The *Haṭha Yoga Pradīpikā* says that 'in *samādhi* a yoga is neither consumed by the processes of time (death) nor is he affected by action nor affected by any influence'.[104] 'The sun and moon divide time into day and night. Suṣumnā is the consumer of time.' [105]

' This means that when the life-force (*prāṇa*) enters the axial channel, the mind stands still and all perception of space and time ceases.' [106]

The *jāgati* metre is mentioned in hymns of the *Rig Veda*. Wendy Doniger cites these two: *The Creation of the Sacrifice* and *The Elements of Sacrifice.*[107] The chanting of *jāgati* during the ritual fire sacrifice is certain to bring benefits and abundance.

Verses 37 to 41: Union of Prāṇa and Apāna

मार्गे बिन्दुं समाबध्य वह्निं प्रज्वाल्य जीवने ।
शोषयित्वा तु सलिलं तेन कायं दृढं भवेत् ॥३७॥
गुदयोनिसमायुक्त आकुञ्चत्येककालतः ।
अपानमूर्ध्वगं कृत्वा समानोऽन्ने नियोजयेत् ॥३८॥
स्वात्मानं च श्रियं ध्यायेदमृतप्लावनं ततः ।
बलं समारभेद्योगं मध्यमद्वारभागतः ॥३९॥
भावयेदूर्ध्वगत्यर्थं प्राणापानसुयोगतः ।
एष योगो वरो देहे सिद्धिमार्गप्रकाशकः ॥४०॥
यथैवापगातः सेतुः प्रवाहस्य निरोधकः ।
तथा शरीरगा छाया ज्ञातव्या योगिभिः सदा ॥४१॥

mārge binduṃ samābadhya vahniṃ prajvālya jīvane
śoṣayitvā tu salilaṃ tena kāyaṃ dṛḍhaṃ bhavet (37)
gudayonisamāyukta ākuñcatyekakālataḥ
apānamūrdhvagaṃ kṛtvā samāno'nne niyojayet (38)
svātmānaṃ ca śriyaṃ dhyāyedamṛtaplāvanaṃ tataḥ
balaṃ samārabhedyogaṃ madhyamadvārabhāgataḥ (39)
bhāvayedūrdhvagatyarthaṃ prāṇāpānasuyogataḥ
eṣa yogo varo dehe siddhimārgaprakāśakaḥ (40)
yathaivāpagātaḥ setuḥ pravāhasya nirodhakaḥ
tathā śarīragā chāyā jñātavyā yogibhiḥ sadā (41)

Vocabulary

samābadhya: observing; *mārge*: in the path; *vahnim*: fire; *prajvālya*: making blaze; *jīvane*: by the vital air; *tena*: thereby; *śoṣayitvā*: drying up; *salilam*: water; *tu*: then; *kāyam*: body; *bhavet*: becomes; *dṛḍham*: strong; *ākuñcati*: having contracted; *eka*: together; *guda-yoni*: anus and yoni; *kālataḥ*: for a long time; *ūrdhvagaṃ kṛtvā*: having raised; *niyojayet*: one combines; *anne*: in the fire; *dhyāyet*: one should contemplate; *sva-ātmānam*: one's own ātman; *śriyam*: as *śrī*;

plāvanam: immersed; *amṛta*: nectar; *tataḥ*: then; *madhyam*: middle; *bhāgataḥ*: part; *advāra*: of the entrance; *samārabhet*: should undertake; *balam*: will; *bhāvayet artham*: one should endeavour; *ūrdhvagati*: to rise up; *suyogataḥ*: complete union; *eṣa*: this; *varaḥ yogaḥ*: auspicious yoga; *prakāśakaḥ*: illuminates; *dehe*: in the body; *siddhi-mārga*: path of psychic powers; *tathaiva*: just as; *setuḥ*: bridge; *āpagātaḥ*: river; *nirodhakaḥ*: obstructs; *pravāhasya*: flow; *tathā*: so; *chāyā*: reflected light; *śarīragā*: of the body; *sadā*: always; *jñātavyā*: should be understood; *yogibhih*: by the yogins.

Translation

Observing the *bindu* in the path, the vital air making the fire blaze, thereby drying up the water, then the body becomes strong. Having contracted together the anus and yoni for a long time [and] raised the *apāna*, [the yogin] unites [it] with the fire of *samāna* [*vayu*]. One should contemplate one's own ātman as *śri*, immersed in nectar, then in the middle part of the entrance should undertake [the practice of] yoga [with all one's] will. One should endeavour to rise up by the complete union of *prāṇa* and *apāna*. This auspicious yoga illuminates in the body the path of psychic powers. Just as a bridge over a river obstructs the flow, so the reflected light of the body should always be understood by the yogins.

Commentary

Swami Muktibodhananda describes the bindu as 'an important aspect of tantra and yoga. *Bindu* means 'point' or 'nucleus', and refers to the nucleus in each individual which contains the potential consciousness and creative force. What is the potential consciousness within the nucleus? It can be compared to the DNA molecule which contains the potential of creating an entire universe in the form of a new being.' [108]

The importance of the union of *prāṇa* and *apāna* is reflected in the following commentaries.

Swami Satsangananda says in her book *Tattwa Shuddhi* that 'The two most influential *vāyus* are *prāṇa* and *apāna.* Prāṇa is the inward moving force which is said to create a field moving upwards from the navel to the throat. Apāna is the outward moving force which is said to create a field, moving downwards from the navel to the anus. They both move spontaneously in the body. The movement of their opposite moving forces needs to be reversed, so that they unite with *samana* in the navel centre, the result of which is the awakening of the kuṇḍalinī.'[109]

Again, the yogin, to emphasise the importance of filling the body with nectar, is instructed to contemplate the Self as *śri*, immersed in nectar.

The verse says 'one should endeavour to rise up by the complete union of *prāṇa* and *apāna*'. This can be done by perfecting the practices of *mūla bandha* (perineal lock for men; cervical lock for women) and *jālandara bandha* (throat lock). These two bandhas force together *prāṇa* and *apāna*, so that they unite in *maṇipura*.

Verses 62 to 65 in *Yoga Kundali Upanishad* emphasises the importance of purifying the mind through prāṇāyāma before attempting these bandhas:
'Thus the practice of prāṇāyāma should always be performed by meditating steadily on purity. Then the mind is dissolved in suṣumnā [and] prāṇa pervades [it]. When the impurities have withered away, and with movement up [the suṣumnā], he then becomes a yogin. Apāna moving downwards should be raised upwards by contracting it with force. This is called mūlabandha. Apāna, having been raised up, moves together with agni to the seat of prāṇa. Then agni, having united prāṇa and apāna, quickly goes to kuṇḍalinī [who is] coiled, fast asleep.'[110]

Verses 42 to 45: Saṃpuṭa Yoga

सर्वासामेव नाडीनामेष प्रकीर्तितः ।

बन्धस्यास्य प्रसादेन स्फुटीभवति देवता ॥४२॥

एवं चतुष्पथो बन्धो मार्गत्रयनिरोधकः ।

एक विकासयन्मार्गं येन सिद्धाः सुसङ्गताः ॥४३॥

उदानमूर्ध्वगं कृत्वा प्राणेन सह वेगतः ।

बन्धोऽयं सर्वनाडीनामूर्ध्वं याति निरोधकः ॥४४॥

अयं च संपुटो योगो मूलबन्धोऽप्ययं मतः ।

बन्धत्रयमनेनैव सिद्ध्यत्यभ्यासयोगतः ॥४५॥

sarvāsāmeva nāḍīnāmeṣa bandhaḥ prakīrtitaḥ
bandhasyāsya prasādena sphuṭībhavati devata (42)
evaṃ catuṣpatho bandho mārgatrayanirodhakaḥ
eka vikāsayanmārgaṃ yena siddhāḥ susaṅgatāḥ (43)
udānamūrdhvagaṃ kṛtvā prāṇena saha vegataḥ
bandho'yaṃ sarvanāḍīnāmūrdhvaṃ yāti nirodhakaḥ (44)
ayaṃ ca saṃpuṭo yogo mūlabandho'pyayaṃ mataḥ
bandhatrayayamanenaiva siddhyatyabhyāsayogataḥ (45)

Vocabulary

eṣa bandhaḥ: this bandha; *prakīrtitaḥ*: is approved; *sarvāsām nāḍīnām*: for all the nāḍīs; *prasādena*: through the grace; *bandhasya-asya*: of this bandha; *devata*: deity; *bhavati*: becomes; *sphuṭī*: manifest; *catuṣ-pathāḥ*: four ways; *nirodhakaḥ*: obstructing; *traya mārga*: three paths; *vikāsayan*: illuminates; *eka mārgam*: one way; *yena*: to which; *siddhāḥ*: sages; *susaṅgatāḥ*: adhere; *kṛtvā*: having caused; *ūrdhvagam*: to rise; *vegataḥ*: quickly; *saha prāṇena*: with *prāṇa vāyu*; *ayam*: this; *sarva-nāḍīnām*: all the nāḍīs; *yāti*: goes; *ūrdhvam*: upwards; *ayam mataḥ*: this is called; *ca api*: and also; *eva*: only; *abhyāsa-yogataḥ*: by the practice of yoga; *yamanena*: by controlling; *siddhyati*: are perfected.

Translation

This *bandha* (union of *prāṇa* and *apāna*) is approved for all the nāḍīs. Through the grace of this bandha the deity becomes manifest. This bandha of the four ways, by obstructing the three paths, illuminates the one way to which the sages adhere. Having caused *udāna vāyu* to rise quickly with *prāṇa vāyu*, this bandha, by obstructing all the nāḍīs, goes upwards. This is called *saṃpuṭa yoga*, and also *mūlabandha*. Only by the practice of yoga, controlling the three bandhas, are they perfected.

Commentary

'*Saṃpuṭa*' means 'shaped like a hemispherical bowl'. According to Georg Feuerstein it symbolises 'the perfect self-containedness of the ultimate Reality, which is called Shiva'.[111] The deity is the inner consciousness.

The means to *saṃpuṭa yoga* is through the bandha of the four ways, where the four nāḍīs, *viz* suṣumnā, iḍā, piṅgalā and kuhu meet. It is also called mūlabandha. Thus the three *nādis* of *idā, piṅgala* and *kuhu* are blocked, merging into the one path of the enlightened ones, which is suṣumnā. Then *udāna vāyu*, the prānic air flowing in the area of the throat and face, quickly rises.

Verses 46 to 49: Benefits of Saṃpuṭa Yoga

दिवारात्रमविच्छिन्नं यामेयामे यदा यदा ।

अनेनाभ्यासयोगेन वायुरभ्यसितो भवेत् ॥४६॥

वायावभ्यसिते वह्निः प्रत्यहं वर्धते तनौ ।

वह्नौ विवर्धमाने तु सुखमन्नादि जीर्णते ॥४७॥

अन्नस्य परिपाकेन रसवृद्धिः प्रजायते ।

रसे वृद्धिं गते नित्यं वर्धन्ते धातवस्तथा ॥४८॥

धातूनां वर्धनेनैव प्रबोधो वर्धते तनौ ।

दह्यन्ते सर्वपापानि जन्मकोट्यर्जीतानि च ॥४९॥

divārātramavicchinnaṃ yāmeyāme yadā yadā
anenābhyāsayogena vāyurabhyasito bhavet (46)
vāyāvabhyasite vahniḥ pratyahaṃ vardhate tanau
vahnau vivardhamāne tu sukhamannādi jīrṇate (47)
annasya paripākena rasavṛddhiḥ prajāyate
rase vṛddhiṃ gate nityaṃ vardhante dhātavastathā (48)
dhātūnāṃ vardhanenaiva prabodho vardhate tanau
dahyante sarvapāpāni janmakoṭyarjītāni ca (49)

Vocabulary

divārātram: day and night; *yāmeyāme*: every hour; *avicchinnam*: without interruption; *yadā yadā*: whenever; *vāyuḥ*: vital air; *bhavet*: becomes; *abhyasitaḥ*: controlled; *anena-abhyāsa-yogena*: by this practice of yoga; *vahniḥ*: fire; *vardhate*: increases; *pratyaham*: every day; *tanau*: in the body; *vivardhamāne*: with the increase; *vahnau*: of fire; *anna*: food; *sukham*: well; *jīrṇate*: digested; *paripākena*: with the full digestion; *annasya*: of food; *vṛddhi*: increase; *rasa*: juice; *prajāyate*: is generated; *rase*: when the juice; *gate vṛddhim*: is increased; *nityam*: every day; *tathā*: then; *dhātavaḥ*: vital forces; *vardhante*: increase; *prabodhaḥ*: understanding; *sarva-pāpāni*: all sins; *arjītāni*: accumulated; *koṭi*: crores; *janma*: births; *dahyante*: are burned.

Translation

Day and night, every hour without interruption, at any time, the vital air becomes controlled by this practice of yoga. When the vital airs are controlled, the fire increases every day in the body. With the increase of fire, food etc is well-digested. With the full digestion of food, an increase of juice is generated. When the juice is increased every day, then the vital forces increase. With the increase of the vital forces alone, understanding increases in the body [and] all sins accumulated in crores of births are burned.

Commentary

The regular practice of *saṃpuṭa yoga* gives energy and physical health. The most important benefit is the ascension of kuṇḍalinī to *sahasrāracakra,* at the crown of the head. Then there arises the knowledge of the one Brahman, where the knower attains liberation.

Verses 50 to 53: Parā Śaktiḥ in Mūlādhāra

गुदमेढ्रान्तरालस्थं मूलाधारं त्रिकोणकम् ।
शिवस्य बिन्दुरूपस्य स्थानं तद्धि प्रकाशकम् ।।५०।।
यत्र कुण्डलिनी नाम परा शक्तिः प्रतिष्ठिता ।
यस्मादुत्पद्यते वायुर्यस्माद्वह्निः प्रवर्धते ।।५१।।
यस्मादुत्पद्यते बिन्दुर्यस्मान्नादः प्रवर्धते ।
यस्मादुत्पद्यते हंसो यस्मादुत्पद्यते मनः ।।५२।।
मूलाधारादिषट्चक्रं शक्तिस्थानमुदीरितम् ।
कण्ठादुपरि मूर्धान्तं शांभवं स्थानमुच्यते ।।५३।।

gudameḍhrāntarālasthaṃ mūlādhāraṃ trikoṇakam
śivasya bindurūpasya sthānaṃ taddhi prakāśakam (50)
yatra kuṇḍalinī nāma parā śaktiḥ pratiṣṭhitā
yasmādutpadyate vāyuryasmādvahniḥ pravardhate (51)
yasmādutpadyate bonduryasmānnādaḥ pravardhate
yasmādutpadyate haṃso yasmādutpadyate manaḥ (52)
mūlādhārādiṣaṭcakraṃ śaktisthānamudīritam
kaṇṭhādupari mūrdhāntaṃ śāṃbhavaṃ sthānamucyate (53)

Vocabulary

antarālastham: intermediate space; *guda-meḍhrāt*: between the anus and the genitals; *trikoṇakam*: triangular; *tat prakāśakam*: it illumines; *sthānam*: seat; *śivasya*: of Śiva; *bindu-rūpasya*: of the form of bindu; *yatra*: there; *pratiṣṭhitā*: is situated; *nāma*: with the name of; *yasmāt*: from which; *vāyuḥ*: vital air; *utpadyate*: rises, originates, is born, is produced; *vahniḥ*: fire; *pravardate*: increases, expands; *nādaḥ*: inner sound; *haṃsaḥ*: soul; *manaḥ*: mind; *ṣaṭ-cakram*: six cakras; *ādi*: beginning with; *udīritam*: are said to be; *śakti*-sthānam: seat of śakti; *upari*: above; *kaṇṭhāt*: from the throat; *mūrdhāntam*: crown of the head; *ucyate*: is said to be; *śāṃbhavaṃ sthānam*: seat of Śambhu.

Translation

In the intermediate space between the anus and the genitals [is] the triangular *mūlādhāra*. It illumines the seat of Śiva of the form of the bindu. There is situated the *parā śaktiḥ* with the name of *kuṇḍalinī*, from which the vital air rises, from which the fire increases, from which the bindu originates, from which the inner sound expands, from which the soul is born, from which the mind is produced. The six cakras beginning with mūlādhāra are said to be the seat of śakti. From above the throat to the crown of the head is said to be the seat of Śambhu.

Commentary

Mūlādhāra is the 'base prānic centre in the human body situated in the perineum in men and the cervix in women and also connected to the coccygeal plexus, it is the seat of *kuṇḍalinī* (the primal evolutionary energy in human beings).' 'Its bīja mantra is *lam*, pertaining to the earth element.'[112]

'Its centre contains the radiant triangle, within which is found the golden phallus (*linga*) of Śiva. This cakra is the source of suṣumnā nāḍī, the central channel of the life force and resting place of the 'serpent power', *kuṇḍalinī śakti.*' [113]

Here Śiva is manifest in his seed form. *Parā śaktiḥ* is the Supreme Power or Transcendent Energy, the counterpart of Śiva, also known as Śambhu, meaning 'born of peace'.

The seat of Śambhu is described thus in *Haṭha Yoga Pradīpikā*:

'In the middle of the eyebrows is the place of Śiva, there the mind is quiescent. That state is known as *turīya* or the fourth dimension. There, time is unknown.'

Verses 54 to 59a: Prāṇa, the abode of the Jīva

नाडीनामाश्रयः पिण्डो नाद्यः प्राणस्य चाश्रयः ।
जीवस्य निलयः प्राणो जीवो हंसस्य चाश्रयः ॥५४॥
हंसः शक्तेरधिष्ठानं चराचरमिदं जगत् ।
निर्विकल्पः प्रसन्नात्मा प्राणायां समभ्यसेत् ॥५५॥
सम्यग्बन्धत्रयस्थोऽपि लक्ष्यलक्षणकारणम् ।
वेद्यं समुद्धरेन्नित्यं सत्यसंधानमाबसः ॥५६॥
रेचकं पूरकं चैव कुम्भमध्ये निरोधयेत् ।
दृश्यमाने परे लक्ष्ये ब्रह्मणि स्वयमाश्रितः ॥५७॥
बाह्यस्यविषयं सर्वं रेचकः समुदाहृतः ।
पूरकं शास्त्रविज्ञानं कुम्भकं स्वगतं स्मृतम् ॥५८॥
एवमभ्यासचित्तंचेत्स मुक्तो नात्र संशयः ।५९।

nāḍīnāmāśrayaḥ piṇḍo nādyaḥ prāṇasya cāśrayaḥ
jīvasya nilayaḥ prāṇo jīvo haṃsasya cāśrayaḥ (54)
haṃsaḥ śakteradhiṣṭhānaṃ carācaramidaṃ jagat
nirvikalpaḥ prasannātmā prāṇāyāṃ samabhyaset (55)
samyagbandhatrayastho'pi lakṣyalakṣaṇakāraṇam
vedyaṃ samuddharennityaṃ satyasaṃdhānamānasaḥ (56)
recakaṃ pūrakaṃ caiva kumbhamadhye nirodhayet
dṛśyamāne pare lakṣye brahmaṇi svayamāśritaḥ (57)
bāhyasyaviṣayaṃ sarvaṃ recakaḥ samudāhṛtaḥ
pūrakaṃ śāstravijñānaṃ kumbhakaṃ svagataṃ smṛtam (58)
evamabhyāsacittaṃcetsa mukto nātra saṃśayaḥ (59a)

Vocabulary

piṇḍaḥ: body; *āśrayaḥ*: base; *nāḍīnām*: of the nāḍīs; *ca nāḍyaḥ*: and the nāḍīs; *prāṇasya*: of prāṇa; *nilayaḥ*: abode; *haṃsasya*: of the soul; *adhiṣṭhānam*: seat; *śakteḥ*: of śakti; *idam jagat*: this world; *carācaram*: all creations; *prasanna*: lucid; *nirvikalpaḥ*: free from differences; *samabhyaset*: one should practise; *prāṇāyām*: breath control; *api*: although; *samyak sthaḥ*: well established; *bandha-traya*: three bandhas; *nityam*: always; *samuddharet*: one should uplift; *mānasaḥ*: mind; *saṃdhāna*: attached to; *satya*: truth; *vedyam*: that which should be known; *kāraṇam*: reason; *lakṣaṇa*: goal; *lakṣya*: is recognised; *nirodhayet*: one should abstain from; *pūrakam*: inhaling; *ca recakam*: and exhaling; *kumbha-madhye*: in the middle of kumbhaka; *āśritaḥ*: depending; *svayam*: by oneself; *brahmaṇi*: on Brahman; *pare*: highest; *dṛśyamāne lakṣye*: visible goal; *sarvam viṣayam*: all matter; *bāhasya*: external; *samudāhṛtaḥ*: is called; *śāstra-vijñānam*: wisdom of the śāstras; *smṛtam*: remembering; *svagatam*: in oneself; *evam*: thus; *cet*: if; *cittam*: mind; *abhyāsa*: practises; *atra*: here; *na saṃśayaḥ*: without doubt; *saḥ muktaḥ*: one is liberated.

Translation

The body is the base of the nāḍīs and the nāḍīs are the base of prāṇa. The prāṇa is the abode of the *jīva* and the jīva is the base of the soul. The soul is the seat of śakti. This world [is the cause of] all creations. The ātman is lucid [and] free from differences. One should practise breath control. Although well established in the three bandhas, one should always uplift, [with] mind attached to the truth, that which should be known, [and is] the reason by which the goal is recognised. One should abstain from inhaling and exhaling in the middle of kumbhaka, depending by oneself on Brahman, the highest visible goal. All matter which is external is called exhalation. The wisdom of the *śāstras* is inhalation. Remembering [it] in oneself is retention. Thus if the mind practises here, one is without doubt liberated.

Commentary

The body, the nāḍīs, the prāṇa, the jīva (the individual living being) and the *haṃsa* (soul, ātman) are all linked and support each other. Śakti, the divine energy, rests in the soul. This

world is full of a variety of creations, whereas the ātman, the basis of all beings, is the same in all creations.
Prāṇāyām, breath control, means 'using the breath to control the flow of prāṇa within the body, thus expanding the range of vital energy'.[115] This is achieved through the practice of the three bandhas, mūla, jālandhara and uḍḍiyāna. At the same time, the yogin should concentrate on attaining the True Reality, the ātman, only retaining the breath without inhaling and exhaling, and depend solely on Brahman, 'the only real entity, [who] cannot be attained by any other means than removal of ignorance through knowledge of the Self'. [116]

The removal of ignorance is exhalation. The study of the knowledge of the *śāstras*, spiritual texts, is inhalation, and the absorption of their wisdom is retention. Thus one attains liberation.

Verses 59b to 61a: Kumbhaka

कुम्भकेन समारोप्य कुम्भकेनैव पूरयेत् ॥५९॥
कुम्भेन कुम्भयेत्कुम्भं तदन्तस्थः परं शिवम् ।
पुनरास्फलायेदद्य सुस्थिरं कण्ठमुद्रया ॥६०॥
वायूनां गतमावृत्य धृत्वा पूरककुम्भकै ।६१।

kumbhakena samāropya kumbhakenaiva pūrayet (59b)
kumbhena kumbhayetkumbhaṃ tadantasthaḥ paraṃ śivam
punarāsphalāyedadya susthiraṃ kaṇṭhamudrayā (60)
vāyūnāṃ gatamāvṛtya dhṛtvā pūrakakumbhakai (61a)

Vocabulary

samāropya: causing to rise; *kumbhakena*: through kumbhaka; *pūrayet*: it should be filled; *kumbhakena-eva*: by kumbhaka alone; *kumbhayet*: one should control; *kumbham*: pot; *kumbhena*: through the pot; *tat-antasthaḥ*: within it is; *param śivam*: Supreme Śiva; *susthiram*: stable; *phalāyet*: is the result; *adya punarāḥ*: daily repetition; *kaṇṭha-mudrayā*: of the throat posture; *āvṛtya*: turning towards; *gatam*: course; *dhṛtvā*: holding; *pūraka*: in-breath;

Translation

[The mind], having been caused to rise through kumbhaka, should be filled by kumbhaka alone. One should control the pot through the pot. Within it is the Supreme Śiva. A stable [pot] is the result of daily repetition of the throat posture, turning towards the course of the vāyus [and] holding the in-breath in kumbhaka.

Commentary

'Kumbhaka' literally means 'potlike'. Here kumbhaka refers to retention of the breath, when the body is filled with life energy (prāṇa), which is retained as a pot (kumbha) retains liquid.' [117]

Swami Satyadharma says that 'when the senses are withdrawn into the mind, and then restrained by the practice of kumbhaka, breath retention, the mind becomes absolutely still.'[118] Remaining in that stillness, one becomes Brahman.

Daily repetition of jālandhara bandha, the throat lock leading to the union of prāṇa and apāna, and kumbhaka, breath retention, is necessary to stabilise the mind. Then one attains Śiva.

Verses 61b to 68a: Raising the Vital Air

समहस्तयुगं भूमै समं पादयुगं तथा ।।६१।।
वेधकक्रमयोगेन चतुष्पीथं तु वायुना ।
आस्फालयेन्महामेरुं वायुवक्रे प्रकोटिभः ।।६२।।
पुटद्वयं समाकृष्य वायुः स्फुरति सत्वरम् ।
सोमसूर्याग्निसंबन्धाज्जानीयादमृताय वै ।।६३।।
मेरुमध्यगता देवाश्चलन्ते मेरुचालनात् ।
आद्य संजायते क्षिप्रं वेधोऽस्य ब्रह्मग्रन्थितः ।।६४।।
ब्रह्मग्रन्थिं ततो भित्त्वा विष्णुग्रन्थिं भिनत्त्यसौ ।
विष्णुग्रन्थिं ततो भित्त्वा रुद्रग्रन्थिं भिनत्त्यसौ ।।६५।।
रुद्रग्रन्थिं ततो भित्त्वा छित्त्वा मोहमलं तथा ।
अनेकजन्मसंस्कारगुरुदेवप्रसादतः ।।६६।।
योगाभ्यासात्ततो वेधो जायते तस्य योगिनः ।
इडापिङ्गलयोर्मध्ये सुषुम्नानाडिमण्डले ।।६७।।
मुद्राबन्धविशेषेण वायुमूर्ध्वं च कारयेत् ।६८।

samahastayugaṃ bhūmai samaṃ pādayugaṃ tathā (61b)
vedhakakramayogena catuṣpīthaṃ tu vāyunā
āsphālayenmahāmeruṃ vāyuvakre prakoṭibhaḥ (62)
puṭadvayaṃ samākṛṣya vāyuḥ sphurati satvaram
somasūryāgnisaṃbandhājjānīyādamṛtāya vai (63)
merumadhyagatā devāścalante merucālanāt
ādya saṃjāyate kṣipraṃ vedho'sya brahmagranthitaḥ (64)
brahmagranthiṃ tato bhittvā viṣṇugranthiṃ bhinattyasau
viṣṇugranthiṃ tato bhittvā rudragranthiṃ bhinattyasau (65)
rudragranthiṃ tato bhittvā chittvā mohamalaṃ tathā
anekajanmasaṃskāragurudevaprasādataḥ (66)
yogābhyāsāttato vedho jāyate tasya yoginaḥ
iḍāpiṅgalayormadhye suṣumnānāḍimaṇḍale (67)
mudrābandhaviśeṣena vāyumūrdhvaṃ ca kārayet (68a)

Vocabulary

tathā: then; *sama*: together; *hasta-yugam*: both hands; *pāda-yugam*: both feet; *samam*: evenly; *bhūmai*: on the ground; *krama*: gradually; *vedaka*: making known; *catuṣpītham*: four seats; *vāyunā*: through the vāyu; *vedaka yogena*: through Vedaka Yoga; *āsphālayet*: one should shake; *prakoṭibhaḥ*: with the forces; *vāyu-vakre*: in the course of the vāyu.

saṃbandhāt: because of the conjunction; *soma*: moon; *sūrya*: sun; *agni*: fire; *puṭa-dvayam*: two pockets; *samākṛṣya*: having been drawn together; *satvaram*: immediately; *sphurati*: throbs; *jānīyāt*: may know; *amṛtāya*: immortality; *merucālanāt*: through the movement of *Meru*; *devāḥ*: gods; *gatāḥ*: having gone to; *meru-madhya*: centre of Meru; *calante*: move about.

ādya: at first; *vedhaḥ*: hole; *kṣipram*: directly; *saṃjāyate*: appears; *tataḥ*: then; *bhittvā*: having pierced; *asau bhinatti*: one pierces; *chittvā*: having split; *malam*: dirt; *moha*: delusion; *prasādataḥ*: through the grace; *guru-deva*: god and guru; *saṃskāra*: mental impressions; *aneka-janma*: many births; *yoga-abhyāsāt*: through the practice of yoga; *jāyate*: one is born as; *yoginaḥ*: yogin; *maṇḍale*: in the region; *madhye*: between; *kārayet ūrdhvam*: is made to rise; *viśeṣena*: especially with.

Translation

Then [placing] both hands and both feet together evenly on the ground, gradually [attaining] the four seats [and] the vāyu through Vedhaka Yoga, one should shake *Mahāmeru* with the forces in the course of the vāyu.

Because of the conjunction of the moon, sun and fire, the two pockets having been drawn together, the vāyu immediately throbs [and the yogin] may know immortality. Through the movement of *Meru* the gods, having gone to the centre of Meru, move about.

At first a hole directly appears in the *brahma-granthi*. Then having pierced the Brahma knot, one pierces the Viṣṇu knot. Then having pierced the Viṣṇu knot, one pierces the Rudra knot. Having pierced the Rudra knot [and] split the dirt of delusion [and] through the grace of God and guru, the mental impressions [of] many births, then through the practice of yoga one is born as a yogin of Vedha [Yoga]. In the region of *suṣumnā nāḍī* between *iḍā* and *piṅgalā*, the vāyu is made to rise, especially with mudrā and bandha.

Commentary

The posture described is *padmāsana*, the lotus pose. The four seats, sacred sites in India, are *kāmarūpa pūrṇagiri*, *jālandhara* and *uḍḍīyāna*. Here they may refer to mūlādhāra, maṇipura, *viśuddhi* (at the throat) and *ājña* (at the eyebrow centre) cakras.

'Mount Meru, in Hindu mythology, is a golden mountain that stands in the centre of the universe and is the axis of the world. It is the abode of gods, and its foothills are the Himalayas. It reaches down below the ground, into the nether regions, as far as it extends into the heavens.'[119] In the lowest world of Mount Meru lives the snake Vasuki, symbolised in the body by the *kuṇḍalinī*.

Here Meru refers to suṣumnā nāḍī, the spinal column, often called *meru-danda* (*meru*-staff). [120]

The moon represents *iḍā nāḍī*, and the sun *piṅgalā nāḍī*. The fire is the fire of the kuṇḍalinī. When they merge, the yogin experiences the pulsation of the prāṇa which has absorbed the *amrita*, nectar. Swami Satyananda says that 'he who meditates on this awakened chakra sees a flaming lamp shining as the morning sun and he dwells within the regions of fire, sun and moon, and realises his unity with Brahman.' [121]

Vedhaka Yoga is the yoga of piercing through the knots (*granthis*). There are three *granthis*, energy blockages or attachments which obstruct the upward flow of kuṇḍalinī along suṣumnā nāḍi. They can be unblocked by the practice of *maha bandha*, the great lock, a combination of jālandhara, uḍḍīyāna and mūla bandha, with external kumbhaka.

Swami Niranjananda describes the three granthis thus:
'*Brahma granthi* in mūlādhāra cakra which creates attachments to material objects, sensual pleasures and selfishness.
Viṣnu granthi in anāhata cakra which creates bondage to other people, emotional relationships and attachment to psychic experiences and emotional situations.
Rudra granthi in ājña cakra which represents the obstacles created by the power of the intellect, along with attachment to siddhis and other higher psychic experiences.
The practice of bandhas creates a build-up of prāṇa to untie or release these knots of bondage, so that the *sadhaka* (aspirant, yogin) is free to attain what lies beyond all attachment.'[122]

Verses 68b to 71a: Three Kinds of Praṇava

ह्रस्वो दहति पापानि दीर्घो मोक्षदायकः ॥६८॥
आप्यायनः प्लुतो वापि त्रिविधोञ्छारणेन तु ।
तैलधारामिवाच्छिन्नं दीर्घघण्टानिनादवत् ॥६९॥
अवाच्यं प्रणवस्याग्रं यस्तं वेद स वेदवित् ।
ह्रस्वं बिन्दुगतं दैर्घ्यं ब्रह्मरन्ध्रगतं प्लुतम् ।
द्वादशान्तगतं मन्त्रं प्रसादं मन्त्रसिद्धये ॥७०॥
सर्वविघ्नहरश्चायं प्रणवः सर्वदोषहा ।७१।

hrasvo dahati pāpāni dīrgho mokṣadāyakaḥ (68b)
āpyāyanaḥ pluto vāpi trividhoñchāraṇena tu
tailadhārāmivācchinnaṃ dīrghaghaṇṭāninādavat (69)
āvācyaṃ praṇavasyāgraṃ yastaṃ veda sa vedavit
hṛsvaṃ bindugataṃ dairghyaṃ brahmarandhragataṃ plutam
dvādaśāntagataṃ mantraṃ prasādaṃ mantrasiddhaye (70)
sarvavighnaharaścāyaṃ praṇavaḥ sarvadoṣahā (71a)

Vocabulary

uñchāraṇena: in the group; *trividha*: of three kinds; *hrasvaḥ*: short; *dahati*: burns; *pāpāni*: sins; *dīrghaḥ*: long; *mokṣa-dāyakaḥ*: gives liberation; *plutaḥ*: very long; *āpyāyanaḥ*: strength; *iva-acchinnam*: like the incessant; *dhārām*: flow; *taila*: oil; *dīrgha*: lingering; *nināda-vat*: like the sound; *ghaṇṭā*: bell; *āgram*: origin; *praṇavasya*: of *praṇava*; *avācyam*: cannot be spoken; *yaḥ*: whoever; *veda*: knows; *tam*: this; *vedavit*: knower of the Veda; *dvādaśānta*: end of the twelfth; *prasādam*: grace; *mantra-siddhaye*: from the power of mantra; *sarva*: all; *ca ayam*: and this; *vighnaharaḥ*: remover of obstacles; *doṣa-hā*: disorders.

Translation

In the group of three kinds [of *praṇava*], the short one burns

[all] sins; the long one gives liberation [and] the very long one [gives] strength. Like the incessant flow of oil [and] the lingering sound of a bell, the origin of *praṇava* cannot be spoken. Whoever knows this is a knower of the Veda. The short sound goes to the bindu. The long sound goes to the crown of the head. The very long sound goes to the end of the twelfth. The grace of mantra [is] from the power of mantra. This praṇava [is] the remover of all obstacles and all disorders.

Commentary

The *praṇava* is the mantra AUM. Its origin is the primal sound vibration or primal seed which is the cause of speech. There are three ways of pronouncing the mantra. The short way reaches the bindu in the heart, erasing sins. The long way reaches the opening in the crown of the head, giving liberation. The very long way reaches the twelve digits beyond the crown cakra.

The concluding verse of *Mandukyopanishad* says 'Om is Ātman, the transcendent, the beyond understanding, the cessation of all phenomena, the blissful, the non-dual. The knower of this final Truth is merged in Ātman and attains the final goal, which is Brahman'. [123]

Verses 71b to 75: Four States of Nāda Yoga

आरम्भश्च घटश्चैव पुनः परिचयस्तथा ।।७१।।
निष्पत्तिश्चेति कथिताश्चतस्रस्तस्य भूमिकाः ।
कारणत्रयसंभूतं बाह्यं कर्म परित्यजन् ।।७२।।
अन्तरं कर्म कुरुते यत्रारम्भः स उच्यते ।
वायुः पश्चिमतो वेधं कुर्वन्नापूर्य सुस्थिरम् ।।७३।।
यत्र तिष्ठति सा प्रोकता घटाख्या भूमिका बुधैः ।
न सजीवो न निर्जीवः काये तिष्ठति निश्चलम् ।
यत्र वायुः स्थिरः खे स्यात्सेयः परिचयभूमिका ।।७४।।
यत्रात्मनो सृष्टिलयौ जीवन्मुक्तिदशागतः ।
सहजः कुरुते योगं सेयं निष्पत्तिभूमिका ।।७५।।

ārambhaśca ghaṭaścaiva punaḥ paricayastathā (71b)
niṣpattiśceti kathitāścatasrastasya bhūmikāḥ
kātaṇatrayasaṃbhūtaṃ bāhyaṃ karma parityajan (72)
antaraṃ karma kurute yatrārambhaḥ sa ucyate
vāyuḥ paścimato vedhaṃ kurvannāpūrya susthiram (73)
yatra tiṣṭhati sā proktā ghaṭākhyā bhūmikā budhaiḥ
na sajīvo na nirjīvaḥ kāye tiṣṭhati niścalam
yatra vāyuḥ sthiraḥ khe syātseyaḥ paricayabhūmikā (74)
yatrātmano sṛṣṭilayau jīvanmuktidaśāgataḥ
sahajaḥ kurute yogaṃ seyaṃ niṣpattibhūmikā (75)

Vocabulary

tasya: its; *catasraḥ*: four; *bhūmikāḥ*: states; *kathitāḥ*: are described; *ca punaḥ*: and then; *ucyate*: is said to be; *yatra*: where; *parityajan*: abandoning; *bāhyam*: external; *saṃbhūtam*: produced; *traya kāraṇa*: three causes; *kurute*: one makes; *antaram*: inner; *bhūmikā*: state; *ākhyā*: called; *proktā*: is declared; *budhaiḥ*: by the wise; *vāyuḥ*: vital air; *kurvan*: by making; *vedham*: opening; *paścimataḥ*: from behind; *āpūrya*: having filled; *tiṣṭhati*: remains; *susthiram*: fixed; *yatra*: there;

syāt: is; *na sajīvaḥ*: neither alive; *na nirjīvaḥ*: nor lifeless; *niścalam*: immobile; *sthiraḥ*: fixed; *khe*: in the ether; *kāye*: in the body; *sṛṣṭi-layau*: creation and dissolution; *ātmanaḥ*: through the ātman; *āgataḥ*: having reached; *daśā*: state; *kurute*: performs; *sahajaḥ*: innate nature.

Translation

Its four states are described: *ārambha* and *ghaṭa*, then *paricaya* and *niṣpatti*. Ārambha is said to be where, abandoning the external karma produced [by] the three causes, one makes inner karma. The state called ghaṭa, declared by the wise, [is] that the vital air, by making an opening from behind [and] having filled [it], remains fixed there. The paricaya state is where the vital air, neither alive nor lifeless, remains immobile and fixed in the ether in the body. The niṣpatti state [after] creation and dissolution, through the ātman, having reached the state of *jīvanmukti*, performs the yoga of one's innate nature.

Commentary

These verses describe the four states of yogic accomplishment. Swami Muktibodhananda describes them as 'the four stages of progressive experience of *nāda* [which] are known as *bhava* or spontaneous unfoldment. Each stage is more subtle and refined than the preceding one. They are said to apply to all yogic practices, but the *Shiva Samhita* applies them particularly to prāṇāyāma'. [124]

Ārambha avasthā is the beginning stage, where the yogin gives up external actions caused by mind, speech and body, and functions inwardly instead.

The *Haṭha-Yoga-Pradīpikā* describes it thus:
'The Brahma granthi being pierced, the feeling of bliss arises from the void; wondrous, tinkling sounds and the unstruck sound (*anāhata*) are heard within the body.

When the yogi experiences ārambha in the void of the heart, his body becomes lustrous and brilliant with a divine smell and diseaseless.' [125]

Ghaṭa avasthā is the second stage. 'The *Shiva Samhita* defines it as that stage in which the inbreath, the outbreath, the inner sound, the seed, the individuated self and the transcendental Self are all united. According to the *Haṭha-Yoga-Pradīpikā*, this coincides with the piercing of *viṣnu granthi.*' [126]

'When the *viṣnu granthi* is pierced, the greatest bliss is revealed. Then from the void the sound of the kettledrum manifests.' [127]

Ghaṭa is a vessel for holding water. The vessel immersed in water has water both inside and outside. This can be compared to 'the same nāda which flows through the entire universe flows throughout our entire being. In the second stage, mind is like a vessel; consciousness is able to perceive the flow of nāda within and without. When *viṣnu granthi* in *anāhata cakra* is untied, the mind becomes attuned to the subtler sound frequencies'. [128]

Paricaya avasthā (accumulation state):
'In the third stage is the experience of the sound of the drum.
Then there is the great void and one enters the place of total perfection or siddhi.
Then the bliss of citta being attained, natural or spontaneous ecstasy arises.
Imbalance of the three humors or doshas, pain, old age, disease, hunger, sleep are overcome.' [129]

Niṣpatti avasthā (state of completion):
This is the fourth and final state in which both creation and dissolution take place through the ātman and in which the

yogin spontaneously reaches the state of a jīvanmukta, similar to *nirvikalpa samādhi*.

The *Shiva Samhita* says that now 'the yogi drinks amrita (the nectar of immortality), having destroyed the seeds of his karma'. [130]

'If the *rudra granthi* is pierced, the fire of prāṇa is moved to the place of Īshwara. Then in the stage of consummation is the tinkling sound of the flute resonating like a *vīṇā*.'[131]

'When the rudra granthi is pierced the kuṇḍalinī moves to sahasrāra cakra, the abode of *paramśiva*, the *mahabindu*. This is above the state of manifested or differentiated Shakti. Here Shiva and Shakti abide together. It is *turīyātita*, even beyond the fourth dimension.'[132]

Epilogue

इति ।

एतदुपनिषदं योऽधीते सोऽग्निपूतो भवति ।

स वायुपूतो भवति ।

सुरापानात्पूतो भवति ।

स्वर्णस्तेयात्पूतो भवति ।

स जीवन्मुक्तो भवति ।

तदेतदृचाभ्युक्तम् ।

तद्विष्णोः परमं पदं सदा पश्यन्ति सूरयः ।

दिवीव चक्षुराततम् ।

तद्विप्रासो विपन्यवो जागृवांसः समिन्धते ।

विष्णोर्यत्परमं पदमित्युपनिषत् ।

इति पञ्चमोऽध्यायः ।।५।।

iti
etadupaniṣadaṃ yo'dhīte so'gnipūto bhavati
sa vāyupūto bhavati
surāpānātpūto bhavati
svarṇasteyātpūto bhavati
sa jīvanmukto bhavati
tadetadṛcābhyuktam
tadviṣṇoḥ paramaṃ padaṃ sadā paśyanti sūrayaḥ
divīva cakṣurātatam
tadviprāso vipanyavo jāgṛvāṃsaḥ samindhate
viṣṇoryatparamaṃ padamityupaniṣat
iti pañcamo'dhyāyaḥ (5)

Vocabulary

iti: thus; *yaḥ*: whoever; *etat*: this; *adhīte*: studies; *bhavati*: becomes; *pūtaḥ*: purified; *agni*: fire; *surāpānāt*: from drinking spirituous liquor; *steyāt*: from the theft; *svarṇa*:

gold; *tat etat uktam*: this [is] what is said; *ṛcābhi*: by the *Ṛgveda*; *sūrayaḥ*: sages; *sadā*: always; *paśyanti*: see; *paramam padam*: supreme seat; *viṣṇoḥ*: of Viṣṇu; *iva*: as if; *cakṣuṣ*: eyes; *ātatam*: stretched; *divi*: heaven; *jāgṛvāṃsaḥ*: watchful; *vipanyavaḥ*: joyful; *samindhate*: they illuminate; *viprāsaḥ*: might.

pañcamaḥ: fifth; *adhyāyaḥ*: section, chapter.

Translation
Thus, whoever studies this upaniṣad becomes purified by the fire. One becomes purified by the air. One becomes purified from drinking spirituous liquor. One becomes purified from the theft of gold. One becomes a jīvanmukta. This is what is said by the *Ṛgveda*. The sages always see the supreme seat of Viṣṇu, as if their eyes are stretched to heaven. Watchful [and] joyful they illuminate [with their] might the supreme seat of Viṣṇu.

Thus [ends] the fifth section.

इति वराहोपनिषत्समाप्ता ॥
iti varāhopaniṣat samāptā

Thus ends the Varāha Upaniṣad.

APPENDICES

A. End Notes

1. Feuerstein, Georg *The Yoga Tradition* (Hohm Press, Prescott, Arizona, 2001) p.85
2. *ibidem*
3. Swami Muktibodhananda *Haṭha Yoga Pradīpikā* (Bihar School of Yoga, Munger, Bihar, India 1998) Chapter 1, Verse 40
4. *ibidem* Verse 39
5. Feuerstein, Georg *The Encyclopedia of Yoga and Tantra* (Shambala Publications, Boulder, USA 2011) p.342
6. *ibidem* p.372
7. Paramahamsa Niranjanananda *Yoga Darshan* (Sri Panch-dashnam Paramahamsa Alakh Bara, Deoghar, India 1993) p.242
8. Swami Yogakanti *Sanskrit Glossary of Yogic Terms* (Yoga Publications Trust, Munger, Bihar, India 2007) p.78
9. Swami Satyananda Saraswati *Four Chapters on Freedom* (Bihar School of Yoga, Munger, Bihar, India 1984) Chapter 2, Verse 27, p.125
10. Swami Yogakanti *Sanskrit Glossary of Yogic Terms* (Yoga Publications Trust, Munger, Bihar, India 2007) p.204
11. *ibidem* p.25
12. Swami Sivananda Saraswati *Samatvam: The Yoga of Equanimity* (Yoga Publications Trust, Munger, Bihar, India 2009) p.34
13. *ibidem* p.34
14. Feuerstein, Georg *The Encyclopedia of Yoga and Tantra* (Shambala Publications, Boulder, USA 2011) p.297
15. *ibidem* p.4
16. Swami Satyananda Saraswati *Ishavasya Upanishad* ((Bihar School of Yoga, Munger, Bihar, India 1984) pp.19-20
17. Swami Sarvapriyananda *Lamp of Bliss* (youtube 2024)
18. Swami Satyadharma Saraswati *Yoga Kundali Upanishad* (translated by Ruth Perini) 2019 Ch.3 Vs.25b-26
19. Swamis Sivananda & Satyananda *Maha Samadhi: Antardhyana* (Yoga Publications Trust, Munger, Bihar, India. 2010) p.258

20. Frawley, David *Vedic Yoga: The Path of the Rishi* ((Lotus Press, Twin Lakes, Wisconsin 2014) p.247
21. Swami Satyananda Saraswati *Nine Principal Upanishads* (Yoga Publications Trust, Bihar 1975) p.144
22. Paramahamsa Niranjanananda *Yoga Darshan* (Sri Panchdashnam Paramahamsa Alakh Bara 1993) p.28
23. *ibidem* p.105
24. *ibidem* p.188
25. Swami Yogakanti Saraswati *Living Shankara* (Yoga Publications Trust, Bihar 2018) pp.400-1
26. Paramahamsa Niranjanananda *Yoga Darshan* (Sri Panchdashnam Paramahamsa Alakh Bara 1993) p.54
27. Swamis Sivananda & Satyananda *Maha Samadhi: Antardhyana* (Yoga Publications Trust, Munger, Bihar, India. 2010) p.256
28. Swami Satyananda Saraswati *Nine Principal Upanishads* (Yoga Publications Trust, Bihar 1975) *Ishavasya Upanishad* Vs. 6 and 7. p.91-92
29. *ibidem. Muṇḍaka-Upanishad* Section 2 Part 2 Vs 8 p.76
30. Paramahamsa Niranjanananda *Yoga Darshan* (Sri Panchdashnam Paramahamsa Alakh Bara 1993) p.238
31. Frawley, David *Vedic Yoga: The Path of the Rishi* ((Lotus Press, Twin Lakes, Wisconsin 2014) p.233
32. Swamis Sivananda & Satyananda *Maha Samadhi: Antardhyana* (Yoga Publications Trust, Munger, Bihar, India. 2010) p.109
33. Swami Satyadharma Saraswati *Yoga Darshana Upaniṣad* (2018 translated by Ruth Perini) Vs.I0.1-5 Commentary p.223
34. *Bhagavad Gita* Srinivas Fine Arts Ltd (nightingale.co.in 2009) Ch3 Vs.6-7
35. Swami Sivananda *Raja Yoga* (Divine Life Society 1984) Ch.11
36. *Bhagavad Gita* Srinivas Fine Arts Ltd (nightingale.co.in 2009) Ch.13 Vs.13
37. Swami Sivananda *Raja Yoga* (Divine Life Society 1984) Ch.11
38. Swami Yogakanti *Sanskrit Glossary of Yogic Terms* (Yoga Publications Trust, Munger, Bihar, India 2007) p.78
39. *ibidem* p.119
40. Swamis Sivananda & Satyananda *Maha Samadhi: Antardhyana* (Yoga Publications Trust, Munger, Bihar, India. 2010) p.26

41. Swami Satyadharma Saraswati *Yoga Darshana Upaniṣad* (2018 translated by Ruth Perini) Vs.I0.1-5 Commentary p.224
42. Feuerstein, Georg *The Encyclopedia of Yoga and Tantra* (Shambala Publications, Boulder, USA 2011) p.361
43. Swami Satyananda Saraswati *Nine Principal Upanishads* (Yoga Publications Trust, Bihar 1975) *Mandukya Upanishad* Vs.6. p.54
44. Swami Yogakanti *Sanskrit Glossary of Yogic Terms* (Yoga Publications Trust, Munger, Bihar, India 2007) p.135
45. Swami Satsangananda *Light on the Guru & Disciple Relationship* (Satyananda Ashram, Gosford, Australia 1983) *The Grace of Guru* p.37
46. *The Complete Works of Swami Vivekananda* pdf (Advaita Ashrama, Kolkata (Calcutta) 1989) p.315
47. *ibidem* p.3498
48. Swamis Sivananda & Satyananda *Maha Samadhi: Antardhyana* (Yoga Publications Trust, Munger, Bihar, India. 2010) Swami Niranjananda p.1
49. *ibidem* p.254
50. *ibidem* p.260
51. Swami Yogakanti Saraswati *Living Shankara* (Yoga Publications Trust, Bihar 2018) p.404
52. *ibidem* p.409
53. *The Complete Works of Swami Vivekananda* pdf (Advaita Ashrama, Kolkata (Calcutta) 1989) p.629
54. Swami Sivananda *Raja Yoga* (Divine Life Society 1984) Ch.11 *Destruction of Vrittis Leads to Mental Strength.*
55. Swami Satyadharma Saraswati *Yoga Tattwa Upanishad* (2nd edition 2018) (translated by Ruth Perini) Vs. 76-78a commentary pp.115-116.
56. Swami Sarvapriyananda *Jīvanmukti* (youtube 2024)
57. Swami Yogakanti *Sanskrit Glossary of Yogic Terms* (Yoga Publications Trust, Munger, Bihar, India 2007) p.78
58. Swami Satyananda *Four Chapters on Freedom* (Bihar School of Yoga, Munger, Bihar, India 1976) Sutra 27 p.125
59. Swami Satyananda Saraswati *Nine Principal Upanishads* (Yoga Publications Trust, Bihar 1975) *Mandukya Upanishad*, Introduction p.51
60. Swami Sarvapriyananda *Turīya* (youtube 2024)
61. Swami Mukundananda *holy-bhagavad-gita.org* Vs.2.62

62. *ibidem* Vs.2.71
63. *ibidem* Vs.2.64
64. *ibidem* Vs.14.5-14.6
65. *ibidem* Vs.14.6 commentary
66. Swami Yogakanti *Sanskrit Glossary of Yogic Terms* (Yoga Publications Trust, Munger, Bihar, India 2007) p.192
67. Feuerstein, Georg *The Encyclopedia of Yoga and Tantra* (Shambala Publications, Boulder, USA 2011) p.167-8
68. Swami Mukundananda *holy-bhagavad-gita.org* Vs.2.56, 2.57 and 2.59
69. Feuerstein, Georg *The Encyclopedia of Yoga and Tantra* (Shambala Publications, Boulder, USA 2011) p.167
70. *ibidem* p.168
71. Swami Yogakanti *Sanskrit Glossary of Yogic Terms* (Yoga Publications Trust, Munger, Bihar, India 2007) p.42
72. Sarma, K. Lakshmana *Maha Yoga* (Sri Ramanasramam, Tiruvannamalai, India 1996) p.100
73. Smith, John D. *The Mahābhārata* (Penguin Classics 2009) p.658
74. Swami Yogakanti *Sanskrit Glossary of Yogic Terms* (Yoga Publications Trust, Munger, Bihar, India 2007) p.216
75. Smith, John D. *The Mahābhārata* (Penguin Classics 2009) p.660
76. *wisdom.lib.org*
77. Swami Mukundananda *holy-bhagavad-gita.org* Vs.4.35, 15.5 and 6.21
78. Swami Satyadharma Saraswati *Yoga Darshana Upanishad* (translated by Ruth Perini 2018) First Section Vs.9-10
79. Paramahamsa Niranjanananda *Yoga Darshan* (Sri Panchdashnam Paramahamsa Alakh Bara 1993) p.307
80. Feuerstein, Georg *The Yoga Tradition* (Hohm Press, Prescott, Arizona, 2001) p.319
81. Swami Satyadharma *Yoga Chudamani Upanishad* (Yoga Publications Trust, Munger, Bihar, India 2003) Vs.48-49 commentary p.122
82. Swami Muktibodhananda Saraswati *Haṭha Yoga Pradīpikā* Bihar School of Yoga, Munger, Bihar, India 1998) Chapter 3, Vs.55-56 p.299

83. Swami Yogakanti *Sanskrit Glossary of Yogic Terms* (Yoga Publications Trust, Munger, Bihar, India 2007) p.105
84. Paramahamsa Niranjanananda *Yoga Darshan* (Sri Panchdashnam Paramahamsa Alakh Bara, Deoghar 1993) p.213
85. Feuerstein, Georg *The Deeper Dimension of Yoga* (Shambhala Publications 2003) p.22
86. Paramahamsa Niranjanananda *Yoga Darshan* (Sri Panchdashnam Paramahamsa Alakh Bara, Deoghar 1993) p.460
87. Feuerstein, Georg *The Deeper Dimension of Yoga* (Shambhala Publications 2003) p.81
88. Swami Yogakanti *Sanskrit Glossary of Yogic Terms* (Yoga Publications Trust, Munger, Bihar, India 2007) p.97
89. Feuerstein, Georg *The Encyclopedia of Yoga and Tantra* (Shambala Publications, Boulder, USA 2011) p.207
90. Paramahamsa Niranjanananda *Yoga Darshan* (Sri Panchdashnam Paramahamsa Alakh Bara, Deoghar 1993) p.232
91. Swami Muktibodhananda Saraswati *Haṭha Yoga Pradīpikā* (Bihar School of Yoga, Munger, Bihar, India 1998) Chapter 4, Vs.34 p.464
92. Swami Satyadharma Saraswati *Yoga Darshana Upanishad* (translated by Ruth Perini 2018) First Section Vs.6 commentary p.27
93. *ibidem* Second Section Vs.1-2 commentary p.56
94. *ibidem* Sixth Section Vs.12b-13 commentary p.164
95. Swami Satyananda Saraswati *Kundalini Tantra* (Bihar School of Yoga, Munger, Bihar, India 1996) Chapter 5 p.35
96. Swami Satyadharma Saraswati *Yoga Darshana Upanishad* (translated by Ruth Perini 2018) Fourth Section Vs.1-2 p.102
97. *ibidem* Fourth Section Vs.3-5a commentary p.105
98. Swami Satyadharma *Yoga Chudamani Upanishad* (Yoga Publications Trust, Munger, Bihar, India 2003) Vs.4b-6a Commentary p.40
99. Perini, Ruth *Shandilya Upanishad* (2020) Fourth Section Vs.12-14 p.66-7
100. Feuerstein, Georg *The Encyclopedia of Yoga and Tantra* (Shambala Publications, Boulder, USA 2011) p.25
101. *ibidem* p.86

102. Swami Muktibodhananda *Haṭha Yoga Pradīpikā* (Bihar School of Yoga, Munger, Bihar, India 1998) Chapter 4. Vs.53 p.489
103. Feuerstein, Georg *The Encyclopedia of Yoga and Tantra* (Shambala Publications, Boulder, USA 2011) p.176
104. Swami Muktibodhananda Saraswati *Haṭha Yoga Pradīpikā* (Bihar School of Yoga, Munger, Bihar, India 1998) Chapter 4, Vs.108 p.530
105. *ibidem* Chapter 4, Vs.17 p.441
106. Feuerstein, Georg *The Encyclopedia of Yoga and Tantra* (Shambala Publications, Boulder, USA 2011) p.176
107. Doniger, Wendy *The Rig Veda* (Penguin Books 1981) p.33, p.78
108. Swami Muktibodhananda Saraswati *Haṭha Yoga Pradīpikā* (Bihar School of Yoga, Munger, Bihar, India 1998) Chapter 3 Vs.64 commentary p.308
109. Swami Satsangananda Saraswati *Tattwa Shuddhi* (Bihar School of Yoga, Munger, Bihar, India 1992) Chapter 5, p.27
110. Swami Satyadharma Saraswati *Yoga Kundali Upanishad* (translated by Ruth Perini 2019) Ch.1 Vs.62-65
111. Feuerstein, Georg *The Encyclopedia of Yoga and Tantra* (Shambala Publications, Boulder, USA 2011) p.313
112. Swami Yogakanti *Sanskrit Glossary of Yogic Terms* (Yoga Publications Trust, Munger, Bihar, India 2007) p.111, p.97
113. Feuerstein, Georg *The Encyclopedia of Yoga and Tantra* (Shambala Publications, Boulder, USA 2011) p.232
114. Swami Muktibodhananda Saraswati *Haṭha Yoga Pradīpikā* (Bihar School of Yoga, Munger, Bihar, India 1998) Ch. 4 Vs.48
115. Swami Yogakanti *Sanskrit Glossary of Yogic Terms* (Yoga Publications Trust, Munger, Bihar, India 2007) p.138
116. Swami Satyananda Saraswati *Nine Principal Upanishads* (Yoga Publications Trust, Bihar 1975) *The Essence of the Upanishads* no.46 p.4
117. Feuerstein, Georg *The Encyclopedia of Yoga and Tantra* (Shambala Publications, Boulder, USA 2011) p.200
118. Swami Satyadharma Saraswati *Yoga Tattwa Upanishad* (translated by Ruth Perini) (2nd edition 2018) Vs.142 commentary p.186
119. *Britannica.com*

120. Feuerstein, Georg *The Encyclopedia of Yoga and Tantra* (Shambala Publications, Boulder, USA 2011) p.228
121. Swami Satyananda Saraswati *Kundalini Tantra* (Bihar School of Yoga, Munger, Bihar, India 1996) Chapter 3 p.120
122. Swami Niranjananda Saraswati *Prana Pranayama Prana Vidya* (Bihar School of Yoga, Munger, Bihar, India 1996) Chapter 11 A. p.120
123. Swami Satyananda Saraswati *Nine Principal Upanishads* (Yoga Publications Trust, Bihar 1975) *Mandukyopanishad* p.56
124. Swami Muktibodhananda Saraswati *Haṭha Yoga Pradīpikā* (Bihar School of Yoga, Munger, Bihar, India 1998) Chapter 4 Vs.69 commentary p.505
125. *ibidem* Chapter 4 Vs.70-71 p.506
126. Feuerstein, Georg *The Encyclopedia of Yoga and Tantra* (Shambala Publications, Boulder, USA 2011) p.130
127. Swami Muktibodhananda Saraswati *Haṭha Yoga Pradīpikā* (Bihar School of Yoga, Munger, Bihar, India 1998) Chapter 4 Vs.73 p.507
128. *ibidem* Chapter 4 Vs.72-73 commentary p.507
129. *ibidem* Chapter 4 Vs.74-75 p.508
130. *ibidem* Chapter 4 Vs.76 commentary p.511
131. *ibidem* Chapter 4 Vs.76 p.511
132. *ibidem* Chapter 4 Vs.76 commentary p.511

B. References

Aiyar, K. Narayanasvami *Thirty Minor Upaniṣads* (Parimal Publications, Delhi India 2009)

Ayyaṅgār, T.R.Ś. *The Yoga Upaniṣads* (The Adyar Library 1938)

Bhagavad Gita Srinivas Fine Arts Ltd (nightingale.co.in 2009)

Doniger, Wendy *The Rig Veda* (Penguin Books 1981)

Feuerstein, Georg, **Kak** Subash & **Frawley** David *In Search of the Cradle of Civilization* (Quest Books, Illinois USA 2001)

Feuerstein, Georg *The Deeper Dimension of Yoga* (Shambhala Publications 2003)

Feuerstein, Georg *The Encyclopedia of Yoga and Tantra* (Shambala Publications, Boulder, USA 2011)

Feuerstein, Georg *The Yoga-Sūtra of Patañjali* (Inner Traditions International, Vermont USA 1979)

Feuerstein, Georg *The Yoga Tradition* (Hohm Press, Prescott, Arizona, 2001)

Frawley, David *The Ancient Yoga of the Sun* (vedanet.com)

Frawley, David *Gods, Sages and Kings* (Passage Press, Salt Lake City, Utah USA 1991)

Frawley, David *Vedic Yoga: The Path of the Rishi* ((Lotus

Press, Twin Lakes, Wisconsin 2014)

Joshi Bimali Trivedi *112 Upaniṣads* (Parimal Publications, Delhi India 2007)

Paramahamsa Niranjananda *Yoga Darshan* (Sri Panchdashnam Paramahamsa Alakh Bara 1993)

Perini, Ruth *Shandilya Upanishad* (2020)

Sarma, K. Lakshmana *Maha Yoga* (Sri Ramanasramam, Tiruvannamalai, India 1996)

Smith, John D. *The Mahābhārata* (Penguin Classics 2009)

Swami Muktibodhananda *Haṭha Yoga Pradīpikā* (Bihar School of Yoga, Munger, Bihar, India 1998)

Swami Mukundananda *holy-bhagavad-gita.org*

Swami Niranjanananda Saraswati *Prana Pranayama Prana Vidya* (Bihar School of Yoga, Munger, Bihar, India 1996)

Swami Sarvapriyananda youtube

Swami Satsangananda *Light on the Guru & Disciple Relationship* (Satyananda Ashram, Gosford, Australia 1983)

Swami Satsangananda Saraswati *Tattwa Shuddhi* (Bihar School of Yoga, Munger, Bihar, India 1992)

Swami Satyadharma Saraswati *Yoga Chudamani Upanishad* (Yoga Publications Trust, Munger, Bihar, India 2003)

Swami Satyadharma Saraswati *Yoga Darshana Upaniṣad* (2018)

Swami Satyadharma Saraswati *Yoga Tattwa Upanishad* (2nd edition 2018)

Swami Satyananda Saraswati *Four Chapters on Freedom* (Bihar School of Yoga, Munger, Bihar, India 1984)

Swami Satyananda Saraswati *Ishavasya Upanishad* ((Bihar School of Yoga, Munger, Bihar, India 1984)

Swami Satyananda Saraswati *Kundalini Tantra* (Bihar School of Yoga, Munger, Bihar, India 1996)

Swami Satyananda Saraswati *Nine Principal Upanishads* (Yoga Publications Trust, Bihar 1975)

Swamis Sivananda & Satyananda *Maha Samadhi: Antardhyana* (Yoga Publications Trust, Munger, Bihar, India. 2010)

Swami Sivananda *Raja Yoga* (Divine Life Society 1984)

Swami Sivananda Saraswati *Samatvam: The Yoga of Equanimity* (Yoga Publications Trust, Munger, Bihar, India 2009)

Swami Vivekananda *Raja Yoga* (Advaita Ashrama, Calcutta, India 1923)

Swami Vivekananda *The Complete Works* (Advaita Ashrama, Kolkata 1989)

Swami Yogakanti Saraswati *Living Shankara* (Yoga Publications Trust, Bihar 2018)

Swami Yogakanti *Sanskrit Glossary of Yogic Terms* (Yoga Publications Trust, Munger, Bihar, India 2007)

C. Pronunciation Guide

a	nut
ā	father
i	bit
ī	knee
u	hook
ū	sue
ṛ	hurt
e	net
ai	time
o	got
au	house
ṃ	hum
ḥ	h + preceding vowel
k	paprika
kh	ink horn
g	ago
gh	big hut
ṅ	anger
c	chat
ch	much harm
j	jog
jh	raj house
ñ	engine
ṭ	borscht
ṭh	borscht home
ḍ	fresh dill
ḍh	flushed heart
ṇ	rainy
t	tarp
th	scout hall
d	modern
dh	mud hut

n	banal
p	papa
ph	top half
b	maybe
bh	mob hall
m	chroma
y	young
r	merit
l	alas
v	lava
ś	shin
ṣ	sunshine
h	hut

D. Sanskrit Text

वराह उपनिषद्

श्रीमद्वाराहोपनिषद्वद्याखङ्डसुखाकृति ।
त्रिपान्नारातणाख्यं तद्रामचन्द्रपदं भजे ।।१।।
ॐ सहनाववत्विति शानति ।।

।। प्रथमोऽध्यायः ।।

हरिः ॐ ।
अथ ऋभुर्वै महामुनिर्देवमानेन द्वादशत्सरं तपश्चार ।
तदवसाने वराहरूपी भगरान्प्रादुरभूत ।
स होवाचोत्तिष्ठोत्तिष्ठ वरं वृणेष्वेति ।
सोदतिष्ठत् ।
तस्मै नमस्कृत्योवाच भगवन्कामिभिर्यद्यत्कामितं
ततत्त्वत्सकाशात्स्वप्नेऽपि न याचे ।
समस्तवेदशास्त्रेतिहासपुराणानि समस्त्विद्याजालानि
ब्रह्मादयः सुराः सर्वे त्वद्रूपज्ञान्मुकतिमाहुः ।
अतस्त्वद्रूपप्रातिपदिकं ब्रह्मविद्यां ब्रूहीति होवाच ।
तथेति स होवाच वराहरूपी भगवान् ।
चतुर्विंशतितत्त्वानि केचिदिच्छन्ति वादिनः ।
केचित्षद्त्रिंशत्तत्त्वानि केचित्षण्णवतीनि च ।।१।।

तेषां क्रं प्रवक्ष्यामि सावधानमनाः शृणु ।
ज्ञानेन्द्रियाणि पञ्चैव श्रोत्रत्वग्लोचनादयः ।।२।।

कर्मेन्द्रियाणि पञ्चैव वाक्पाण्यङ्घ्र्यादयः क्रमात् ।
प्राणादतस्तु पञ्चैव पञ्च शब्दादयस्तथा ।।३।।
मनोबुद्धिरहंकारश्चित्तं चेति चतुष्टयम् ।
चतुर्विंशतितत्तवानि तानि ब्रह्मविद् विदुः ।।४।।

एतैस्तत्त्वैः समं पञ्चीकृतभूतानि पञ्च च ।
पृथिव्यापस्तथा तेजो वायुराकाशमेव च ।।५।।
देहत्रयं स्थूलसुक्ष्मकारणानि विदुर्बुधाः ।
अवस्था त्रितयं चैव जाग्रत्स्वप्न सुषुप्तयः ।।६।।
आहत्य तत्त्वजातानां षट्त्रिंशन्मुनयो विदुः ।
पूर्वोक्तैस्तत्त्वजातैस्तु समं तत्त्वानि योजयेत् ।।७।।

षद्भावविकृतिश्चास्ति जायते वर्धतेऽपि च ।
परिणामं क्षयं नाशं षड्भावविकृतिं विदुः ।।८।।
अशना च पिपासा च शोकमोहै जरा मृतिः ।
एते षडूर्मयः प्रोक्ताः षट्कोशानतह वच्मि ते ।।९।।
त्वक्च रक्तं मांसमेदोमज्जास्थानी निबोधत ।
कामग्रोधै लोभमोहै मदो मात्सर्यमेव च ।।१०।।
एतेऽरिषड्वा विश्वश्च तैजसः प्राज्ञ एव च ।
जीवत्रयं सत्त्वरजस्तमांसि च गुणज्ञयम् ।।११।।
प्रारब्धागामीसञ्चितानि कर्मत्रयमितीरितम् ।
वचनादानगमनविसर्गानन्दपञ्चकम् ।।१२।।
संकल्पोऽध्यवशयश्च अभिमानोऽवधारणा ।
मुदिता करुणा मैत्री उपेक्शा च चतुष्टयम् ।।१३।।

दिवाकरप्रचेतोऽश्विनौवह्नीन्द्रेपेन्द्रमृत्युकाः ।
तथा चन्द्रश्चतुर्वक्त्रो रुद्रः क्षेत्रज्ञ ईश्वरः ।।१४।।

आहत्य तत्त्वजातानां षण्णवत्यस्तु कीर्तिताः ।
पूर्वोक्ततत्त्वजातानां वैलक्षण्यमनामयम् ।।१५।।
वराहरूपिणं मां ये भजन्ति मयि भक्तितः ।
विमुक्ताज्ञतत्कार्या जीवन्मुक्ता भवन्ति ते ।।१६।।
ये षण्णवतितत्त्वज्ञा यत्र कुत्राश्रमे रतः ।
जटी मुण्डी शिकही वापि मुच्यते नात्र संशयः ।।१७।।

।।द्वितीयोऽध्यायः।।
ऋभुर्नाम महायोगी क्रोडरूप रमापतिम् ।
वरिष्ठां ब्रह्मविद्यां त्वमधीहि भगवन्मम ।
एवं स पृष्टो भगवान्प्राह भक्तार्तिभञ्जनः ।।१।।
स्ववर्णाश्रमधर्मेण तपसा गुरुतोषणात् ।
साधनं प्रभवेत्पुंसा वैराग्यदिचतुष्टयम् ।।२।।
नित्यानित्यविवेकश्च इहामुत्र विरागता ।
शमादिषड्कसंपत्तिर्मुमुक्षा तां समभ्यसेत् ।।३।।

एवं जितेन्द्रियो भूत्वा सर्वत्र ममतामतिम् ।
विहाय साक्षिचैतन्ये मयि कुर्यादहंमतिम् ।।४।।
दुर्लभं प्राप्य मानुष्यं तत्रापि नरविग्रहम् ।
ब्राह्मण्यं च महाविष्णोर्वेदान्तश्रवणादिना ।।५।।
अतिवर्णाश्रं रूपं सच्चिदानन्दलक्षणम् ।

यो न जानाति सोऽविद्वान्कदा मुक्तो भविष्यति ।।६।।

अहमेव सुखं नान्यदन्यच्चेत्रेव तत्सुखम् ।
अमदर्थं न हि प्रेयो मदर्थं न स्वतः प्रियम् ।।७।।
परप्रेमास्पदतया मा न भूवमहं सदा ।
भूयासमिति यो द्रष्टा सोऽहं विष्णुर्मुनीश्वर ।।८।।
न प्रकाशोऽहमित्युक्तिर्यत्प्रकाशैकबन्धना ।
स्वप्रकाशं तमात्मानमप्रकाशः कथं स्पृशेत् ।।९।।
स्वयं भातं निराधारं ये जानन्ति सुनिश्चितम् ।
ते हि विज्ञानसंपन्ना इति मे निश्चिता मतिः ।।१०।।

स्वपूर्णात्मातिरेकेण जगज्जीवेश्वरादयः ।
नसन्ति नास्ति माया च तेभ्यश्चाहं विलक्षणः ।।११।।
अज्ञानान्धतमोरूप कर्मधर्मादिलक्षणं ।
स्वयंप्रकाशात्मानं नैव मां स्प्रष्टुमर्हति ।।१२।।
सर्वसाक्षिणमात्मानं वर्णाश्रमविवर्जितम् ।
ब्रह्मरूपतया पश्यन्ब्रह्मैव भवति स्वयम् ।।१३।।
भासमानमिदं सर्वं मानरूपं परं पदम् ।
पश्यन्वेदान्तमानेन सद्य एव विमुच्यते ।।१४।।
देहात्मज्ञानवज्ज्ञानं देहात्मज्ञानबाधकम् ।
आत्मन्येव भवेद्यस्य स नेच्छन्नापि मुच्यते ।।१५।।
सत्यज्ञानान्दपूर्णालक्षणं तमसः परम् ।
ब्रह्मानन्दं सदा पश्यन्कथं बध्ये कर्मणा ।।१६।।
त्रिधामसाक्षिणं सत्यज्ञानानन्दादिलक्षणां ।

तवमहंशब्दलक्ष्यार्थमसक्तं सर्वदोषता ।।१७।।
सर्वगं सत्चिदात्मानं ज्ञानच्क्षुर्निरीक्षते ।
अज्ञानच्क्षुर्नेक्षेत भास्वन्तं भानुमन्धवत् ।।१८।।
प्रज्णानमेव तद्ब्रह्म सत्रप्रज्ञानलक्षणम् ।
एवं ब्रह्मपरिज्ञानादेव मर्त्योऽमृतो भवेत् ।।१९।।

तद्ब्रह्मानन्दमद्वन्द्वं निर्गुणं सत्यचिद्धनम् ।
विदित्वा स्वात्मनो रूपं न बिभेति कुश्चन ।।२०।।
चिन्मात्रं सर्वगं नित्यं संपूर्णं सुखमद्वयम् ।
साक्षाद्ब्रह्मैव नान्योऽस्तीत्येवं ब्रह्मविदां स्थितिः ।।२१।।
अज्ञास्य दुःखौघमयं ज्ञास्यानन्दमयं जगत् ।
अन्धं भुवनमन्धस्य प्रकाशं तु सुचक्षुषाम् ।।२२।।
अनन्ते सच्चिदानन्दे मयि वाराहरूपिणि ।
स्थितेऽद्वितीयभावः स्यात्को बन्धः कष्च मुच्यते ।।२३।।
स्वरूपं तु चिन्मात्रं सर्वदा सर्वदेहिनाम् ।
नैव देहादिसंघातो घटवद्दृशिगोचरः ।।२४।।
स्वात्मनोऽन्यदिवाभातं चराचरमिदं जगत् ।
स्वात्ममात्रतया बुद्ध्वा तदस्मीति विभावय ।।२५।।
स्वस्वरूपं स्वं भुङ्क्ते नास्ति भोज्यं पृथक् स्वतः ।
अस्ति चेदस्तितारूपं ब्रह्मैवास्तित्वलक्षणम् ।।२६।।
ब्रह्मविज्ञानसंपन्नः प्रतीतमखिलं जगत् ।
पश्यन्नपि सदा नैव पश्यति स्वात्मनः पृथक् ।।२७।।
मत्स्वरूपपरिज्ञानात्कर्मभिर्न स बधयते ।।२८।।

यः शरीरेन्द्रियादिभ्यो विहीनं सर्वसाक्षिणम् ।
परमार्थैकविज्ञानं सुखात्मानम् स्वयम्प्रभम् ।।२९।।
स्वस्वरूपतया सर्वं वेद स्वानुभवेन यः ।
स धीरः स तु विज्ञेयः सोऽहं तत्त्वं ऋभो भव ।।३०।।
अतः प्रपञ्चानुभवः सदा न हि स्वरूपबोधानुभवः
सदा खलु ।
इति प्रपश्यन्परिपूर्णवेदनो न बन्धमुक्तो न च बद्ध
एव तु ।।३१।।

स्वस्व रूपानुसंधानान्नृत्यन्तं सर्वसाक्षिणम् ।
मुहूर्तं चिन्तेन्मां यः सर्वबन्धैः प्रमुच्यते ।।३२।।
सर्वभूतान्तरस्थाय नित्यमुक्तचिदात्मने ।
प्रत्यक्चैतन्यरूपाय मह्यमेव नमोनमः ।।३३।।
त्वं वाहमस्मि भगवो देवतेऽहं वै त्वमसि ।
तुभ्यं मह्यमनन्ताय मह्यं तुभ्यं चिदात्मने ।।३४।।
नमो मह्यं परेशाय नमस्तुभ्यं शिवाय च ।
किं करोमि क्व गच्छमि किं गृह्णामि त्यजामि किम् ।।३५।।
यन्मया पूरितं विश्वं महाकल्पाम्बुना यथा ।
अन्तःसङ्गं बहिःसङ्गमात्मसङ्गं च यस्त्यजेत् ।
सर्वसङ्गनिवृत्तात्मा स मामेति न संशयः ।।३६।।
अहिरिव जनयोगं सर्वदा वर्जयेद्यः कुणपमिव
सुनारीं त्यक्तुकामो विरागी ।
विषमिव विषयादीन्मन्यमानो दुरन्ताञ्जगति
परमहंसो वासुदेवोऽहमेव ।।३७।।

इदं सत्यमिदं सत्यं सत्यमेतदिहोच्यते ।
अहं सत्यं परं ब्रह्म मत्तः किंचिन्न विद्यते ।।३८।।

उप समीपे यो वासो जीवात्मपरमात्मनोः ।
उपवासः स विज्ञेयो न तु दायस्य शोषणम् ।।३९।।
कायशोषणमात्रेण का तत्र ह्यविवेकिनाम् ।
वल्मीकताडनादेव मृतः किं नु महोरगः ।।४०।।
अस्ति ब्रह्मेति चेद्वेद परोक्षज्ञानमेव तत् ।
अहं ब्रह्मेति चेद्वेद साक्षात्कारः स उच्यते ।।४१।।
यस्मिन्काले स्वमात्मानं योगी जानाति केवलम् ।
तस्मात्कालात्समारभ्य जीवन्मुक्तो भयेदसौ ।।४२।।
अहं ब्रह्मेति नियतं मोक्षहेतुर्महात्मनाम् ।
द्वे पदे बन्धमोक्षाय निर्ममेति ममेति च ।।४३।।
ममेति बध्यते जन्तुर्निर्ममेति विमुच्यते ।
बाह्याचिन्ता न कर्तव्या तथैवान्तरचिन्तिका ।
सर्वचिन्तां समुत्सृज्य स्वस्थो भव सदा ऋभो ।।४४।।

संकल्पमात्रकलनेन जगत्समग्रं संकल्पमात्रकलने हि
जगद्विलासः ।
संकल्पमात्रमिदमुत्सृज निर्विकल्पमाश्रित्य मामकपदं
हृदि भावयस्व ।।४५।।
मच्चिन्तनं मत्कथनमन्योन्यं मत्प्रभाषणम् ।
मदेकपरमो भूत्वा कालं नय महामते ।।४६।।
चिदिहास्तीति चिन्मात्रमिदं चिन्मयमेव च ।

चित्त्वं चिदहमेते च लोकाश्चिदिति भावय ।।४७।।
रागं नीरागतां नीत्वा निर्लेपो भव सर्वदा ।४८।

अज्ञानजन्यकर्त्रादिकारकोत्पन्नकर्मणा ।।४८।।
श्रुत्युत्पन्नात्मविज्ञानप्रदीपो बाध्यते कथम् ।
अनात्मतां परित्यज्य निर्विकारो जगात्स्थितौ ।।४९।।
एकनिष्ठत्वयान्तस्थसंदचिन्मात्रपरो भव ।५०।

घटाकाशमठाकाशौ महाकाशे प्रतिष्ठितौ ।।५०।।
एवं मयि चिदाकशे जीवेशौ परिकल्पतौ ।
या च प्रागात्मनो माया तथान्ते च तिरस्कृता ।।५१।।
ब्रह्मवादिमिरुद्गीता सा मायेती विवेकतः ।
मायातत्कार्यविलये नेश्वरत्वं न जीवता ।।५२।।
ततः शुद्धश्चिदेवाहं व्योमवन्निरुपाधिकः ।
जीवेश्वरादिरूपेण चेतनाचेतनात्मकम् ।।५३।।
ईक्षणादिप्रवेशान्ता सृष्टिरीशेन कल्पता ।
जाग्रदादिविमोक्षान्तः संसारो जीवकल्पितः ।।५४।।

त्रिणाचिकादियोगान्ता ईश्वरभ्रान्तिमाश्रिताः ।
लोकायतादिसांख्यान्ता जीवविश्रान्तिमाश्रिताः ।।५५।।
तस्मान्मुमुक्षुभिर्नैव मतिर्जीवेशवादयोः
लार्या किंतु ब्रह्मतत्त्वं निश्चलेन विचार्यताम् ।।५६।।
अद्वितीयब्रह्मतत्त्वं न जानन्ति यथा तथा ।
भ्रान्ता एवाखिलास्तेषां क्व मुक्तिः क्वेह वा सुखम् ।।५७।।

उत्तमाधमभावश्चेत्तेषां स्यादस्ति ते किम् ।
स्वप्नस्थराज्यभिक्षाभ्यां प्रबुद्धः स्पृशते खलु ।।५८।।
अज्ञाने बुद्धिविलये निद्रा सा भण्यते बुधैः ।
विलीनाज्ञानतत्कार्ये मयि निद्रा कथं भवेत् ।।५९।।
बुद्धेः पूर्णविकासोऽयं जागरः परिकीर्त्यते ।
विकारादिविहीनत्वाज्जगरो मे न विद्यते ।।६०।।
सूक्ष्मनाडिषु संचारो बुद्धेः स्वप्नः प्रजायते ।
संचारधर्मरहिते मयि स्वप्नो न विद्यते ।।६१।।
सुषुप्तिकाले सकले विलीने तमसावृते ।
स्वरूपं महदानन्दं बुङ्क्ते विश्वविवर्जितः ।।६२।।
अविशेषेण सर्वं तु यः पश्यति चिदन्वयात् ।
स एव साक्षाद्विज्ञानीं स शिवः स हरिर्विधि ।।६३।।

दीर्घस्वप्नमिदं यत्तद्दीर्घं वा चिदत्तविभ्रमम् ।
दीर्घं वापि मनोराज्यं संसारं दुःखमागरम् ।
सुप्तेरुत्थाय सुप्त्यन्तं ब्रह्मैकं प्रविविन्त्यताम् ।।६४।।
आरोपितस्य जगतः प्रविलापनेन चित्तं मदात्मकतया
परिकल्पितं नः ।
शत्रून्निहस्य गुरुषट्कगणान्निपाताद्गन्धद्विपो भवति
केवलमद्वितीयः ।।६५।।

अद्यास्तमेतु वपुरशशङ्कतारकास्तां कस्तावत्वापि मम
चिद्वपुषो विशेषः ।
कुम्भे विनाश्यति चिरं समवस्थिते वा कुम्भाम्बरस्य

नहि कोऽपि विशेषलेशः ॥६६॥
अहिनिर्व्लयनी सर्पनिर्मोके जीववर्जितः ।
वल्मीके पतितस्तिष्ठेत्तं सर्पो नाभिमन्यते ॥६७॥
एवं स्थूलं च सूक्ष्मं च शरीरं नाभिमन्यते ।
प्रत्यग्ज्ञानशिखिध्वंसो मिथ्याज्ञाने सहेतुके ।
नेति नेतीति रूपत्वादशरीरे भवत्ययम् ॥६८॥
शास्त्रेण न स्यात्परमार्थदृष्टिः कार्यक्षमं पश्यति
चापरोक्षम् ।
प्रारब्धनाशात्प्रतिभाननाश एवं त्रिधा नश्यति
चात्ममायस ॥६९॥
ब्रह्मत्वे योजिते स्वामिञ्जीवभावो न गच्छति ।
अद्वैते बोधिते तत्त्वे वासना विनिवर्तते ॥७०॥
प्रारब्धान्ते देहहानिर्मायेति क्षीयतेऽखिला ।७१।

अस्तीत्युक्ते जगत्सर्वं सद्रसं ब्रह्म तद्भवेत् ॥७१॥
भातीत्युक्ते जगत्सर्वं भानं ब्रह्मैव केवलम् ।
मरुभूमौ जलं सर्वं मरुभूमात्रमेव तत् ।
जगत्त्रयमिदं सर्वं चिन्मात्रं स्वविचारतः ॥७२॥
अज्ञानमेव न कुतो जगतः प्रसङ्गे जीवेशदेशिकविकल्प-
कथातिदूरे ।
एकान्तकेवलचिदेकरसस्वभावे ब्रह्मैव केवलमहं
परिपूर्णमस्मि ॥७३॥
बोधचन्द्रमसि पूर्णविग्रहे मोहराहुमुषितात्मतेजसि ।
स्नानदानयजनादिकाः क्रिया मोचनावधि वृथैव यिष्ठते ॥७४॥

सलिले सैन्धवं यद्वत्साम्यं भवति योगतः ।
तथात्ममनसोरैक्यं समाधिरिति कथ्यते ।।७५।।
दुर्लभो विषयत्यागो दुर्लभं तत्त्वदर्शनम ।
दुर्लभो सहजावस्था सद्गुरोः करुणां विना ।।७६।।
उत्पन्नशक्तिबोधस्य त्यक्निःशेषकर्मणः ।
योगिनः सहजावस्था स्वयमेव प्रकाशते ।।७७।।
रसस्य मनसश्चैव चञ्चलत्वं स्वभावतः ।
रसो बद्धो मनो बद्धं किं न सिद्ध्यति भूतले ।।७८।।

मूर्छितो हरति व्याधिं मृतो जीवयति स्वयम् ।
बद्धः खेचरतां धत्ते ब्रह्मत्वं रसचेतसि ।।७९।।
इन्द्रियाणां मनो नाथो मनोनाथस्तु मारुतः ।
मारुतस्य लयो नाथस्तन्नाथं लयमाश्रय ।।८०।।
निश्चेष्टो निर्विकारश्च लयो जीवति योगिनाम् ।
उच्छिन्नसर्वसंकल्पो निःशेषाशेषचेष्टितः ।
स्वावगम्यो लयः कोऽपि मनसां वागगोचरः ।।८१।।
पुङ्खनुपुङ्खविषयेक्षणतत्परोऽपि
ब्रह्मावलोकनधियं न जहाति योगी ।
सङ्गीततालयावाद्यवशं गतापि मौलिस्यकुम्भपरि-
रक्षणन्नर्तकीव ।।८२।।
सर्वचिन्तां परित्यज्य सावधानेन चेतसा ।
नाद एवानुसंधेयो योगसाम्राज्यमिच्छता ।।८३।।

तृतीयोऽध्यायः

नहि नानास्वरूपं स्यादेकं वस्तु कदाचन ।
तस्मादखङ्ड एवास्मि यन्मदन्यन्न किंचन ।।१।।
दृङ्यते ङ्र्यते यद्यद्ब्रह्मणोऽन्यन्न तद्भवेत् ।
नित्यशुद्धविमुक्तैकमखङ्डानन्दमद्वयम् ।
सत्यं ज्ञानमनन्तं यत्परं ब्रह्माहमेव तत् ।।२।।
आनन्दरूपोऽहमखङ्डबोधः परात्परोऽहं घनचित्प्रकाशः ।
मेघा यथा व्योम न च स्पृशन्ति संसारदुःखानि न मां
स्पृशन्ति ।।३।।
सर्वं सुखं विद्धि सुदुःखनाशात्सर्वं सद्रूपमसत्यनाशात् ।
चिद्रूपमेव प्रतिभानयुक्तं तस्मादखण्डं मम रूपमेतत् ।।४।।
नहि जनिर्मरणं गमनागमौ न च मलं विमलं न च वेदनम् ।
चिन्मयं हि सकलं विराजते स्पुटतरं परमस्य तुयोगिनः ।।५।।

सत्यचिद्धनमखण्डमद्वयं सर्वदृश्यरहितं निरामयम् ।
यत्परं विमलमद्वयं शिवं तत्सदाहमिति मौनमाश्रय ।।६।।
जन्ममृत्युसुखदुःखवर्जितं जातिनीतिकुलगोत्रदूरगम् ।
चिद्विवर्तजगतोऽस्य कारणं तत्सदाहमिति मौनमाश्रय ।।७।।
पूर्णमद्वयमखण्डचेतनं विश्वभेदकलनादिवर्जितम् ।
अद्वितीयपरसंविदंशकं तत्सदाहमिति मौनमाश्रय ।।८।।

केनाप्यबाधितत्वेन त्रिकालेऽप्येकरूपतः ।
विद्यमानत्वमस्त्येतत्सद्रूपत्वं सदा मम ।।९।।
निरुपाधिकनित्यं यत्सुप्तौ सर्वसुखात्परम् ।

सुखरूपत्वमस्त्येतदानन्दत्वं सदा मम ।।१०।।

दिनकरकिरणैर्हि शार्वतं तमो न निबिडतरं झटिति प्रणाशमेति
।
घनतरभवकारणं तमो यद्धरिदिनकृत्प्रभया न चान्तरेण।।११।।
मम चरणस्मरणेन पूजया च स्वकतमसः परिमुच्यते हि
जन्तुः ।
नहि मरणप्रभवप्रणाशहेतुर्मम चरणस्मरणादृतेऽस्ति किंचित्
।।१२।।
आदरेण यथा स्तुति धनवन्तं धनेच्छया ।
तथा चेद्विश्वकर्तारं को न मुच्यते बन्धनात् ।।१३।।

आदित्यसंनिधौ लोकश्चष्टते स्वयमेव तु ।
तथा मत्संनिधावेव समस्तं चेष्टते जगत् ।।१४।।
शुक्तिकाया यथा तारं कल्पितं मायया तथा ।
महदादि जगन्मायामयं मय्येव केवलम् ।।१५।।
चण्डालदेहे पश्वादिस्थावरे ब्रह्मविग्रहे
अन्येशु तारतम्येन स्थितेषु न तथा ह्यहम् ।।१६।।
विनष्टदिग्भ्रमस्यापि यथापूर्वं विभाति दिक् ।
तथा विज्ञानविध्वस्तं जगन्मे भाति तन्न हि ।।१७।।
न देहो नेन्द्रियप्राणो न मनोबुद्ध्यहंकृति ।
न चित्तं नैव माया च न च व्योमादिकं जगत् ।।१८।।
न कर्ता नैव भोक्ता च न च भोजयिता तथा ।
केवलं चित्सदानन्दब्रह्मैवाहं जनार्दनः ।।१९।।

जलस्य चलनादेव चञ्चलत्वं तथा रवेः ।
तथाहं कारसंबन्धादेव संसार आत्मनः ॥२०॥
चित्तमूलं हि संसारस्तत्प्रयत्नेन शोधयेत् ।
हन्त चित्तमहत्तायां कैषा विश्वासता तव ॥२१॥
क्व धनानि महीपानां ब्राह्मणः क्व जगन्ति वा ।
प्राक्तनानि प्रयातानि गताः सर्गपरम्पराः ।
कोटयो ब्रह्मणां याता भूपा नष्टाः परागवत् ॥२२॥
स चाध्यात्माभिमानोऽपि विदुषोऽयासुरत्वतः ।
विदुषोऽप्यासुरश्चेत्स्यान्निष्फलं तत्त्वदर्षनम् ॥२३॥
उत्पाद्यमाना रागाद्या विवेकज्ञानवह्निना ।
यदा तदैव दह्यन्ते कुतस्तेषां प्ररोहणम् ॥२४॥

यथा सुनिपुनः सम्यक् परदोषेक्षने रतः ।
तथा चेन्निपुणः स्वेषु को न मुच्यते बन्धनात् ॥२५॥
अनात्मविदमुक्तोऽपि सिद्धिजालानि वाञ्छति ।
द्रव्यमन्त्रक्रियाकालयुक्त्याप्नोति मुनीश्वरः ॥२६॥
नात्यमञ्जस्यैष विषय आत्मज्ञो ह्यात्ममात्रदृक् ।
आत्मनात्मनि संतृप्तो नाविद्यामनुधावति ॥२७॥
ये केचन जगद्भावस्तानविद्यामयान्विदुः ।
कथं तेषु किलात्मज्ञस्त्यक्ताविद्यो निमज्जति ॥२८॥
द्रव्यमन्त्रक्रियाकालयुक्तयः साधुसिद्धिदाः ।
परमात्मपदप्राप्तौ नोपकुर्वन्ति काश्चन ॥२९॥
सर्वेच्छाकलनाशानतावात्मलाभोदयाभिधः ।

स पुनः सिद्धिवाञ्छायां कथमर्हत्यचित्ततः ।।३०।।

चतुर्थोऽध्यायः

अथ ह ऋभुं भगवन्तं निदाघः पप्रच्छ जीवन्मुक्ति-लक्षणमनुब्रीति ।

तथेति स होवाच । सप्तभूमिषु जीवन्मुक्तश्चत्वारः ।
शुभेच्छा प्रथमा भुमिका भवति । विचारणा द्वितीया ।
तनुमानसी तृतीया । सत्त्वापत्तिस्तुरीया ।
असंसक्तिः पञ्चमी । पदर्थभावना षष्ठी । तुरीयगा सप्तमी ।
प्रणवात्मका भूमिका अकारोकारमकारार्धमात्रात्मिका ।
स्थूलसूक्ष्मबीजसाक्षिभेदेनाकारादयश्चतुर्विधाः ।

तदवस्था जाग्रत्स्वप्नसुषुप्तितुरीयाः ।
अकारस्थूलांशे जाग्रद्विश्वः । सुक्ष्मांशे तत्तैजसः ।
बीजांशे तत्प्राज्ञः । साक्ष्यंसे तत्तुरीयः ।
उकारस्थूलांशे स्वप्नविश्वः । सुक्ष्मांशे तत्तैजसः ।
बीजांशे तत्प्राज्ञः । साक्ष्यंसे तत्तुरीयः ।
मकारस्थूलांशे सुषुप्तविश्वः । सुक्ष्मांशे तत्तैजसः ।
बीजांशे तत्प्राज्ञः । साक्ष्यंशे तत्तुरीयः ।
अर्धमात्रास्थूलांशे तुरीयविश्वः । सुक्ष्मांशे तत्तैजसः ।
बीजांशे तत्प्राज्ञः । साक्ष्यंशे तुरीयतुरीयः ।

अकारतुरीयांशाः प्रथमद्वितीयतृतीयभूमिकाः ।
उकारतुरीयांशा चतुर्थी भूमिकाः ।

मकारतुरीयांशा पञ्चमी ।
अर्धमात्रातुरीयांशा षष्ठी । तदतीता सप्तमी ।
भूमित्रयेषु विहरन्मुमुक्षुर्भवति ।
तुरीयभूम्यां विहरन्ब्रह्मविद्भवति ।
पञ्चमभूम्यां विहरन्ब्रह्मविद्वरो भवति ।
षष्ठभूम्यां विहरन्ब्रह्मविद्वरीयान्भवति ।
सप्तभूम्यां विहरन्ब्रह्मविद्वरिष्ठो भवति ।
तत्रैते श्लोका भवन्ति ।
ज्ञानभूमिः शुभेच्छा स्यात्प्रथमा समुदीरिता ।
विचारणा द्वितीया तु तृतीया तनुमानसा ।।१।।
सत्त्वापत्तिश्चतुर्थी स्यात्ततोऽसंसक्तिनामिका ।
तदर्थभावना षष्थी सप्तमी तुरियगा स्मृता ।।२।।

स्थितः किं मूढ एवास्मि प्रेक्ष्योऽहं शास्त्रसज्जनैः ।
वैराग्यपूर्वमिच्छेति शुभेच्छेत्युच्यते बुधैः ।।३।।
शास्त्रसज्जनसंपर्कवैरग्याभ्यासपूर्वकम् ।
सदाचार प्रवृत्तिर्या प्रोच्यते सा विचारणा ।।४।।
विचारणाशुभेच्छामिन्द्रियार्थेषुरक्तता ।
यत्र सा तनुतामेति प्रोच्यते तनुमानसी ।।५।।

भूमिकात्रितयाभ्यासाच्चित्तेऽर्थविरतेर्वशात् ।
सत्वात्मनि स्थिते शुद्धे सत्त्वापत्तिरूदाहृयता ।।६।।
दशाचतुष्टयाभ्यासादसंसर्गफला तु या ।
रूढसत्वचमत्कारा प्रोक्ता असंसक्तिनामिका ।।७।।

भूमिकापञ्चकाभ्यासात्स्वात्मारामतया भृशम् ।
आभ्यन्तराणां बाह्यानां पदार्थनामभावनात् ।।८।।
परप्रयुक्तेन चिरं प्रत्ययेनावबोधनम् ।
पदर्थभावना नाम षष्ठी भवति भूमिका ।।९।।

षड्भूमिकाचिराभ्यासाद्भेदस्यानुपलम्भनात् ।
यत्स्वभावैकनिष्ठत्वं सा ज्ञेया तुरयगा गतिः ।।१०।।
शुभेच्छादित्रयं भूमिभेदाभेदयुतं स्मृतम् ।
यथावद्वेद बुद्ध्येदं जगज्जाग्रति दृश्यते ।।११।।
अद्वैते स्थैर्यमायाते द्वैते च प्रशमं गते ।
पश्यन्ति स्वप्नवल्लोकं तुर्यभूमिसुयोगतः ।।१२।।
विच्छिन्नशरदभ्राम्शविलयं प्रविलीयते ।
सत्वावशेष एवास्ते हे निदाघ दृढीकुरु ।।१३।।

पञ्चभूमिं समारुह्य सुषुप्तिपदनामिकाम् ।
शान्ताशेषविशेषांशस्तिष्ठत्यद्वैतमात्रके ।।१४।।
अन्तर्मुखतया नित्यं बहिर्वृत्तिपरोऽपि सन् ।
परिश्रान्ततया नित्यं निद्रालुरिव लक्ष्यते ।।१५।।

कुर्वन्नभ्यासमेतस्यां भूम्यां सम्यग्विवासनः ।
साप्तमी गूढसुप्त्याख्या क्रमप्राप्ता पुरातनी ।।१६।।
यत्र नासन्न सद्रूपो नाहं नाप्यनहंकृतिः ।
केवलं क्षीणमनन स्तेऽद्वैऽतिनिर्भयः ।।१७।।
अन्तःशून्यो बहिःशून्यः शूनयाकुमगह इवाम्बरे ।

अन्तःपूर्णो बहिःपूर्णः पूर्णकुम्भ इवार्णवे ।।१८।।
मा भव ग्राह्यभावात्मा ग्राहकात्मा च मा भव ।
भावनामखिलां त्यक्त्वा यच्छिष्टं तन्मयो भव ।।१९।।
द्रष्टृदर्शनदृश्यानि त्यक्त्वा वासनया सह ।
दर्शनप्रथमाभासमात्मानं केवलं भज ।।२०।।

यथास्थितमिदं यस्य व्यवहारवतोऽपिच ।
अस्तंगतं स्थितं व्योम स जीवन्मुक्त उच्यते ।।२१।।
नोदेति नास्तमायाति सुखे दुःखे मनःप्रभा ।
यथाप्राप्तस्थितिर्यस्य स जीवन्मुक्त उच्यते ।।२२।।
यो जागर्ति सुषुप्तिस्थो यस्य जाग्रन्न विद्यते ।
यस्य निर्वासनो बोधः स जीवन्मुक्त उच्यते ।।२३।।
रागद्वेषभयादीनामनुरूपं चरन्नपि ।
योऽन्तर्व्योमवदच्छन्नः स जीवन्मुक्त उच्यते ।।२४।।
यस्य नाहंकृतो भावो बुद्धिर्यस्य न लिप्यते ।
कुर्वतोऽकुर्वतो वापि स जीवन्मुक्त उच्यते ।।२५।।
यस्मान्नोद्विजते लोको लोकान्नोद्विजते च यः ।
हर्षामर्षभयोन्मुक्तः स जीवन्मुक्त उच्यते ।।२६।।
यः समस्तार्थजालेषु व्यवहार्यपि शीतलः ।
परार्थेष्विव पूर्णात्मा स जीवन्मुक्त उच्यते ।।२७।।
प्रजहाति यदा कामान्सर्वांश्चित्तगतान्मुने ।
मयि सर्वात्मके तुष्टः स जीवन्मुक्त उच्यते ।।२८।।
चैत्यवर्जितचिन्मात्रे पदे परमपावने ।
अक्षुब्धचित्तो विश्रान्तः स जीवन्मुक्त उच्यते ।।२९।।

इदं जगदहं सोऽयं दृशयजातमवास्तवम् ।
यस्य चित्ते न स्फुरति स जीवन्मुक्त उच्यते ॥३०॥

सद्ब्रह्माणि स्थिरे स्फारे पूर्णे विषयवर्जिते ।
आचार्यशास्त्रमार्गेण प्रविश्याशु स्थिरे भव ॥३१॥
शिवो गुरुः शिवो वेदः शिव देवः शिवः प्रभुः ।
शिवोऽस्म्यहं शिवः सर्वं शिवादन्यन्न किंचनन ॥३२॥
तमेव धीरो विज्ञाय प्रज्ञां कुर्वीत ब्राह्मणः
नानुध्यायाद्वहुञ्छब्दान्वाचो विग्लापनं हि तत् ॥३३॥

शुको मुक्तो वामादेवोऽपि मुक्तस्ताभ्यां विना मुक्तिभाजो न सन्तिः ।
शुकमार्गं येऽनुसरन्ति धीराः सद्यो मुक्तास्ते भवन्तीह लोके ॥३४॥
वामदेवं येऽनुसरन्ति नित्यं मृत्वा जनित्वा च पुनःपुनस्तत
ते वै लोके क्रममुक्ता भवन्ति योगैः सांख्यैः
कर्मभिः सत्त्वयुक्तैः ॥३५॥
शुकश्च वामदेवश्च देव सृती देवनिर्मिते ।
शुको विहङ्गमः प्रोक्तो वामदेवः पिपीलिका ॥३६॥
अतद्व्यावृत्तिरूपेण साक्षाद्विधिमुखेन वा ।
महावाक्यविचारेण सांख्ययोगसमाधिना ॥३७॥
विदित्वा स्वात्मनो रूपं संप्रज्ञातसमाधितः ।
शुकमार्गेण विरजाः प्रयान्ति परमं पदम् ॥३८॥
यमाद्यासनजायासहठाभ्यासात्पुनःपुनः
विघ्नबाहुल्यसंजात अणिमादिवशादिह ॥३९॥

अलब्ध्वापि फलं सम्यक्पुनर्भूत्वा महाकुले ।
पुनर्वास्न्यैवायं योगाभ्यासं पेनश्चरन् ।।४०।।
अनेकजन्माभ्यासेन वामदेवेन वे पक्ष ।
सोऽपि मुक्तिं समाप्नोति तद्विष्णो परं पदम् ।।४१।।
द्वाविमावपि पन्थानौ ब्रह्मप्राप्तिकरौ शिवौ ।
सद्यौ मुक्तिप्रदश्चैकः क्रममुक्तिप्रदः परः ।४२।

अत्र को मोहः कः शोक एकत्वमनुपश्यतः ।।४२।।
यस्यानुभवपर्यन्ता बुद्धिस्तत्त्वे प्रवर्तते ।
तद्दृष्टिगोचराः सर्वे मुच्यन्ते सर्वपातकैः ।।४३।।
खेचरा भूचराः सर्वे ब्रह्मविद्दृष्टिगोचराः
सद्य एव विमुच्यन्ते कोटिजन्मार्जितैरदैः ।।४४।।

पञ्चमोऽध्यायः
अथ इमं ऋभुं भगवन्तं निदाघः पप्रच्छ योगाभ्यास-
विधिमनुब्रूब्रूहीति ।
तथेति स होवाच ।
पञ्चभूतात्मको देहः पञ्चमण्डलपूरितः ।
काठिन्यं पृथिवीमेका पानीयं तद्द्रवाकृति ।।१।।
दीपनं च भवेत्तेजः प्रचारो वायुलक्षणम ।
आकाशः सत्त्वतः सर्वं ज्ञातव्यं योगमिच्छता ।।२।।
षट्शतान्यधिकान्यत्र सहस्त्राण्येकविंशतिः ।
अहोरात्रवहैः श्वासैर्वायुमण्डलघाततः ।।३।।

तत्पृथ्वीमण्डले क्षीणे वलिरायाति देहिनाम् ।

तद्वदाहो गणापाये केशाः स्युः पाण्दुराः क्रमात् ।।४।।
तेजःक्क्षये क्षुधा कान्तिर्नश्यते मारुतक्षये ।
वेपशुः संभवेन्नित्यं नाम्भसेनैव जीवति ।।५।।
इत्थंभूतं क्षयान्नित्यं जीवितं भूतधारणम् ।६।

उड्याणं कुरुते यस्मादविश्रान्तं महाखगः ।।६।।
उड्डियाणं तदेव स्यात्तत्र बन्धोऽभिधीयते ।
उड्डियाणे ह्यसै बन्धो मृत्युमातङ्गकेशरी ।।७।।
तस्य मुक्तिस्तनोः कायात्तस्य बन्धो हि दुष्करः ।
अग्नै तु चलिते कुक्षै वेदना जायते भृशम् ।।८।।
न कार्या क्षुधि तेनापि नापि विण्मूत्रवेगिना
हितं मितं च भोक्तव्यं स्तोकं स्तोकमनेकधा ।।९।।

मृदुमध्यममन्त्रेषु क्रमानमन्त्रं लयं हठम् ।
लयमन्त्रहठा योगा योगो ह्यष्टाङन्गसंयुतः ।।१०।।
यमश्च तथा चासनमेव च ।
प्राणायामस्तथा पश्चात्याहारस्तथा परं ।।११।।
धारणा च तथा ध्यानं समाधिश्चाष्टमो भवेत् ।१२।

अहिंसा सत्यमस्तेयं ब्रह्मचर्यं दयार्जवम् ।।१२।।
क्षमा धृतिर्मिताहारः शौचं चेति यमा दश ।
तपः सन्तोषमस्तिक्यं दानमीश्वरपूजनम् ।।१३।।
सिद्धान्तश्रवणं चैव ह्रीर्मतिश्च जपो व्रतम् ।
एवे हि नियमाः प्रोक्ता दशधैव महामते ।।१४।।

एकदशासनानि स्युश्चक्रादि मुनिसत्तम ।
चक्रं पद्मासनं कूर्मं कुक्कुटं तथा ।।१५।।
वीरासनं स्वास्तिकं च भद्रं सिंहासनं तथा ।
मुक्तासनं गोमुखं च कीर्तितं योगवित्तमैः ।।१६।।
सव्योरु दक्षिणे गुल्पे दक्षिणं दक्षिणेतरे ।
निदध्यादृजुकायस्तु चक्रासनमिदं मतम् ।।१७।।

पूरकः कुम्भकस्तद्वद्रेचकः पूरकः पुनः ।
प्राणायामः स्वनाडीभिस्तस्मान्नाडीः प्रचक्षते ।।१८।।

शरीरं सर्वजन्तूनां षण्णवत्यङ्गुलात्मकम् ।
तन्मध्ये पायुदेशात्तु द्व्तङ्गुलात्परतः परम् ।।१९।।
मेढ्रदेशादधस्तात्तु द्वङ्गुलान्मध्यमुच्यते ।
मेढ्रान्नवाङ्गुलादूर्ध्वं नाडीनां कन्दमुच्यते ।।२०।।
चतुरङ्गुलमुत्सेधं चतुरङ्गुलमायतम् ।
अण्डाकारं परिवृतं मेदोमज्जास्थिशोणितैः ।।२१।।

तत्रैव नाडीचक्रं तु द्वादशारं प्रतिषठितम् ।
शरीरं धृयते येन वर्तते तत्र कुण्डली ।।२२।।
ब्रह्मरन्ध्रं सुषुम्णा या वदनेन पिधाय सा ।
अलम्बुसा सुषुम्नायाः कुरूर्नाडी वसत्यसौ ।।२३।।
अनन्तरारयुग्मे तु वारूणा च यशस्विनी ।
दक्षिणारे सुषुम्नायाः पिङ्गला वर्तते क्रमात् ।।२४।।

तदन्तरारयोः पूषा वर्तते च पयस्विनी ।
सुषुम्ना पश्चिमे चारे स्थिता नाडी सरस्वती ।।२५।।
शङ्खिनी चैव गान्धारी तदनन्तरयोः स्थिते ।
उत्तरे तु सुषुम्नाया इडाख्या निवसत्यसै ।।२६।।
अनन्तरं हस्तिजीह्वा ततो विश्वोदरी स्थिता ।
प्रदक्षिणक्रमेणैव चक्रस्यारेषु नाड्यः ।।२७।।

वरन्ते द्वादश ह्येता द्वादशानिलवाहकाः ।
पटवत्संस्थिता नाड्यो नानावर्णाः समीरिताः ।।२८।।
पटमध्यं तु यत्स्थानं नाभिचक्रं चदुच्यते ।
नादाधारा समाख्याता ज्वलन्ती नादरूपिणी ।।२९।।
पररन्ध्रा सुषुम्ना च चत्वारो रत्नपूरिताः ।
कुण्डल्या पिहितं शश्वद्ब्रह्मरन्ध्रस्य मध्यमम् ।।३०।।
एवमेतासु नाडीषु धरन्ति दश वायवः ।३१।

एवं नाडीगतिं वायुगतिं ज्ञात्वा विचक्षणः ।।३१।।
समग्रीवशिरःकायः संवृतास्यः सुनिश्चलः ।
नासाग्रे चैव हृन्मध्ये बिन्दुमध्ये तुरीयकम् ।।३२।।
स्रवन्तममृतं पश्येन्नेत्राभ्यां सुसमाहितः ।३३।

अपानं मुकुलीकृत्य पायुमाकृष्य चैन्मुखम् ।।३३।।
प्रणवेन समुत्थाप्य श्रीबीजेन निवर्तयेत् ।
स्वात्मानं च श्रियं ध्यायेदमृतप्लावनं ततः ।।३४।।
कालवञ्चनमेतद्धि सर्वमुख्यं प्रचक्षते ।
मनसा चिन्तितं कार्यं मनसा येन सिध्यति ।।३५।।

जलेऽग्निज्वलनाच्छाखापल्लवानि भवन्ति हि ।
नाधन्यं जागतं वाक्यं विपरीता भवेत्क्रिया ।।३६।।

मार्गे बिन्दुं समाबध्य वह्निं प्रज्वाल्य जीवने ।
शोषयित्वा तु सलिलं तेन कायं दृढं भवेत् ।।३७।।
गुदयोनिसमायुक्त आकुञ्चत्येककालतः ।
अपानमूर्ध्वगं कृत्वा समानोऽन्ने नियोजयेत् ।।३८।।
स्वात्मानं च श्रियं ध्यायेदमृतप्लावनं ततः ।
बलं समारभेद्योगं मध्यमद्वारभागतः ।।३९।।
भावयेदूर्ध्वगत्यर्थं प्राणापानसुयोगतः ।
एष योगो वरो देहे सिद्धिमार्गप्रकाशकः ।।४०।।
यथैवापगातः सेतुः प्रवाहस्य निरोधकः ।
तथा शरीरगा छाया ज्ञातव्या योगिभिः सदा ।।४१।।

सर्वासामेव नाडीनामेष प्रकीर्तितः ।
बन्धस्यास्य प्रसादेन स्फुटीभवति देवता ।।४२।।
एवं चतुष्पथो बन्धो मार्गत्रयनिरोधकः ।
एक विकासयन्मार्गं येन सिद्धाः सुसङ्गताः ।।४३।।
उदानमूर्ध्वगं कृत्वा प्राणेन सह वेगतः ।
बन्धोऽयं सर्वनाडीनामूर्ध्वं याति निरोधकः ।।४४।।
अयं च संपुटो योगो मूलबन्धोऽप्ययं मतः ।
बन्धत्रययमनेनैव सिद्ध्यत्यभ्यासयोगतः ।।४५।।

दिवारात्रमविच्छिन्नं यामेयामे यदा यदा ।
अनेनाभ्यासयोगेन वायुरभ्यसितो भवेत् ।।४६।।

वायावभ्यसिते वह्निः प्रत्यहं वर्धते तनौ ।
वह्नौ विवर्धमाने तु सुखमन्नादि जीर्णते ॥४७॥
अन्नस्य परिपाकेन रसवृद्धिः प्रजायते ।
रसे वृद्धिं गते नित्यं वर्धन्ते धातवस्तथा ॥४८॥
धातूनां वर्धनेनैव प्रबोधो वर्धते तनौ ।
दह्यन्ते सर्वपापानि जन्मकोट्यर्जीतानि च ॥४९॥

गुदमेढ्रान्तरालस्थं मूलाधारं त्रिकोणकम् ।
शिवस्य बिन्दुरूपस्य स्थानं तद्धि प्रकाशकम् ॥५०॥
यत्र कुण्डलिनी नाम परा शक्तिः प्रतिष्ठिता ।
यस्मादुत्पद्यते वायुर्यस्माद्वह्निः प्रवर्धते ॥५१॥
यस्मादुत्पद्यते बिन्दुर्यस्मान्नादः प्रवर्धते ।
यस्मादुत्पद्यते हंसो यस्मादुत्पद्यते मनः ॥५२॥
मूलाधारादिषट्चक्रं शक्तिस्थानमुदीरितम् ।
कण्ठादुपरि मूर्धान्तं शांभवं स्थानमुच्यते ॥५३॥

नाडीनामाश्रयः पिण्डो नाद्यः प्राणस्य चाश्रयः ।
जीवस्य निलयः प्राणो जीवो हंसस्य चाश्रयः ॥५४॥
हंसः शक्तेरधिष्ठानं चराचरमिदं जगत् ।
निर्विकल्पः प्रसन्नात्मा प्राणायां समभ्यसेत् ॥५५॥
सम्यग्बन्धत्रयस्थोऽपि लक्ष्यलक्षणकारणम् ।
वेद्यं समुद्धरेन्नित्यं सत्यसंधानमाबसः ॥५६॥
रेचकं पूरकं चैव कुम्भमध्ये निरोधयेत् ।
दृश्यमाने परे लक्ष्ये ब्रह्मणि स्वयमाश्रितः ॥५७॥
बाह्यस्यविषयं सर्वं रेचकः समुदाहृतः ।

पूरकं शास्त्रविज्ञानं कुम्भकं स्वगतं स्मृतम् ।।५८।।
एवमभ्यासचित्तंचेत्स मुक्तो नात्र संशयः ।५९।

कुम्भकेन समारोप्य कुम्भकेनैव पूरयेत् ।।५९।।
कुम्भेन कुम्भयेत्कुम्भं तदन्तस्थः परं शिवम् ।
पुनराऽस्फलायेदद्य सुस्थिरं कण्ठमुद्रया ।।६०।।
वायूनां गतमावृत्य धृत्वा पूरककुम्भकै ।६१।

समहस्तयुगं भूमै समं पादयुगं तथा ।।६१।।
वेधकक्रमयोगेन चतुष्पीथं तु वायुना ।
आस्फालयेन्महामेरुं वायुवक्रे प्रकोटिभः ।।६२।।
पुटद्वयं समाकृष्य वायुः स्फुरति सत्वरम् ।
सोमसूर्याग्निसंबन्धाज्जानीयादमृताय वै ।।६३।।
मेरुमध्यगता देवाश्चलन्ते मेरुचालनात् ।
आद्य संजायते क्षिप्रं वेधोऽस्य ब्रह्मग्रन्थितः ।।६४।।
ब्रह्मग्रन्थिं ततो भित्त्वा विष्णुग्रन्थिं भिनत्त्यसौ ।
विष्णुग्रन्थिं ततो भित्त्वा रुद्रग्रन्थिं भिनत्त्यसौ ।।६५।।
रुद्रग्रन्थिं ततो भित्त्वा छित्त्वा मोहमलं तथा ।
अनेकजन्मसंस्कारगुरुदेवप्रसादतः ।।६६।।
योगाभ्यासात्ततो वेधो जायते तस्य योगिनः ।
इडापिङ्गलयोर्मध्ये सुषुम्नानाडिमण्डले ।।६७।।
मुद्राबन्धविशेषेण वायुमूर्ध्वं च कारयेत् ।६८।

ह्रस्वो दहति पापानि दीर्घो मोक्षदायकः ।।६८।।
आप्यायनः प्लुतो वापि त्रिविधोञ्छारणेन तु ।

तैलधारामिवाच्छिन्नं दीर्घघण्टानिनादवत् ।।६९।।
अवाच्यं प्रणवस्याग्रं यस्तं वेद स वेदवित् ।
ह्रस्वं बिन्दुगतं दैर्घ्यं ब्रह्मरन्ध्रगतं प्लुतम् ।
द्वादशान्तगतं मन्त्रं प्रसादं मन्त्रसिद्धये ।।७०।।
सर्वविघ्नहरश्चायं प्रणवः सर्वदोषहा ।७१।

आरम्भश्च घटश्चैव पुनः परिचयस्तथा ।।७१।।
निष्पत्तिश्चेति कथिताश्चतस्रस्तस्य भूमिकाः ।
कारणत्रयसंभूतं बाह्यं कर्म परित्यजन् ।।७२।।
अन्तरं कर्म कुरुते यत्रारम्भः स उच्यते ।
वायुः पश्चिमतो वेधं कुर्वन्नापूर्य सुस्थिरम् ।।७३।।
यत्र तिष्ठति सा प्रोकता घटाख्या भूमिका बुधैः ।
न सजीवो न निर्जीवः काये तिष्ठति निश्चलम् ।
यत्र वायुः स्थिरः खे स्यात्सेयः परिचयभूमिका ।।७४।।
यत्रात्मनो सृष्टिलयौ जीवन्मुक्तिदशागतः ।
सहजः कुरुते योगं सेयं निष्पत्तिभूमिका ।।७५।।

इति ।
एतदुपनिषदं योऽधीते सोऽग्निपूतो भवति ।
स वायुपूतो भवति ।
सुरापानात्पूतो भवति ।
स्वर्णस्तेयात्पूतो भवति ।
स जीवन्मुक्तो भवति ।
तदेतद्दचाभ्युक्तम् ।

तद्विष्णोः परमं पदं सदा पश्यन्ति सूरयः ।
दिवीव चक्षुराततम् ।
तद्विप्रासो विपन्यवो जागृवांसः समिन्धते ।
विष्णोर्यत्परमं पदमित्युपनिषत् ।
इति पञ्चमोऽध्यायः ।।५।।

E. Continuous Translation

Opening Invocation

I worship the name Rāmacandra, called the triple Narāyaṇa, causing endless joy in the words of the holy Varāha-Upaniṣad. Saying thus, may we both have the peace of Om.

First Chapter

1.

Now the great sage Ṛbhu wandered about [performing] austerities for a period of twelve years in honour of the gods. At the end of that time the Lord appeared before [him] in the form of a boar.

He [the Lord] said: "Arise, arise! You may choose a boon!"

He arose. Bowing down to Him he said: "O Lord, I will not ask for whatever is desired by the worldly, even if it appears in a dream. All the Vedas, Śāstras, Itihāsas and Purāṇas [and] mass of spiritual knowledge, from Brahma and divine beings, all say [that] liberation [comes] from the knowledge of your true nature. So [please] explain the supreme knowledge of Brahman [which] expresses your nature." Thus he spoke.

"Very well," said the boar-shaped Lord. "Some like to assert [that there are] twenty-four elements, some thirty-six and some ninety-six.

2 to 4.

I shall relate [them] in their order. Listen with an attentive mind. [There are] five sensory organs: ear, skin, eye and so on. [There are] in order five organs of action: mouth, hand, foot and so on; then five vital airs beginning with sound and the others [are] five. Manas, buddhi, ahaṃkāra and citta are four. [Whoever] knows these twenty-four principles knows Brahman.

5 to 7.
The wise know [that] as well as these principles [there are] five quintuplicated elements: earth, water, fire, air and ether; three bodies: gross, subtle [and] causal; and three states of consciousness: waking, dreaming and sleeping. The sages know [that] the total collection of tattvas is thirty-six. These principles are combined with the collection spoken of previously.

8 to 14.
And [within the tattwas] there are six changes in existence. One is born and also grows. The wise [know that] in the six changes in existence, [there are] transformation, decay and destruction. Hunger, thirst, pain, delusion, age and death are said to be the six waves of existence. Know [that] the six sheaths are skin, blood, flesh, fat marrow [and] bones. Passion, anger, greed, delusion, pride and jealousy, these are indeed the six enemies. *Viśva, Taijasaḥ* and *Prājña* [are] the three [parts] of the *jīva. Sattva, rajas* and *tamas* are known as the *guṇas*.

It is said [that] *prārabdha, āgāmī* [and] *sañcita* [are] the three karmas. Talking, grasping, walking, voiding [and sensual] pleasure [are] the five [actions]; volition, perseverance, arrogance, determination, and this set of four: sympathetic joy, compassion, friendliness [and] indifference; [four] directions, Vāyu, Sun, Varuṇa, Aśvins, Agni, Indra, Upendra and Mṛtyu; then the Moon, Brahma, Rudra, Kṣetrajña [and] Īśvara.

15 to 17.
Altogether there are said to be an aggregate of ninety-six tattvas. Those who worship me [with] devotion in me [as] the form of the boar, [who], without disease, diverges from the aforesaid aggregate of tattwas, this having been done, they become *jīvanmuktas*, freed from ignorance. Those who know the ninety-six tattvas, intent on whichever stage of life, [their

hair] matted, shaven or even [in] a tuft, without a doubt become liberated here.

Second Chapter

1 to 3.

The great yogin called Ṛbhu [asked] the spouse of Lakshmi in the form of a boar: "O Lord, please reveal to me the transcendent Brahma Vidyā". Having been asked thus, the Lord, [who] removes the suffering of his devotees, instructed: "Through one's duty [according to] caste [and] stage of life, through austerity [and] through the act of pleasing the guru, the four spiritual disciplines, non-attachment etc, arise in a person. [They are] discrimination [between] the permanent and impermanent, indifference to [what is] in this world and others, the six virtues, equanimity etc, [and] the desire for final liberation. One should practise these.

4 to 6.

Having become one who has control over the senses [and] given up the concept [of] 'mine' at all times, [your] concept [of] 'I' should be in me, the witnessing consciousness. Having attained with great difficulty the human state, even in the form of a man [who is] a brāhmaṇa, whoever does not learn, through hearing vedānta and others, the goal of existence-consciousness-bliss, the great Viṣṇu, [as] the form beyond caste and stage of life, when will he, ignorant, become liberated?

7 to 10.

I alone [am] happiness, nothing else. If there is, then that happiness [which is] not for my sake is not dear [to me]. [That happiness which is] for my sake [and] not for oneself is dear [to me]. Because [I am] the abode of Supreme Love, existence is not mine. I am one who has always been. I am Viṣṇu, the silent witness, the Supreme Consciousness.

How can the non-light touch that ātman with its own light? This statement 'I am not the Light' is produced [by] the one Light. Those who know with certainty [that I am] my own light, without support, are endowed with supreme wisdom. This is my definite conviction.

11 to 19.

With the exception of the ātman [which is] complete by itself, the world [of] living beings, the Supreme Lord and others do not exist and nor does *māyā* exist. I do not have those characteristics. [Whatever has] the form of the intense darkness of ignorance in the character of *karma* [and] *dharma* etc does not deserve to touch me, the self-shining ātman. Seeing the ātman, the witness of all, free from caste and life stages, in the formation of Brahman, one becomes Brahman oneself. Seeing through the testament of Vedānta this appearance of light [as] the whole form of the Supreme Seat, one is instantly liberated.

Whoever, refuting knowledge of the kind [that] the ātman [is] in the body, has knowledge of the ātman alone is liberated even if not desiring [it]. Always seeing the nature of truth, knowledge, bliss and fullness [which is furthest] from darkness, the supreme bliss of Brahman, how can one be bound by karma? [One who has] the eyes of spiritual wisdom perceives the omnipresent spirit [as] the witness of the three states, with the characteristics [of] truth, wisdom, bliss and so on, [which is] the inner meaning of the words 'your' [and] 'I' [and] detached from all faults. [One whose] eyes are without spiritual wisdom does not see the radiant light of the splendour of the sun. Supreme knowledge alone [is] that Brahman [with] the characteristics of truth [and] wisdom. Only through knowing Brahman thus, does a mortal become immortal.

20 to 28.

Knowing one's own ātman [as] the form [of] that non-dual

bliss of Brahman, without qualities, possessing true consciousness, one does not fear any threat.

The conviction of the knowers of Brahman [is] thus: clearly there is nothing else, only Brahman, consciousness alone, all-pervading, eternal, complete [and] ultimate joy. The material world is a flood of suffering to the ignorant [and] full of bliss to the wise, [just as] the earth is dark to the blind but bright to those with good vision. [Whoever] has faith in me, in the form of a boar, infinite existence, consciousness, bliss, is in the non-dual state. [Therefore] what is bondage and who is to be liberated?

The true nature of all bodies is always consciousness alone. The combination of the body and its parts is not like a pot perceived through the eyes. Knowing [that] this moving and fixed world appears as [something] other than one's own Self, [yet is] not more or less than one's own ātman, reflect on 'That I am'. One enjoys by oneself one's own real form. There is no enjoyment apart from one's own Self. If there is a form of reality, [then] Brahman alone [has] the attribute of reality. One who is endowed with knowledge of Brahman, even when seeing the whole recognised world, never sees [it] apart from one's ātman. Through complete knowledge [of] My form, one is not bound by karma.

29 to 31.

Whoever knows [Brahman] free from sense organs and body, witness of all, the one knowledge [of] the highest truth, the self-shining blissful ātman, whoever [knows this] through direct experience the state of one's true nature, that [one] should be known as [a person of] courage. O Ṛbhu, become 'I Am That'. Hence, understanding [that] the perception of the visible world is not always true, indeed the experience of the realisation of one's true form [is] always [true and possessing] full knowledge [of the ātman], one is neither liberated from bondage nor at all bound.

32 to 38.
One who meditates through concentration on one's own real form for a *muhurta*, on me, dancing as the witness of all, is liberated from all bondage. Salutations to me alone who am within all beings, of the nature of consciousness, ever liberated, the form of innermost consciousness. I am truly you. You are I, o Glorious Divine one, to you [and] me the infinite, to me [and] you the nature of consciousness. Reverence to me, the transcendent Lord, and reverence to you, the auspicious one.

What shall I do? Where shall I go? What shall I take? What shall I renounce? Just as the universe is filled by me with the ocean of the great cycle of time, so whoever gives up attachment to the internal, attachment to the external and attachment to the self, the ātman devoid of all attachments, that one without doubt reaches me.

Whoever wishes to leave the worldly life should always avoid like a snake the company of men, [be] indifferent to a beautiful woman as if to a corpse, [and] regard endless sensual enjoyments as poison. [This is] the *paramahaṃsa* [who says] 'I [am] Vāsudeva alone'. This is the Truth. This is the Truth. This is the Truth spoken here. I am the Truth, the Supreme Brahman. Nothing exists [apart] from me.

39 to 44.
Upavāsaḥ should be known as that which abides near *param-ātman* and *jīvātman*, not as the withering of the body. What then [is the use] of the mere drying up of the body for the ignorant? Does the great serpent die just by beating the ant-hill alone? If one knows 'this is Brahman', that [is] only indirect knowledge. One is said [to have] direct knowledge if one knows 'I am Brahman'.

At whatever time the yogin knows his own ātman [to be] the one Self, beginning from that time that [person] becomes a *jīvanmukta*. Always in the state 'I am Brahman' is the cause of liberation for the high souls. [There are] two words for bondage and liberation. They are 'mine' and 'non-mine'. A person is bound by 'mine' and freed by 'non-mine'. External anxieties are not to be had [and] similarly any inner anxieties. Having given up all anxiety, be always at ease, o Ṛbhu!

45 to 48a.
The entire world [exists] through the effect of the extent of volition. Hence the extent of volition is the cause of the shining forth of the world. Having abandoned this volition, taking refuge in *nirvikalpa*, meditate on My abode in [your] heart. O wise one, having become Me, the one Supreme, spend your time thinking about Me, singing about Me [and] conferring about Me with one another. Know that in this universe there is consciousness, pure intelligence consisting of consciousness alone, and you are consciousness, I am consciousness and [all] these worlds are consciousness. Having changed passion to dispassion, become forever unattached.

48b to 50a.
How can the bright lamp [of] the knowledge of the ātman, stemming from the Vedas, be impaired by any action arising from causes [made by] agents and others [which is] born from ignorance? Having left the *anātman* state, remaining in the world unaffected, devote yourself to the one inner Supreme Intellligence.

50b to 54.
The ether of the pot [and] the ether of the monastery are located in the great ether. Thus living beings are formed in Me, the space of pure unlimited consciousness. Whichever illusive power [exists] before [Me], the ātman, then at the end vanishes. This has been sung as *māyā* by the teachers of

Brahman through their correct understanding. With the death [of] māyā [and] its actions, [there is] neither supremacy nor existence. Thus pure, I [am] consciousness alone, like the ether without attributes, consisting of the sentient and the non-sentient, with the form of *jīva, Īśvara* and others. Creation, beginning with reflection [and] ending with entry, [is] the function of sight. Worldly existence, beginning with waking [and] ending with liberation [is] the function of jīva.

55 to 57.
[Teachings] beginning with *triṇāciketa* [and] ending with yoga rest on confusion about Īśvara. [Philosophies] beginning with *lokāyata* [and] ending with *sāṃkhya* rest on the cessation of jīva. Therefore no thought at all by those desirous of liberation [should be given to] controversies about jīva and *īśa*, but, with a steady [mind], the true nature of Brahman should be investigated. To whatever extent [people] do not know the non-dual nature of Brahman, to that extent [they are] all deluded. Where [is] their liberation? Where in this world [is] happiness?

58 to 63.
If they have the impression [of] high and low, what is that? Is one [who is] woken indeed affected by sovereignty and beggary [experienced] in the dreaming state? When the intellect is dissolved in ignorance, this is called sleep by the wise. How can there be sleep for me, free from ignorance in its deeds? The fully expanded [state] of the intellect is called the waking [state]. The waking [state] does not exist for me, [who am] devoid of change. The dreaming [state] is caused by the movement of the intellect through the subtle nāḍis. The dreaming [state] does not exist in me [who am without] the inner attribute of movement.

Freed from all, enclosed in darkness when all is dissolved at the time of deep sleep, one enjoys the highest bliss of one's own true nature. Whoever sees everything without difference because of the connection with consciousness is indeed one who has direct realisation. He [is] Śiva. He [is] the way of Hari.

64 to 65.

Having risen from sleep, reflecting at the end of sleep on the one Brahman, [one realises that] this mundane existence [is] like a long dream, which [is] a long delusion consuming the mind, [and] also like an ocean of suffering [with] a long reign over the mind.

Through complete dissolution of the apparent world, the mind takes on My form. The enemies having been killed, their destruction [caused] by the six means [through the grace of] *guru*, [the ātman], [like] the scent of an elephant, becomes peerless alone.

66 to 71a.

Let the body exist today or even as long as the moon and stars, consciousness of my body will survive. [Whether] a pot is broken or fully formed for a long time [makes] little difference at all to the ether of the pot. The lifeless cast-off skin of a snake remains cast off over the anthill [and] the snake does not care about it. Thus [the wise person] does not care about the gross and subtle bodies. When false knowledge together with its cause is destroyed [by] the fire [of] inner knowledge, this [person] becomes bodiless through the state of the form of 'not this not this'.

One sees the visible as made enduring, [but] according to the *śāstras* (sacred texts) it does not exist, [only] the perception of the highest truth. Through the removal of *prārabdha karma*, [there is] the destruction of the manifestation [of the world]. Thus in three ways delusion about the ātman is destroyed. The yogin does not go to the state of a jīva when he is attached to the state of Brahman. When the non-dual is known, an affinity for objects ceases. Thus [there is] loss of the body at the end of his karma [and] delusion perishes completely.

71b to 74.
When 'There Is' is uttered, the whole world becomes that essence of Truth, Brahman. When 'It Shines Forth' is uttered, the whole world [becomes] only the light of Brahman alone. All the water in the desert [becomes] only that desert itself. [Through] the enquiry into the nature of the Self, this whole threefold world is consciousness alone.

Ignorance [is] in the context of the world alone, nowhere [else]. At a great distance from the accounts of the differences [between] *jīva, īśvara* and *guru*, I am the completely full Brahman whose being is the one alone absolute consciousness.

When the radiance in the full moon of consciousness is obscured by the shadow of delusion, the rites [of] ablution, donation and sacrifice and so on remain futile for the duration [of the eclipse] until the end.

75 to 78.
Just as rock-salt in water becomes the same, so [when] through yoga the mind and ātman [become] one, it is said to be *samādhi*. Without the grace of a true guru, the giving up of sensual pleasure [is] very difficult, the perception of Truth [is] hard to obtain, [and] the natural state [is] rare. The natural state of a yogin shines of its own accord [and] in whom the awakened *śakti* has arisen, [and in whom] all the karmas [have been] relinquished. Fluctuation is the innate tendency of quicksilver and the mind. [If] quicksilver [is] bound [and] mind [is] bound, what cannot be accomplished on [this] earth?

79 to 83.
[Whoever] is filled [with prāṇa] removes disease. The dead is

restored to his own life. [Whoever] has bound [the mind or intellect] is given the power of flying. Then mercury and mind [are in] the state of Brahman. The lord of the sense organs is the mind. The lord of the mind is the vital air. The lord of the vital air is dissolution. The refuge of dissolution is that lord.

The yogin, viewing all sensual pleasures with feather after feather does not forsake that highest aim of beholding Brahman, like the female dancer, absorbed in [the symphony of] singing and cymbals composed by musical instruments, also maintains the pot on her head.

[If there is] the desire for the power of yoga, the inner sound alone should be meditated on with an attentive mind, all worries having been given up.

Third Chapter

1 to 5.

At no time can the One Reality be of many forms. Therefore, [as there is] no other [besides] myself, I alone am indivisible. Whatever is seen [and] heard, that is no other than Brahman. I alone [am] that Supreme Brahman which [is] eternal, pure, free, the one indivisible bliss, non-dual, truth [and] infinite wisdom. I [am] the nature of bliss, the indivisible intelligence. I [am] the exalted unshakeable light of consciousness and just as clouds do not touch the ether, [so] the sufferings of worldly life do not touch me.

Know [that] all happinesss [is] through the elimination of great suffering; all is of the nature of truth through the elimination of untruth. The nature of consciousness alone is connected with the inner light. Therefore this form of mine is indivisible. To the supreme yogin [there is] no birth or death, no going or coming, no impurity or purity and no knowledge, as [to him] all shines clearly as pure consciousness.

6 to 8.

Always practise silence 'I am that', which [is] the supreme, untainted, unique Śiva, the non-dual, indivisible, permeating consciousness of truth, pure, devoid of the whole visible [world]. Always practise silence 'I am that', consciousness the cause of the illusory manifestation of the world, devoid of birth and death, happiness and suffering, remote from caste, law, clan [and] lineage. Always practise silence 'I am that', the full, non-dual, indivisible consciousness without divisions and other faults [existing in] the universe, forming part of the unique Supreme.

9 to 10.

That [which] exists is composed of the one form throughout the three periods of time, unimpeded by anything, [and is] always the form of My existence. Even the state of happiness which [is] eternal without limits [and] superior to all the happiness in sleep, that is always My bliss.

11 to 13.

Is it not so [that] the very dense gloom of darkness is immediately banished by the rays [of] the sun? The darkness which [is] the cause of the existence of impassable crossing [is dispelled] by Hari, the illumination of the sun, and not by another. A person is freed from his own darkness by remembering and worshipping My feet. Intent on remembering My feet, there is nothing [which is] the cause [of] extinction [and] origin [of] death. Just as [one who] desires [to obtain] wealth [has] praise for a rich man, so if with respect [one praises] the creator of the universe, who is not freed from bondage?

14 to 19.

The world is only active of its own accord in the presence of the sun, and thus in My presence alone does the world act. Just as through mother-of-pearl [is] silver imagined through the power of illusion, so in Me alone [does] the world consist of this power alone, from *mahat* etc.

While others turn to differences in the body of a low-caste [person], an animal etc [and] a vegetable [and] the body of a brahman, I am not so. Just as to one who wanders in the wrong direction [and] the direction appears as before, so the world, disappeared through spiritual wisdom, does not appear to Me thus.

The world [is] not the body, nor the vital energy [of] the organs of sense and action, nor the individual self [with its] rational and discerning mind, nor the individual consciousness, nor illusion and nor ether etc. Neither the creator, nor the enjoyer, nor the cause of enjoyment, thus I am Janārdana, Brahman alone, nothing but consciousness, existence, bliss.

20 to 24.

Because of the movement of water, [there are] ripples in the [reflected] sun, so [is the appearance of] the ātman in mundane existence because of its connection [with] the individual self. The root of the mind, in mundane existence, should be purified with effort. Alas! What is this confidence of yours in the greatness of the mind?

Where is the wealth of the kings? Where are the Brahmanas and the worlds? The previous ones have vanished and gone to future creations. Crores of Brahmanas have gone. Kings have disappeared like dust.

When generated desires and so on are burnt by the fire [of] the wisdom [of] discrimination, then how [can] they begin to grow?

25 to 30.

Just as a very clever person takes pleasure in seeing the

exact faults [of another], thus if he [is aware] of his own, who will not be liberated from bondage?

O Lord of sages, [whoever is] without knowledge of the ātman [and] also not liberated, longs for the traps of siddhis, [which] he attains through drugs, mantra, religious rites, time [and] practice. To one who knows the ātman this is a matter of absolute ignorance. [Whoever has] his sight solely on the ātman, satisfied with the ātman in his ātman, does not pursue ignorance.

Whoever exists [in] the world, the wise [know] them [to be] [of] the nature of ignorance. How then can the knower of ātman, having abandoned ignorance, be immersed [in it]? Drugs, mantra, religious rites, time [and] practice can give strong powers, [yet] they do not in any [way] lead to the attainment of the seat of the Supreme Spirit. How can he [who is] beyond the mind, in the peace of the knowledge of existence [where] all desires [and their] actions are burned, again crave powers?

Fourth Chapter
1-2.
Then Nidāgha asked Lord Ṛbhu: "please relate [to me] the definition of *jīvanmukti*". He answered in the affirmative.

"[There are] four *jīvanmuktas* in the seven stages [of wisdom]. The first stage is desire for happiness. Inquiry [is] the second; the third fine-minded; the fourth abundance of sattwa; the fifth non-attachment; the sixth right perception; the seventh entrance into the fourth state. The stage in the form of *praṇava* is based on the sounds A, U, M [and] the half-syllable. The sound A and others [are] of four kinds because of the difference between gross, subtle, causal [and] witness.
These states [are] waking, dreaming, sleeping and *turīya*. The waking *viśva* is in the gross part of A. The *taijasa* is in the

subtle part. The *prājña* is in the seed part. The *turīya* is in the witness part. The dreaming viśva is in the gross part of U. The taijasa is in the subtle part. The prājña is in the seed part. The turīya is in the witness part. The sleeping viśva is in the gross part of M. The taijasa is in the subtle part. The prājña is in the seed part. The turīya is in the witness part. The turīya viśva is in the gross part of the half-syllable. The taijasa is in the subtle part. The prājña is in the seed part. The turīya of the turīya is in the witness part.

The turīya part of A [includes] the first, second and third stages. The turīya part of U [includes] the fourth stage. The turīya part of M [includes] the fifth stage. The turīya part of the half-syllable [includes] the sixth stage. Beyond this [is] the seventh stage. Moving in the [first] three stages one becomes a seeker of liberation. Moving in the fourth stage, one becomes a knower of Brahman. Moving in the fifth stage, one becomes a wise knower of Brahman. Moving in the sixth stage, one becomes an exalted knower of Brahman. Moving in the seventh stage one becomes a most exalted knower of Brahman. There are verses with reference to this. The first stage of knowledge is said to be the desire for happiness, the second inquiry, the third fine-minded, the fourth abundance of *sattwa*; then there is [the fifth,] non-attachment, right perception, the sixth [and] rememberance of the entrance to turīya the seventh.

3 to 5.

The desire [which arises] from prior detachment, [namely] ‘why do I remain ignorant? I am regarded by the teachings [and] the virtuous’ is said by the wise to be virtuous desire. A leaning [towards] good conduct, previous constant practice of detachment, contact [with] the teachings [and] the virtuous, this is known as inquiry. Where passionate [attachment] to sensual objects is reduced by virtuous desire [and] inquiry, this is known as fine-minded.

6 to 9.

When the mind is fixed on the pure nature of existence because of the practice of the three stages [and] the cessation [of desires] for [sensual] objects, this is widely known as abundance of *sattwa*. The manifestation of sattwa, which has then risen without attachment [to] the fruits [of actions] of the practice of the four stages is known by the name of detachment. [That stage where] due to practice of the five stages, through taking great pleasure in the Self [and] correct perception of the internal [and] external, [and] having been taught for a long time through beneficial explanation, the sixth stage is called right perception.

10 to 13.

That should be known as the way, having gone to the fourth, to absolute devotion to one's natural state, because of the non-perception of difference due to practice for a long time of the six stages. The triad [of stages], beginning with virtuous desire, is known as stages with and without differences. In which manner one perceives [the world] through the intellect, [so] this world is seen in the waking state. When the non-dual becomes fixed and the dual has gone to extinction, they see through union with the fourth stage the world as a dream. It vanishes [just as] the autumnal cloud, having dissipated, disappears. O Nidāgha, be convinced there remains only the True Reality.

14 to 15.

Having risen to the fifth stage called the seat of deep sleep, [which is] peaceful, one remains entirely in the non-dual state without special parts. With the [mind] always turned inwards, although engaging in other external activities, one always appears like a sleeping person when fatigued.

16 to 20.

Doing the practice in this stage, [mental tendencies] completely eliminated, the seventh, [which is] ancient [and] called secret sleep, is step by step attained, where there is neither non-existence nor the form of existence, neither the I nor even the not-I. One exists alone in non-duality, thinking diminished [and] without fear.

Like an empty pot in the ether, empty inside [and] empty outside, like a full pot in the ocean, full inside [and] full outside, do not be one who is grasped and do not be one who grasps. Having abandoned all concepts, be absorbed in what remains. Disregarding the seer, sight and seen with their impressions, meditate on the ātman alone, seeing its first light.

21 to 30.

Whoever is occupied with this daily life, and also moves [or] stays firm like the ether, is said to be a *jīvanmukta.* In whom the light [of] the mind neither rises nor perishes in happiness [and] suffering [and] remains firm when [one's desire] is not obtained, is said to be a jīvanmukta. Whoever is awake while in deep sleep, whose waking state is not known [and] whose perception is without impressions, is said to be a jīvanmukta. Whoever, although behaving in accordance with desire, hatred, fear and others, is as pure as the inner space, is said to be a jīvanmukta. One whose state of mind is 'I am not the doer' and whose intellect is not attached to doing or not doing, is said to be a jīvanmukta.

One from whom the world does not shrink and who, unfettered by pleasure, anger [and] fear, does not shrink from the world, is said to be a jīvanmukta. One who, although engaging in all trap-like matters, [remains] cool, while [engrossed] in the highest attainment, the Absolute Consciousness, is said to be a jīvanmukta. When, always content in My True Nature, renouncing all past desires [of] the heart, o Sage, that person is said to be a jīvanmukta. [One whose] mind [is] serene, resting in the most pure state of consciousness, devoid of thought, is said to be a jīvanmukta.

In whose mind does not spring this world having no I, he, this one, [and what is] visible [and] unreal, that person is said to be a jīvanmukta.

31 to 33.

Through the path of the spiritual masters and sacred teachings immediately enter the *sat*, the Brahman [which is] changeless, abundant, full [and] free of sense objects, [and] remain fixed [there]. Śiva is *guru*; Śiva is the *veda*; Śiva is God; Śiva is the Lord; I am Śiva; Śiva is all. There is none other than Śiva. The courageous *brāhmaṇa*, having known him alone, attains wisdom, without remembering many words which fatigue the speech organs.

34 to 42a.

The *Śuka* is liberated; the *Vāmadeva* is liberated too. There are no [others] apart from these two [who have] attained liberation. The courageous [ones] who follow the path of Śuka quickly become liberated here in this world. Those who always follow [the path of] Vāmadeva, dying and born again and again in this world, gradually become liberated through yoga, *sāṃkhya* [and] actions devoted to *sattva*. Śuka and Vāmadeva are the two paths created by the Lord of the *devas*. Śuka is called the bird [path and] Vāmadeva the ant. The purified [ones] enter the highest state through the path of Śuka, having perceived the nature of their own ātman by discerning the *samādhi* state, through the samādhi [of] *sāṃkhyayoga* [or] through investigation of the sacred words, or straight through the mouth of the creator [or] by the way of distinction 'not that'.

Having, through the regular practice of *haṭha* [yoga] its strain caused by postures, restraints and others, become vulnerable to multiple obstacles caused by *aṇima* and other [siddhis] in this world, as well as having not obtained rewards, one is well-born again in a noble family, again practising yoga in relation to one's previous tendencies. Through the practice of yoga in many births one attains liberation, the supreme seat of Viṣṇu, through the Vāmadeva or bird [path]. These two paths leading to the attainment of Brahman [are] auspicious. One bestows immediate liberation; the other gives gradual liberation.

42b to 44.
What [is] delusion [and] what [is] sorrow [to] one who sees oneness here, whose intellect, at the end of experience, is intent on the Truth. All who fall [within] the range [of] this vision are freed from all [sins]. All who move in the ether and on the earth within the range of the vision of the knower of Brahman are immediately released from [sins] accumulated through crores of births.

Fifth Chapter
1 to 3.
Then Nidāgha asked this Lord Ṛbhu: 'Please tell me the rule for the practice of yoga'.
'So be it', he said. 'The body is composed of the five elements, [and] filled with five regions. One, which is hard, is earth. That [which] has a fluid nature is water. [That which] inflames is fire. Movement is the characteristic of air. The essence of ether is everywhere. This should be known by one who desires yoga.

Through the cause of the blowing of the region of air day and night, [there are] twenty-one thousand six hundred breaths [and] more elsewhere.

4 to 6a.
When the earth region is worn away, wrinkles appear in the body, indeed just as in the water region the hair becomes gradually pale white. When the fire element is weakened, hunger [and] radiance disappear. When the air element is weakened, there is constant tremor [and when] the ether [is weakened] there is no life at all. Because of [this] weakness,

the elements [must be] maintained in such a way [that there is] constant life.

6b to 9.
As the great bird can soar incessantly, that is [why] one should practise *uḍḍiyāṇa*. The *bandha* is reflected there [in the name]. The *uḍḍiyāṇa bandha* is definitely the lion of the elephant of death. The release from that [depends on power] from the body [as] this bandha is arduous. Then when the fire in the belly has gone, severe pain is produced. It should not be done by one [who is] hungry nor [by one who has] rapid faeces and urine. Beneficial and moderate [food] should be eaten often little by little.

10 to 12a.
[One should practise] gentle, moderate [and] subtle [yogas which are] respectively *laya, haṭha* [and] *mantra.* Laya, haṭha [and] mantra yogas include these eight limbs: thus *yama, niyama, āsana, prāṇāyama*, then henceforth *pratyāhāra, dhāraṇā, dhyāna* [and] *samādhi* is the eighth.

12b to 14.
The ten yamas are *ahiṃsā*, non-violence; *satya*, truthfulness in speech; *asteya*, honesty in action; *brahmacarya*, abstinence or moderation in sexual conduct; *daya*, kindness or compassion; *ārjava*, straightforwardness; *kṣamā*, patience; *dhṛti*, equanimity; *mitāhāra*, moderate and balanced diet; and *śauca*, cleanliness of body and mind.

O Wise One, the tenfold niyamas are said to be *tapas* (austerity, endurance) *santoṣa* (contentment) *āstikya* (faith in the highest consciousness) *dāna* (charity, giving to others) *īśvara pūja* (worship of the highest consciousness) *siddhānta śravaṇa* (listening to the scriptures) *hrī* (shame or remorse) *mati* (desire for humility) *japa* (repetition of mantra, syllables or words of power) and *vrata* (vow or commitment).

15 to 17.

Beginning with *cakra*, there are eleven postures, o Excellent Sage! Thus *cakra, padmāsana, kūrma, kukkuṭa* and similarly *vīrāsana, svāstika, bhadra, siṃhāsana, muktāsana* and *gomukha* are named by well-known yogins. Placing the left thigh on the right ankle [and] the right [thigh] on the left [ankle], the body upright, then this [is] regarded as the cakra posture.

18.

Inhaling, retaining, thus exhaling, inhaling again through one's own nāḍīs [is] prāṇāyāma. Thus it is regarded as the nāḍīs.

19 to 21.

The body of all people consists of ninety-six digits in length. In its middle, two digits from the place of the anus, then two digits below the place of the genitals is said to be the centre. Nine digits above the genitals is said to be the knot of the nāḍīs, four digits in height, four digits in length, the shape of an egg [and] surrounded by fat, marrow, bone [and] blood.

22 to 27.

The twelve-spoked wheel of nāḍīs is situated there. The *kuṇḍalī* through which the body is supported is there. She covers with her face the *brahmarandhra* of *suṣumṇā*. From suṣumṇā dwells that [spoke of] *alambusā* [and] *kurūḥ* nāḍī. Then in another pair [of spokes are] *vārūṇī* and *yaśasvinī*. *Piṅgalā* is continuously on the right of suṣumṇā. Between them are *pūṣā* and *payasvinī*. On the spoke behind suṣumṇā is *sarasvatī* nāḍī. *Śaṅkhinī* and *gāndhārī* are between the two. North of suṣumṇā lives [the nāḍī] known as *iḍā*. Next is *hastijīhvā*, then *viśvodarī* [and] the nāḍīs in the spokes in the clock-wise order.

28 to 31a.

These twelve nāḍīs are indeed the twelve carriers of vital airs. They are said to be shaped like woven cloth [of] different colours. The middle part [of] this cloth is called the navel plexus. *Jvalantī, nādarūpiṇī, pararandhrā* and *suṣumṇā* are called the support of the *nāda*, and the four are filled with gems. The centre of the *brahmarandhra* is always covered by the *kuṇḍalī*. Thus the ten vital airs flow in these nāḍīs.

31b to 33a.

The wise one, having understood the movement of the nāḍīs and vital airs, [with] neck, head and body aligned, mouth closed, motionless, should contemplate the form of turīya, at the nosetip, in the centre of the heart and the middle of the bindu, with the eyes intent on the nectar flowing [from there].

33b to 36.

Having contracted the entrance to the anus, closing it off, causing *apāna vāyu* to rise through [repetition of] the *praṇava*, one should expel [the prāṇa] by means of the *śrī-bīja.* Then one should meditate on one's own ātman as *śri* [and] be immersed in the nectar. This is *kāla-vañcana*, the illusion of time. It radiates as far-reaching. Whatever thought originates through the mind is accomplished by the mind. By the flame of fire in water, there are sprouts and branches. Should there be speech [or] actions in the *jāgati* metre, [there are] surely no adverse results.

37 to 41.

Observing the *bindu* in the path, the vital air making the fire blaze, thereby drying up the water, then the body becomes strong. Having contracted together the anus and yoni for a long time [and] raised the *apāna*, [the yogin] unites [it] with the fire of *samāna* [*vayu*]. One should contemplate one's own ātman as *śri*, immersed in nectar, then in the middle part of the entrance should undertake [the practice of] yoga [with all one's] will. One should endeavour to rise up by the complete union of *prāṇa* and *apāna*. This auspicious yoga illuminates in the body the path of psychic powers. Just as a bridge over a river obstructs the flow, so the reflected light of the body should always be understood by the yogins.

42 to 45.

This *bandha* (union of *prāṇa* and *apāna*) is approved for all the nāḍīs. Through the grace of this bandha the deity becomes manifest. This bandha of the four ways, by obstructing the three paths, illuminates the one way to which the sages adhere. Having caused *udāna vāyu* to rise quickly with *prāṇa vāyu*, this bandha, by obstructing all the nāḍīs, goes upwards. This is called *saṃpuṭa yoga*, and also *mūlabandha*. Only by the practice of yoga, controlling the three bandhas, are they perfected.

46 to 49.

Day and night, every hour without interruption, at any time, the vital air becomes controlled by this practice of yoga. When the vital airs are controlled, the fire increases every day in the body. With the increase of fire, food etc is well-digested. With the full digestion of food, an increase of juice is generated. When the juice is increased every day, then the vital forces increase. With the increase of the vital forces alone, understanding increases in the body [and] all sins accumulated in crores of births are burned.

50 to 53.

In the intermediate space between the anus and the genitals [is] the triangular *mūlādhāra*. It illumines the seat of Śiva of the form of the bindu. There is situated the *parā śaktiḥ* with the name of *kuṇḍalinī*, from which the vital air rises, from which the fire increases, from which the bindu originates, from which the inner sound expands, from which the soul is born, from which the mind is produced. The six cakras beginning with mūlādhāra are said to be the seat of śakti.

From above the throat to the crown of the head is said to be the seat of Śambhu.

54 to 59a.

The body is the base of the nāḍīs and the nāḍīs are the base of prāṇa. The prāṇa is the abode of the *jīva* and the jīva is the base of the soul. The soul is the seat of śakti. This world [is the cause of] all creations. The ātman is lucid [and] free from differences. One should practise breath control. Although well established in the three bandhas, one should always uplift, [with] mind attached to the truth, that which should be known, [and is] the reason by which the goal is recognised. One should abstain from inhaling and exhaling in the middle of kumbhaka, depending by oneself on Brahman, the highest visible goal. All matter which is external is called exhalation. The wisdom of the *śāstras* is inhalation. Remembering [it] in oneself is retention. Thus if the mind practises here, one is without doubt liberated.

59b to 61a.

[The mind], having been caused to rise through kumbhaka, should be filled by kumbhaka alone. One should control the pot through the pot. Within it is the Supreme Śiva. A stable [pot] is the result of daily repetition of the throat posture, turning towards the course of the vāyus [and] holding the in-breath in kumbhaka.

61b to 68a.

Then [placing] both hands and both feet together evenly on the ground, gradually [attaining] the four seats [and] the vāyu through Vedhaka Yoga, one should shake *Mahāmeru* with the forces in the course of the vāyu.

Because of the conjunction of the moon, sun and fire, the two pockets having been drawn together, the vāyu immediately throbs [and the yogin] may know immortality. Through the movement of *Meru* the gods, having gone to the centre of Meru, move about.

At first a hole directly appears in the *brahma-granthi*. Then having pierced the Brahma knot, one pierces the Viṣṇu knot. Then having pierced the Viṣṇu knot, one pierces the Rudra knot. Having pierced the Rudra knot [and] split the dirt of delusion [and] through the grace of God and guru, the mental impressions [of] many births, then through the practice of yoga one is born as a yogin of Vedha [Yoga]. In the region of *suṣumnā nāḍī* between *iḍā* and *piṅgalā*, the vāyu is made to rise, especially with mudrā and bandha.

68b to 71a.
In the group of three kinds [of *praṇava*], the short one burns [all] sins; the long one gives liberation [and] the very long one [gives] strength. Like the incessant flow of oil [and] the lingering sound of a bell, the origin of *praṇava* cannot be spoken. Whoever knows this is a knower of the Veda. The short sound goes to the bindu. The long sound goes to the crown of the head. The very long sound goes to the end of the twelfth. The grace of mantra [is] from the power of mantra. This praṇava [is] the remover of all obstacles and all disorders.

71b to 75.
Its four states are described: *ārambha* and *ghaṭa*, then *paricaya* and *niṣpatti*. Ārambha is said to be where, abandoning the external karma produced [by] the three causes, one makes inner karma. The state called ghaṭa, declared by the wise, [is] that the vital air, by making an opening from behind [and] having filled [it], remains fixed there. The paricaya state is where the vital air, neither alive nor lifeless, remains immobile and fixed in the ether in the body. The niṣpatti state [after] creation and dissolution, through the ātman, having reached the state of *jīvanmukti*, performs the yoga of one's innate nature.

Epilogue

Thus, whoever studies this upaniṣad becomes purified by the fire. One becomes purified by the air. One becomes purified from drinking spirituous liquor. One becomes purified from the theft of gold. One becomes a jīvanmukta. This is what is said by the *Ṛgveda*. The sages always see the supreme seat of Viṣṇu, as if their eyes are stretched to heaven. Watchful [and] joyful they illuminate [with their] might the supreme seat of Viṣṇu.

Thus [ends] the fifth section.

Thus ends the Varāha Upaniṣad.

F. Swami Satyadharma

On 12th June 2019 on the Central Coast of New South Wales Australia, our beloved Swami Satyadharma left her body. It was the day of Ganga Dussehra, celebrating the descent to Earth of the goddess Ganga, Ganga the mother who gives nourishment to all her children.

Dedication in her commentaries on the Yoga Upanishads have been to all spiritual aspirants. Swami Satyadharma's life was dedicated for over forty years to providing spiritual nourishment and bringing the light of yoga to all those who attended her programs throughout the world.

Swami Satyadharma was born in 1946 to a middle-class family in Connecticut, USA. She was the youngest of three and lived surrounded by nature and animals. She recognised the spiritual energy of nature, and was never attracted to big cities.

In search of purpose and spiritual guidance she travelled for years throughout Europe, Africa and Asia, where she met many enlightened masters. She spent two years in Nepal studying with Tibetan Buddhists lamas. She was an accomplished musician of the flute and guitar, and spent two years at the University of Bengal studying the sitar. In Java, Indonesia, she first studied batik, and then took part in a meditation program in one of the Javanese mystical schools. Her teacher was a mahasiddha who was 'breathtaking, awe-inspiring and transformative'. He specifically singled her out and said 'you have a future if you study earnestly, and after a long time you will attain an elevated consciousness as a yoga teacher, and you'll spend the later part of your life travelling internationally, and you'll teach the highest-level yoga teachings'. She was directed by the master to go to Mungher, Bihar, India, where she would meet a great teacher, Swami

Satyananda, a disciple of Swami Sivananda. There she stayed for thirty-five years.

At the age of 28, she was initiated by Swami Satyananda into *pūrṇa sannyasa* (full renunciation), a Dashnami order connected with the Advaita Vedanta tradition established by Adi Shankaracharya to protect, preserve and propagate spiritual knowledge. She absorbed the teachings and worked hard for the ashram for the first twenty years she spent there.

Then she edited books written by Swami Satyananda and, under his guidance, travelled the world teaching a range of spiritual courses on the Yogic Scriptures. And teach she did in Australia, USA, Canada, India, Nepal, Tibet, China, Japan, Korea, Columbia, Greece, Germany, Hungary, Bulgaria, France, Italy, Indonesia, New Zealand. In all those countries she was invited to come back time and time again. She had a great ability to teach. Her vast knowledge of the ancient scriptures was amazing. It just flowed from her. When she taught it was like she stepped into another zone, where she spoke with profound insight. That is why, if Swami Satyadharma was running a course, people would sign up regardless of the topic. Her deep understanding of yoga was reflected in the numerous topics she taught.

Her later years were devoted to writing commentaries on the Yoga Upanishads. At the end of her life she had completed her commentary on Nādabindu, and had written her commentary on only nine verses of Dhyānabindu. No-one else has completed this commentary, or been asked to do so, as her commentaries were original and unique.

Swami Satyadharma's Programs, Retreats and Lectures

Programs

Awakening Kundalini, Meditations from the Tantras, Dancing with the Divine, Atma Darshan, Intuition, Guru

Tattwa, Shiva Sutras, Mantra Yantra and Mandala, Ashram Life, Sadhana, Chakra Meditation, Spiritual Life.

***Deepening Sadhana* Retreats**

Kriya Yoga, Tattwa Shuddhi, Chakra Shuddhi, Prana Vidya and Mahavidya Sadhana.

Lectures

During the years she lived in Australia, she gave many satsangs and lectures to students enrolled in Yogic Studies courses. Topics included Origins of Yoga, Samkhya Tantra Vedanta, Yoga Sutras, Koshas, Chakras, Gunas, Bhagavad Gita, SWAN Theory, Raja Yoga, Gyan Yoga, Bhakti Yoga, Karma Yoga, Hatha Yoga, Upanishads, Pranava, Shiva Shakti, Mantra & Nada, Mantra Yoga Nada Yoga, Mudra Bandha, Shatkarmas, Kundalini Yoga, Swara Yoga, Prana Pranayama, Pratyahara, Theory & Practice of Antar Mouna, Yoga Psychology, Yoga Philosophy, Yoga in India, Yoga Ecology, Yoga History, Path of the Rishis, Yamas Niyamas, Yoga & Religion, Meditation, Yoga Nidra, Addiction, Purpose in Life, Grief, Body-Mind Therapy, Opening the Heart, Perception, Models of Mind, Mind & Consciousness, Mind Management and Living Consciously.

I was privileged to have worked with Swami Satyadharma for nine years. Her unlimited love and teachings will live on well into the future.

Om Tat Sat
Srimukti

राम-राम
राम-राम

G. Author's Note

I started working with Swami Satyadharma early in 2010, collating teachings on Bhakti Yoga, Rāja Yoga and Jñāna Yoga. I then had a yoga studio is Sydney, Australia, where I would invite senior teachers to give weekend programs. Swami Satyadharma had agreed to give a program on *Prāṇa Prāṇāyama Prāṇa Vidyā.* As usual with her programs, it was booked out well in advance. In 2011 she gave a program on *Managing the Mind through Meditation* and in 2014 *Yoga of the Heart* at a time when she was very supportive to me as my husband was ill in hospital.

Our working relationship and friendship developed over the nine years I worked with her on the teachings project and later as translator of the Yoga Upaniṣads on which she wrote the commentaries. She had asked me what I was going to do with the Sanskrit I had studied. "Look for something to translate, I suppose," I said. "I've got something for you to translate: the Yoga Upaniṣads, there are only twenty-one of them," she said as if the matter had been settled. The project was unique because there were no other published commentaries on the Yoga Upaniṣads, except for *Cūdāmani Upaniṣad* which she had completed in Bihar, where it was published in 2003. Years later she told me she had made a *sankalpa* just before she moved to Australia that she would find a translator here.

Together we collaborated on the *Yoga Tattwa, Yoga Darshana, Yoga Kundali, Nadabindu and Dhyanabindu Upanishads*. Wherever we were, at her home, on a bushwalk or at a beach, we would have long talks about the work we were doing together. She wanted us to work on *Shandilya Upanishad* next, so I started the translation and commentary in August 2019 and it was published on her birthday 26th June 2020. I then did the translation and commentary of *Triśikhī-Brāhmaṇopaniṣad*, published in December 2021, and *Advayatāraka and Maṇḍalabrāhmaṇa Upaniṣads,* published in July 2023.

For many years I was a teacher of yoga and meditation. Already a linguist, having graduated in French, Italian and Japanese from the Universities of Sydney and Queensland, Australia, I undertook four years of studies in Sanskrit at the Australian National University (ANU) with Dr McComas Taylor. I was invited to join the Golden Key Internation Society for outstanding academic achievement, as I was awarded High Distinctions throughout my Sanskrit studies.

Ruth Perini (Srimukti)
7th March 2025
yoga.upanishads@yahoo.com

www.ingramcontent.com/pod-product-compliance
Lightning Source LLC
Chambersburg PA
CBHW071957290426
44109CB00018B/2050
* 9 7 8 0 6 4 8 9 1 0 7 6 3 *